HOW TO GET WORK & make money IN COMMERCIALS & MODELING

HOW TO GET WORK & make money

IN COMMERCIALS & MODELING

by cecily hunt

VNR VAN NOSTRAND REINHOLD COMPANY

NEW YORK CINCINNATI TORONTO LONDON MELBOURNE

All photos, with the exception of the snapshots shown
on page 47, were taken by Cecily Hunt.

Copyright © 1982 by Van Nostrand Reinhold Company

Library of Congress Catalog Card Number 81-14817

ISBN   0-442-23643-3 (cloth)
       0-442-23644-1 (paperback)

Printed in the United States of America

Published by Van Nostrand Reinhold Company
135 West 50th Street, New York, NY 10020, U.S.A.

Van Nostrand Reinhold Limited
1401 Birchmount Road
Scarborough, Ontario, M1P 2E7, Canada

Van Nostrand Reinhold Australia Pty. Ltd.
17 Queen Street
Mitcham, Victoria 3132, Australia

Van Nostrand Reinhold Company Limited
Molly Millars Lane
Wokingham, Berkshire, England

16   15   14   13   12   11   10   9   8   7   6   5   4   3   2   1

Library of Congress Cataloging in Publication Data

Hunt, Cecily.
    How to get work and make money in commercials
and modeling.

    Includes index.
    1. Models, Fashion—Vocational guidance.
2. Acting for television—Vocational guidance.
3. Television advertising—Vocational guidance.
I. Title.
HD6073.M77H85   659.1'52   81-14817
ISBN   0-442-23643-3   AACR2
ISBN   0-442-23644-1 (pbk.)

For Steve and Susan,
Whose dream this was

And Steven and Sue
Who helped it come true

Acknowledgments

Many thanks to the following:

A Plus Agency
Chas Alberts
Carol Appleby
Mary Ann Backland
Bob Banks
Gwen Banta
Inez Barnett
Diane Baron
Lauren Baskin
Brad Bates
Cleve Beauchamp
Bonnie Berg
Bud Beyer
Ralph and Leslie Bishop
Claudia Black
Michael Bloom
Stacy Blustein
Marjorie Bradford
Pat Brannen
Pat Bratcher
Johnny Brown
Jean Caputo
Reed Carnahan
Vic Caroli
JoBe Cerny
Mike Chambliss
Sue Charney
Virginia Christine
Liz Cifani
Ron Cohen
Johnny Conrad
Wilhelmina Cooper
Jane Davenport
The Demo Pad

Bonnie DeShong
Nancy DeVore
Larry Dillard
Ekco
Elite Models
John Fisher
Paula Fishman
Cleveland Fields
Debbie Floom
Eileen Ford
Doug Frew
Ann Geddes
Susan Gordon-Clark
Mary Grace
Shay Griffin
Barb Guarino
Shirley Hamilton
Uve Harden
Annie Harvey
Ann Haskel
Debbie Hayes
Bonnie Herman
Peter Hockman
Pam Hoffman
Jim Hunt
Anne Jacques
Pam Jefferson
Marian Jenkinson
Dorothy Jordan
Jimmy Journey
Adair Keating
The Keefes
Arnie Kleban
Tracy Kleronomos
Althea Knowles
The Langs
Tom Leavens
Elise Leventhal
Ben Long
L'Oreal
Emilia Lorence

Gorman Lowe
Sheila Madigan
Joan Mangum
Midge Marinello
McDonald's
Bob McDonald
David McKenna
Patti McKenny
Kevin McLean
Megan McTavish
Chris Meade
Bob Meitzer
Gianfranco Melli
Beverly Merrill
Deborah Messineo
Jackie Meyers
Cheryl Mitchell
Bob Moomey
Larry Moran
Ann Morgan
Bob Napolitano
Lucile Napolitano
National Talent Network
Carol Ness
Northwestern University
Tony Paddock
Jim Parks
Joanna Patton
Sandy Pesch
Curtis Pettijohn
Pat Phillips
Playboy Models
Gina Pontillo
Linda Price
Proctor and Gamble
Diana Quinn
Karl Raack
Marguerite Ray
Reynolds Aluminum
Janice Rhodes
Mary Ried

Bob Ritchie
Albert J. Rosenthal
  Advertising
Malcolm Rothman
Chuck Rowell
Bob Rumbaugh
Dave Rupprecht
Barrie Rutter
Fred Saas
Barbara Sachs
Jeanette Sachs
SAG and AFTRA
  Chicago and
  New York locals
Don Shelton
Arthur Shone
Jane Skinner
Joe Slattery
Duchyll Smithe
Mario Sperandio
Bea Sprague
Raimonda Stasevicius
Pat Stephenson
Terri Stoff
Sandy Storm
Jo Summers
Nancy Syburg
Peter Tambellini
TeleMation
Chip Tom
Joe Van Slyke
Pat Venegoni
Joel Warren and crew
Althea Watson
Sophia Welch
Westbend
Bill Wineburg
Dagmar Wittmer
Bob and Mary Woeller
Young and Rubicam
  Advertising

Very special thanks to the following, who made very special efforts:

B. J. Armstrong
Barbara Brabec
Harisse Davidson
Alice Dodd
Judy Leyrer
Herb Neuer
Barry Steiner

And to Nancy Dold, who was willing to do the "Before" photos.

Book and cover design by Peggy J. Tanner

Cover concept by Cecily Hunt

Contents

10

Winning the Job: The Selection Process / 115

11

Working / 122

12

Getting Your Child into Modeling and Commercials / 134

13

Money / 145

14

Why You May Need an Accountant / 150

15

The Unions: What You Need to Know / 153

16

17

Introduction

You are special. Whether it's your unique freckled face, long hair, bald head, handlebar moustache, missing front teeth, lopsided grin, cute smile, beautiful hands, long legs or high cheekbones, you have something special to offer. Perhaps you have a voice that sounds funny, one that's big and deep, or a snappy singing style, you're a trained dancer or you just have a flair for moving well, you're a puppeteer or you can pull a rabbit out of a hat, you're gorgeous or you're a born ham — you can put these attributes and abilities to work for you in the businesses of modeling and making commercials.

You don't have to be beautiful. You don't need years of expensive training or a college degree. You do have to have the right look — or the right talent — and the right information on how to go about getting this work.

Have you ever watched television commercials or fashion shows or looked at the advertisements in newspapers and magazines and thought that you'd like to be in them? You *can* get this work. At first, the people who hire you, who are excited about your look or your voice or your talent, will help you learn the ropes. The work itself isn't the difficult part; either you have a flair for modeling and performing or you don't. The difficult part is getting the work, knowing how and where to start, and sustaining your interest and drive if you don't get jobs right away. This book tells you how to get the work. I wish I could spare you the frustration you're bound to face at some point simply by writing about it. Unfortunately it doesn't work that way. But you will discover how these businesses operate, the wide variety of work that is available to you, how to get started, what you will need, and how to develop your curiosity into a career.

Anyone can model. Anyone can make a commercial. Hard to believe? I have taped interviews with modeling and talent agents making these statements. Fashion coordinators in department stores say that if you have the right look and are the right size, they can teach you or have one of their models teach you runway walks, pivots and turns in several half-hour sessions. Producers and directors of commercials say that if you have the look or the voice they want, they'll hand- hold you through the moves, the lines, the timing. If you have what somebody wants, they'll take the time to teach you the maneuvers.

They also are quick to admit that some things just can't be taught or learned. You can't "learn" personality, animation or self-confidence. If you don't already have that certain flair, you can't learn it. Experience and time will improve your skills, your timing, and your professionalism. But you must have something that someone is interested in and believes will work before you start.

The statements above may surprise you, but they're true. It's one of the wonderful, fluky, sad things about this business; many well-trained and stunningly beautiful people won't make it and others, whose talent comes naturally or whose appearance is frankly ordinary or even funny, will. It is partially luck — being in the right place at the right

Everyone is unique . . .

time, knowing the right person, having the right look or the right ability. But it is also knowing how to capitalize on what you do have, accepting it, working with it, developing it to the limit, and finding out how to sell it. You have to make others aware of you and excited about working with you.

It's not enough to have good looks or a marketable talent; you must also know how to sell what you have to offer. Many people who do have potential will never get a chance to develop it because they don't have the information, attitude, professionalism nor the proper tools to interest the professionals who offer the jobs they want. You need to align yourself with the professionals who can get you the jobs, and this guide reveals how to approach them.

This guide tells you where to start, how to determine the kinds of work you're right for, and how to market yourself. In fact, it tells how to cash in on your look and your talents right in your hometown. You may not be aware of the wide range of opportunities available to you, and you may not be aware that such opportunities exist in most cities. As you read and become better informed about the business, you will discover the great varieties of work open to models and performers. There are many job opportunities within the business, and there is need for all kinds of people to fill them.

It is a business that has a great deal to offer a great many people. For some it promises big money, high exposure and a shortcut to Hollywood or Broadway. It can provide travel, excitement, glamour and contact with a variety of interesting and influential people. For others, the business offers an opportunity to work occasionally, make extra money, and have the thrill of being recognized in a fashion show, commercial, or newspaper ad for the local bank.

Whether you want to model in the local department store or go all the way to Chicago, Los Angeles or New York, there are procedures and protocol to guide you. If you are not aware of these business procedures, you most likely will not be taken seriously by the agents, advertisers, fashion coordinators, photographers and production people who are in the positions to hire you. If you already work professionally in your hometown and are considering moving to one of the major markets, you need to know how the business operates in those cities and what preparations to make before you actually move. If you are an actor or a college theater major, you ought to at least consider the possibility of working in commercials and other job areas that utilize performing skills.

What This Book is Going To Do for You

Most of you want to get work, but you don't know how to go about it. This guide will, first of all, help you to understand the business so your expectations are realistic. It will help you determine the kind of modeling best suited to you, find the work available in your hometown, start out with appropriate professional tools, and let you know how things really operate.

In addition to saving you time and legwork as you start to explore the business, this guide will also save you money by alerting you to the many cons and unnecessary seminars, classes, newsletters, management companies and other costly services you may be asked to consider. In short, this is a nuts-and-bolts guide to understanding the business and getting work, and it answers the questions you may not know enough at this point in your career to ask.

There are many books about beauty and cosmetics, guides offering three-day regimens for silky hair, 10-day plans for flawless complexions, and two-week diets for inner loveliness. This guide does not concentrate on what you haven't got or changing what you have. It presumes that you're perfectly fine and that you have something special to offer. You may have the classic features of a high fashion model or the irresistible charm of a winning commercial type and be destined to make it to the top; this guide will get you there faster, pointing out the shortcuts.

Chances are, however, that you're not a flawless beauty. Great! This guide will help you determine what you *do* have to offer — whether you're an Italian grandmother, a black professional woman, an Oriental businessman, an all-American blonde cheerleader, or the average housewife — and how to market that look or skill. You do *not* have to be beautiful to get work in modeling and commercials!

Most guides on modeling concentrate on the fashion scene in New York, which, indeed, is where the fashion business in this country is centered; *this* guide includes valuable information and tips on getting work in your hometown. True, most commercials are produced in Los Angeles, New York and Chicago, but the business certainly does exist in other cities. There is a great deal and a great variety of work for models and performers living in other cities. I traveled to more than 20 American and European cities — from New York to Florence, Italy to Toledo, Ohio — to find out how the business operates. Professionals in New York and Los Angeles encourage beginning models to learn the business and get experience in their hometowns. There is work for you at home, and this guide tells you how to find it.

There may not be a great deal of work, however, that you are right for or that your hometown can offer you. The statistics in this business are frightening; very few actors and full-time models on a national scale make enough at this business to earn a living. So it will be important for you to make a decision at some point about how much you are willing to give and what you can ultimately expect from the business as it exists where you are planning to work. If you are happy to do an occasional job and are not dependent on this work for steady income or your sense of self-worth — and if that satisfies the professionals who use your services — fine. For most of you, that will be the case. Even for these few jobs, you'll still need to know whom to call on, how to behave, how to dress, and what to have with you.

If, however, you do intend to become a full-time professional, you will at some point find yourself in the larger, more brutally paced and fiercely competitive markets. This is where the business is serious, a multibillion-dollar affair. The agents in these towns and the people who hire you will be a great deal more demanding. Your half-hearted interest and your lack of commitment, information or professional tools will not impress these people. You may not get another chance. So you'll have to decide how serious your interest is, how much you're willing to give to it, and how much you can realistically expect from the business.

This guide also includes suggestions and personal comments from people in the business whose names or places of work you will recognize. I've interviewed agents to see how they want to be approached by new people and what they expect from the people they agree to represent. I've asked fashion coordinators what training is necessary for runway work and what look is most marketable. I've asked production people what they want to see from new people and what is expected in job situations. I've asked advertisers how they cast their commercials and choose models for their photographic advertisements. This guide, in some ways, is written by the people who look for those fresh, new faces, the people who cast the jobs you want and with whom you'll be interviewing and auditioning — the insiders whose opinions and advice you want to know.

But most of the information in this guide — the questions asked and the answers found — comes from people just like you. As a commercial photographer working in Chicago for the past 10 years, I have photographed hundreds of models and actors. I have respect for these people. It takes courage to try something new, something unknown, and very often our photo session is the first step to getting ready to make an entrance. They've shared a great deal — their feelings, fears and discoveries — with me. That exchange is the basis for much of what is said in the following pages.

The experienced and successful people I photographed have shared their views of the business, their thoughts on why they've been successful, their hot tips, what they'd do differently if they had a fresh start, and, occasionally, a good piece of industry gossip. Many of those I photographed in Chicago who transferred to Los Angeles or New York have kept in touch to share what they found in different markets. Those just beginning often had horrible stories to tell; their naivete and lack of information had led them into situations where they had been stripped of their money, pressured into unnecessary services or classes, or they'd been stripped of their clothes, manipulated and left without self-respect. These people brushed themselves off, prepared to make second starts, and came in for new photos.

I realized, over the span of years, that the questions and concerns were fairly predictable. Each person's motivation, expectations, abilities, tolerance and drive was different, but they all shared the same concerns, asked the same questions, and eventually reported similar conclusions. I, through my association with the agents and advertisers in town, heard the other side of the story, the other point of view. Both sides have been open with me, and so I heard what the agents wanted to see from new models and talent — and what they didn't want to see, too, stated with much greater emphasis — and what these newcomers thought of it all. As my clients became aware of this book in progress, I was inundated with stories, suggestions, advice and information. It has been an ongoing process, and I hear something new and of value constantly.

This guide is the result of those years of listening, the accumulated insider information, and the interviews conducted nationwide. It offers suggestions, however, not rules. There is no rigidly defined, foolproof ladder to success. The tips and experiences of any 10 working professionals would illustrate 10 different pathways leading to 10 different ideas of success. You'll have to adjust and shape what you learn here to your own situation.

Particularly in this field, you must combine your special look or talent with good information and the confidence and perseverance necessary to sustain

. . . and everyone has something special to offer.

your efforts. You need information in order to get work. And that's how you'll really learn. On the spot. In this business, there is no substitute for experience. There is no teaching situation, no class or seminar or book to approximate the tension, the timing, the total atmosphere of a job situation. This guide aims to help you get the job and prepare you for whatever you may encounter.

Armed with this information, you can at least explore the business and discover your potential in modeling and making commercials. Within this business there is something for everyone. The trick is to identify — to accept, and to get excited about — what you have to offer and to discover the markets for your look or your talent in your hometown. Those jobs are out there — go get 'em!

1

Discover the Opportunities: What the Business Offers You

Whether you were born with your good looks and clear voice or you've spent time learning corrective makeup and how to vocalize, whether your flair comes to you naturally or is an act you've studied and rehearsed, you have something special to offer. In this business, whether you're a fashion type or a commercial type, there will be a call for you at some point in time. There is a job — or many — for which you're right, so consider all the possibilities.

One of the interesting and sometimes confusing aspects of the business is the typing or categorizing of the people who work in it. Broadly, these people are divided into fashion and general commercial types. We all have an idea of the female fashion type: 5'9'', well-defined cheekbones, wide-set eyes, long legs, a perfect size 7 or thereabouts. We all know something about the "commercial" types as well: there's the Ajax man, Josephine the plumber, Mrs. Olson, Florence Henderson for Tang, Orson Welles for Perrier, John Wayne, at one time, for aspirin, and a lot of people who look like you and me and our next-door neighbors selling a wide range of products and services.

And that's why it is that anyone can be a model or at least get work doing some kind of modeling. You don't have to have that high fashion look to be a model. You just have to have a look that sells. You're bald, you wear glasses, you're tremendously overweight, you're thin as a rail, or you just have a nice, ordinary look — you're a character model. You have lovely hands, super legs, beautiful eyes; but the rest of you is not so great. Use those hands, legs or eyes to become a feature model. You've heard it once before — you don't have to be beautiful, or handsome, to get work as a model.

There is still more confusion about what models do. Runway models show clothing in style shows. Print models are in the photographs that advertise clothing. Models are used in trade shows, public and industrial, to add glamour to automobiles and demonstrate new services or wares. There are different skills needed for moving gracefully on a ramp, striking poses during a photography session, and promoting products in large convention halls.

Character models — the ordinary faces and the funny faces — do these jobs as well. The models who are hired are the ones who have the look that is right for the job, be that fashion pretty, average American or just plain silly. If, in addition to having the right look, you also have the right abilities — you sing, dance, do magic, do stunts, have a great speaking voice, and enjoy performing — you are right for commercial work. Such people are often classified as "talent," as opposed to models, print models or fashion types.

So, whether you are that high fashion type, or a pretty girl too short for clothing but perfect for cosmetics and jewelry, a perfect 40R with the right look to model clothes or pose as a bank executive, or a Mr. Peepers type with a squeaky voice, there's something in this business for you.

From Runways To Recording Studios

There are many people in the business who work in several areas. A fashion model might do several shows, some informal modeling and a number of photo bookings all within the space of a week. Some models also get involved in commercial work, as Cheryl Tiegs has done, and use their high exposure to break into film, as have Lauren Hutton and Margeaux Hemingway. Actors and people with natural reacting abilities may use their talents to do a mixture of on-camera commercials, voice-over spots, industrial films, trade shows, industrials, photography and slide film work. Singers can keep quite busy doing the jingles for commercial spots for television and radio. Once you've discovered the opportunities, you may decide this is the business for you.

Below is a list of job areas in which models and commercial talent work.

Style shows — These live presentations of new designs or next season's "look" provide the basis for everyone's idea of modeling. Often elevated on a runway or ramp above the heads of the audience, models effortlessly glide and pivot, pausing to highlight the special features of the fashions they're showing. While women have traditionally done the shows, men and children now also appear. The shows are opening up as well to older and larger models.

Informals — These "mini" fashion presentations are less structured than formal fashion shows in terms of where and when they occur. The models often mingle with customers in the department from which the fashions they're showing have been selected, or they may walk throughout the store. Informal presentations often occur on a scheduled and advertised basis in the restaurants, cafeterias and tearooms of department stores.

Tearoom modeling — Generally occurring between the hours of 11 a.m. and 3 p.m., when the luncheon crowd is at its peak, tearoom modeling provides an opportunity for models to show many outfits informally.

Trunk shows — When the representative of a designer or clothing manufacturer comes into a store with an entire collection and stays several days in one department to present it to customers, models are hired to show the line. In cities such as Chicago and Dallas, where there are clothing and apparel markets, models display fashions to interested buyers and representatives. Often they are requested to model something off the rack or a mannequin when a buyer shows interest.

Perhaps you're a fashion type . . .

. . . or a commercial type.

Designer models — This kind of modeling is mostly done in New York and abroad. A designer employs a model for fitting during the designing of garments, and for showing the finished garments to buyers.

Photography or print work — Fashion models, ordinary people and character faces work in this category, teaming with photographers to create pictures that sell clothing, products and services. These photographs are then seen in newspapers, magazines, catalogs, product packaging, point-of-purchase displays, sales literature, slide films and billboards across the nation.

1. Editorial fashion — This kind of photography appears largely in fashion magazines like *Vogue, Glamour* and *Seventeen*. The photographs will feature one aspect of fashion — the new look in swimsuits, hats to top off this season's outfits, hairstyles for today's pretty athletes, the perfect eye shadows to complement new fashion colors — rather than advertise one particular piece of clothing or cosmetic for one particular designer, store or manufacturer. These photos serve to illustrate stories or current trends rather than to advertise.

Models are often used in groups in editorial fashion photography. The majority of this photography is done in New York where the magazines are headquartered, although many cities have newspapers and local magazines that occasionally run fashion articles requiring editorial photographs.

2. Retail fashion — Models in these photographs are advertising one particular garment or accessory. Such photographs appear in catalogs, magazines, newspapers, promotional literature sent out through the mail, hang tags on the clothing on sales racks and other packaging of the garment, and wherever the manufacturer sees fit to use photographic illustration.

These photographs are meant to sell the apparel being advertised, not the model. Models who work in retail fashion photography know how to highlight the fashions they're showing. They must know how to draw attention to features that make the garment unique or beautiful.

3. Feature photography — There are models who feature just one portion of their bodies, and that one portion is what will appear in the advertising photographs. Someone with striking hands may be kept busy advertising cosmetics, jewelry and other hand-held products that are photographed close-up. Only that model's hands will be seen. There are models whose legs are excellent, who will be called to advertise pantyhose. Perfect feet will model

shoes. Distinctive eyes and lips will demonstrate cosmetic products, and beautiful heads of hair will show off hair care products. There are even models who keep their hair cropped short, or who shave it off entirely, to feature wigs.

4. Catalogs — Models are often hired to show certain products in merchandise catalogs. They demonstrate exercise machines and kitchen appliances, hold athletic equipment and barbecue tools, and relax on outdoor furniture. Attractive people who are too short for fashion modeling may be just right for this kind of work; a model 5'3" will make a lounge chair appear more spacious than a model who is 5'9".

5. Advertisements — Models and talent of all ages and appearances are called upon to advertise a wide range of products and services. A retiring couple might be photographed expressing their contentment about finding just the right retirement village, and that photograph might appear in local magazines and in the company's sales literature. A rugged-looking young man might convey enjoyment of a certain brand of cigarette. That photograph will appear in magazines and on billboards nationwide. A cute little girl with pigtails is photographed, grinning, eating a bowl of cereal, and her photograph winds up on the cereal box. An attractive young housewife smiles at finding how easy it is to vacuum with a certain vacuum cleaner, the camera clicks, and that model and her vacuum cleaner appear in appliance catalogs.

Some advertising photography receives nationwide or regional exposure. Usually these significant accounts are handled in large cities. Advertisement of some products and services, particularly banks, car dealerships and area industries, is usually done locally.

6. Slide films — Models and talent are often used in educational and training slide film presentations. Such presentations may be used in a store or at a trade show to demonstrate a product's wide versatility to potential buyers. A slide film might be used within a company to introduce new employees to facilities, policy and benefits, or to illustrate a new sales approach to sales representatives. Slide films are widely used in schools, and models are sometimes used in these presentations.

Doing a slide film is like doing any other still photography, except that the photographs are set up and ultimately exhibited as a series.

Promotion — Models are often hired to hand out samples of products that are new or are being tested. Cosmetic departments in large stores, in particular, employ models for this purpose. This kind of promotional work requires a good sense of public relations,

You might be asked to distribute literature . . .

. . . or demonstrate products at a trade show . . .

. . . while singing and dancing abilities are important for industrial shows.

an aggressive and confident attitude, and an enjoyment of sales and meeting new people. In some cities, there are companies who exclusively list models interested in this kind of part-time work.

Trade shows — Models and talent are regularly employed at trade shows and conventions to show products, deliver short narrations, distribute literature, and present a first-class image for the company that has hired them. Exhibitors set up booths to demonstrate and sell their wares and services to industry representatives or, in an open show, to the general public. Whether a model is gracing next year's Chevrolet at the Auto Show, demonstrating the world's best potato peeler at the Housewares Show, or convincing buyers that her company's paneling is the industry's finest at the Builders Show, this kind of work requires intelligence, enthusiasm and tact. Performing skills are also a definite plus. It's important to project to an audience, memorize a script quickly, and to deliver it with freshness and enthusiasm several times per hour in order to draw crowds to a booth and hold their attention. Magicians, puppeteers, clowns and other performers are sometimes used to perform the above functions.

Industrial shows — Large companies often convene all of their sales representatives or executives in order to explain a new process, product or change within the company, and talent is hired to perform in a show that has been written specifically for this purpose. A company may celebrate the president's 50th year with the company with a production, complete with singing and dancing, recounting high spots of his life and work. These performances may occur once or several times during the course of the meeting. The audiences may consist of the entire company, en masse, or of smaller groups that rotate to different seminars. Strong performing skills are needed for this kind of work.

Films — A great many actors find employment in films that the general public will probably never see. Not produced for movie theaters or television, these 10 to 30-minute-long films are made for individual companies, and religious and educational institutions.

1. Industrial or training films — Actors play the roles of company spokesmen in films used to train incoming personnel or to advise employees of changes, benefits or other company policies. A film for a pharmaceutical firm might utilize talent to portray doctors and technicians, or an actress might be hired to play a senior officer in training films for bank tellers.

This photo might accompany a story describing the fashionable western look.

2. Educational films — These films are produced for use in schools, museums and wherever visual instruction is used. Talent might be hired to represent historical figures and demonstrate historical events, such as in the 1950s series of ''You Are There'' films, or they might act as teachers raising questions about or explaining the subject being discussed in the film.

3. Other films — Colleges and technical institutes with film departments often use local talent in the production of short documentary or creative films. While these productions are not ''commercial,'' they may provide additional experience for interested models and talent. Such endeavors are frequently artistically but not financially rewarding.

4. Feature films — More feature films are being shot outside of Hollywood studios than ever before. Because of current interest in Arizona, Texas, Georgia, Florida and the Midwest, models and talent living in these areas are being hired for small parts and as extras. Production assistants are also often hired locally. This expansion provides one more job area you might explore.

All kinds of people sell products.

Commercials — Models and talent, including singers, are hired to do the visual or audio or both the visual *and* audio segments of commercials that will air on television, and to record the advertisements heard on radio. Many cities have advertising agencies and production facilities that produce the commercials aired locally, while most regionally and nationally aired commercials are made in large cities that have first-rate production houses and talent.

1. On-camera — The talent who work "on camera" are those actually seen in a television commercial. Their voices may or may not be included, and they may be featured principals or extras, background people whose faces are not clearly seen. These visual segments are filmed or videotaped.

2. Voice-over — The audio portions of television commercials and advertisements aired on radio are recorded by talent specializing in voice-over. Narrators, spokespeople, announcers, character voices, singers and sound effects artists deliver spoken or sung commercial messages. These are often recorded independently of the filming of the visual segment of the commercial.

Singers are used singly or in groups to record jingles and to provide background vocals for the segments using music. The commercial sound is specialized, requiring a special vocal brightness and ability to blend.

3. Testimonial commercials — With the new wave of truth in advertising, a banker who says he uses a certain aspirin must actually be a banker who uses that particular aspirin. "Real people" used in commercials are paid professional rates.

Programming — The same talent who use their vocal abilities to do commercial voice-over are also used to record non-broadcast programming. Such audio recordings are used in many areas. They accompany slide films, demonstrations at trade shows, and are used to make announcements in public places such as shopping malls, zoos and amusement parks. Prerecorded announcements are used as telephone messages, such as Dial-A-Prayer and Dial-A-Joke.

Professional voices are also used to narrate industrial, training, documentary and educational films. Educational cassette programs, such as studies in foreign languages, are recorded by voice-over talent, as are recordings of great literature, poetry and dramatic works.

Few occupations offer such great variety. You might start out simply with the right look, and with experience and instruction, develop other skills to make you more marketable. Indeed, there are many opportunities to work in modeling and commercials.

*It takes a special kind of
talent to do a voiceover . . .*

. . . or make a commercial.

2

Finding What Is Right for You: What You Have to Offer

With all of these different job opportunities, there must be some area in which you have interest and would like to get work. You know what the business has to offer; now it is time to discover what you have to offer it. As I said before, everybody has something special, something that can be developed and made appealing to a limited or wide range of buyers. It is essential, however, that you zero in on what it is you have to offer and find the best way to market it.

The Right Look

How you look is going to be a primary consideration in a business so emphatically concerned with appearance and visual appeal. If you don't satisfy the physical requirements of set fashion types or have a marketable commercial look for the city in which you're trying to find work, you may have difficulty getting jobs. You fit exact sizes, or you don't. You photograph well, are animated and project personality, or you don't. You can be assisted with your makeup and hair and taught how to pose, but you can't go from 5'3'' to 5'9'' and you can't be a funny commercial character if you don't have that look.

Particularly for fashion modeling, both live and photographic, you are going to have to satisfy certain requirements. The look they want, says a spokesperson for the Eileen Ford Agency, "is clean and fresh and doesn't really have an age attached to it. It's not teenage, but it's not over 25 either. It's just a very fresh, clean, natural look, with wide eyes and blondish or medium brown hair. Those are the girls who usually will work the quickest — there's always room for one more of those girls. The moment the advertisers and catalogs see a girl like that — a new face — in a magazine, they'll be on the phone to us asking who she is. And that's what makes a new New York girl look."

A fresh look.

Although the requirements for fashion modeling will vary from city to city by a few pounds or an inch or so, certain guidelines have been established. Women should be between 5'7" and 5'9" and wear a perfect size 6, 8, or 9. Since the clothing worn in style shows is not altered, it must look good on you as it comes off the rack. You need to have the proper proportions. In some cities, attractive women who wear half sizes are now finding work in live modeling.

Other physical aspects agents are looking for in female fashion and photography models are wide-set eyes, a clear complexion and good legs, well proportioned from knee to ankle. Wide hips and full busts — curves — are not assets in fashion modeling. They are looking for teeth that are white and even, with no chips or discoloration. A gap, though, can be an advantage, and has been for Lauren Hutton. Hair should be manageable, well-styled and not bleached. An extreme or faddish style will decrease your chances for many jobs — one fashion coordinator says she's seen enough of the Farrah Fawcett hairstyle, particularly on faces totally wrong for it, to last a lifetime! A style that can be worn in a variety of ways increases your marketability.

Age is also a determining factor for certain aspects of fashion modeling. The Eileen Ford Agency is not interested in seeing anyone over 22, and, for some girls, even that is late. Other agencies say 24 is the upper limit for women wanting to model. In some cities, women well into their 30s do runway and other live work, such as trade shows and catalog and advertising photography.

For men, in some instances, older is better. The wrinkles that bring an end to a woman's career can be an asset to a man's face. Those lines of character and maturity and those little gray hairs can add years to a man's modeling career. Men interested in modeling should be between 5'10" and 6'0" tall and wear a size 40 Regular. While the majority of modeling work is done by men in their late 20s, a man can work well into his 40s if he chooses.

The acceptability of facial hair on men varies from year to year and city to city. Conservative cities will require a conservative look for their advertisements, and even a moustache may raise a few eyebrows. A haircut that might bring raves one year will be totally wrong the next. Much of what is expected in a model's appearance is determined by the custom and taste of the city in which he is going to work. The agents are not likely to want to debate the merits of your facial hair with you, regardless of their personal feelings. They have to provide what the community wants. So, says an agency owner in

A look that works.

Dayton, Ohio, "If your beard is more important to you than trying to get work, keep the beard!"

You've got to have the right look. What sells in New York and on the cover of *Vogue* may not sell in Charleston, West Virginia. Smaller cities lean toward a prettier, healthier, more conservative and less severe look than what usually sells in New York. The customers must be able to relate to the models and what they are advertising, so a look that is exotic or bizarre is not appropriate for most cities. The more middle-American and average you look, the more likely you are to get certain kinds of work in most places.

Now if you're 5'0" tall and real sparkly and cute, or if you weigh 250 pounds and look like an Italian mama, or if you're balding and wear glasses and have a funny voice, or if you're Oriental or Jewish or black or seven years old or 77 years old, or if you have flaming red hair or no hair at all, or if you have freckles on your face or bucked teeth,

Personality and an interesting face make you right for commercial work.

This actor got more commercial work when he reduced the size of his afro.

chances are you have the perfect look for some sort of commercial work. Advertisers are not so much interested in a beautiful face as an interesting face. We have gone through an era of plastic prettiness followed by an era of outrageous characters in advertisements. Now we seem to be in an era of realism, evidenced by the increasing use of real people, "live testimonial," type commercials. Ordinary folks are who we're seeing in today's advertising.

Needless to say, the physical requirements for "ordinary folks" are not as rigorous as those for fashion modeling. Height is not a factor. In fact, shorter people are often hired for certain product advertising, furniture, for example, to make the product appear larger. Age is no obstacle. One New York agent says he is always looking for good grandmother and grandfather types. Many agents across the country mention that they could use more older people. They are constantly looking for a different, fresh face. That could be you!

There is work for minority people, although the amount and kinds of work seem to vary from year to year and, certainly, from city to city. If there is a large minority population in a major city, chances are the advertising will reflect the need to appeal to that large market.

Many agents say that black males with reasonable-sized hairdos that aren't disproportionate photographically, with minimal or no facial hair, who are good in front of a camera are few and far between. "That's a type that's hard to find, and that's a type that's needed."

One black actress in Los Angeles says that the minority people who work most often are the ones who have a strong, marketable ethnic look. "A good commercial type is an all-American look. For black people, it has to be a black look. My look goes in cycles. I'm considered too pretty. One friend of mine who has the same agency and goes out on all the same calls gets many more jobs than I do. She is an attractive girl, but she also has a more black look, a more ethnic look. Her features are more Negroid. She's good, and her look is the right look so she gets a lot more commercials."

Ah. "Her look is the right look." Look in a mirror. Don't you have the right look, too?

The Right Talents

It could be that you have an ability, a skill, an aptitude that makes you right for this business. It might be something you were born with, something in you that enjoys being in the spotlight, something that makes you a natural for the business. You may have the right voice, the right way of moving, the right presence in front of a camera or a live audience. Or it may be that you have spent time and money learning the skills that are right, studying acting technique, dance and voice. You might be charmingly cute or strikingly attractive; couple your right look with the right talents and you have an unbeatable combination.

Whether you are doing a live fashion presentation, a 30-second on-camera commercial spot or an industrial show, the ability to move well is a definite plus. You don't necessarily have to be a dancer, although having a dance background does make you right for more kinds of work. Someone who moves well is someone who is comfortable with his body, who has a sense of timing and pacing, who can react on cue in a smooth, believable, realistic manner. Someone who moves well has coordination and grace. The funny people in commercials who appear to be klutzes really aren't; it takes a keen sense of timing and the ability to juggle speech, movement and effective on-camera presentation.

Perhaps you have a beautiful or striking voice. A wide variety of voices are used in the making of commercials: soft, silky, sexy ones; abrasive and grabbing ones; voices that convince you of their authority and sincerity; the ones in whom you can have confidence; funny, laughable voices that imitate all kinds of animals; deep, masterful announcer voices. If you combine a voice that has the right commercial sound with the ability to breathe life into commercial copy and deliver it within the time frame, chances are you can do some kind of voice-over work.

Perhaps you have a beautiful and striking singing voice. The voices who sing jingles and provide the background vocals for television and radio commercials have a particularly commercial quality. It is a "pop" sound, and one that is likeable. "The commercial sound," says a top jingle singer, "is one that wears well." It must be one you can listen to time after time without really being aware of it. For that reason, it is important that the sound be anonymous, blended into the entire commercial presentation. You don't want to be so intrigued with or drawn to a singer's voice that you don't hear the

Dance ability is an asset.

commercial message! Jingle singers should also have musicianship as well as the right commercial sound. It is important that you be able to sight read so you can concentrate on creating sounds and establishing moods instead of worrying about notes.

Another skill you should have or develop is the ability to sell. The importance of this ability can't be too greatly stressed. You need to be able to sell, whether you're convincing an agent to sign you, an interviewer to hire you, or a photographer to test with you. You need to know how to promote yourself and how to promote goods and services at a trade show booth. You must be able to convince an audience to buy a product when you make a commercial and you must be able to convince professionals to work with you. If you have the right look and the right talent but you are too shy, lazy or unaggressive about marketing it, you will be disappointed with the business and it will be unaware of you. You need the look, the skills, the right attitude and the right sales ability in order to work to your potential.

Agents are looking for people with instinctive sales aptitude who speak with authority as well as sincerity, who are outgoing and able to interact well with other people, who are capable of handling themselves in any kind of situation, and who have poise. One woman who formerly worked as a model at trade shows and who now writes, produces and hires for them says she is interested in models and talent "who are aggressive — someone who is a little zany, someone who will invent ways of making people stop, who can take material that isn't working and be creative enough to make it work. Someone who can get the people interested, discover little jokes, and has a desire to keep an audience will work a lot."

What makes a winner? It is an inner quality, more than anything else.

"The looks in the business change. They change at the whim of the people in power. Not us, the agency heads, but the magazine editors, the magazine publishers, the top designers. There are a few people out there who can begin to create an important look, there are people who have a winning drive and personality and projection. Those are the winners!" states a modeling agent in New York.

Whether your technique has been learned and practiced or it comes to you naturally, agents, advertisers and producers are looking for exciting new faces. They are looking for people with energy and animation, models and talent who have a certain style. It is a personal presence that is evident in an office, audition, or on-camera. It is apparent in the way you carry yourself, your dress, your look, your way of speaking. It reflects confidence and an obvious enjoyment of what you're doing. If you have "it" — this flair or style or presence — and acquire an understanding of how to market "it," your success in the business is assured.

What the Different Work Opportunities Offer

You may have the right look and the right movements to do runway work but have greater interest in some other aspect of the business. You may do well in printwork but want to get involved in making commercials. Different job areas in the business will be attractive to you for different reasons: the financial rewards are said to be particularly attractive in one area; job security in a business not known for security is common in another; still another offers

such predictable scheduling that you can arrange the time when you will work and when you will be free months in advance. You may enjoy using makeup and working with your hair or you may be attracted to the end of the business where appearance is not so important. You may have a flair for dressing well and enjoy creating different looks; you may prefer working with the public doing promotional work. Your range of skills and your look may be broad enough that you will be able to choose the job areas in which you want to concentrate, so it is important that you know what they have to offer.

Many models and talent like working trade shows because, if they are pleased with the client and the client is pleased with their work, they are asked to do the show year after year and a pleasant working relationship is developed. If you work long enough and build up a list of satisfied clients from enough different shows, you can make up your schedule a year in advance and know when you will be working and when you will be free. This "guaranteed" work is uncommon in this business. Chances are that a client who is pleased with your work in Dallas might ask you to go with the show to Denver. If you enjoy travel, this field provides such opportunities.

Another advantage of working year after year for the same clients is that they may ask you to expand into other areas. People who began by working trade shows as models and narrators develop new skills and earn more money by writing, directing and managing the shows for their clients. They also become involved in hiring new models and costuming. If you are bright and clever, this field does have room for expansion.

Those interested in doing fashion shows who are right for this kind of work will be glad to know that the stores will train you if they like your look and think you have potential. If they intend to use you in their informal shows or on the runway and you have had no experience, they will work on the walk and the turns with you. In some cases the coordinator herself will work with you. Often they will ask an experienced model to spend time with you.

The stores may hold clinics a few times each year to train the novices breaking in and allow the experienced models to polish their routines. Such clinics may be held for a week at a time, four or five hours per day, with five to ten models in each class. These classes, taught by active professionals, are often free to the models the store is trying to develop.

Some people are born hams and will enjoy working in commercials. Others will find themselves tongue-tied with the idea of performance and, therefore, much prefer doing an occasional print job. Some people will want to work with their voices if they have the right commercial sound. The voice-over field is reputed in the business to be where the big money is. Talent are paid residuals, as are those actually seen in commercials, but the exposure and recognition are much less. People recognize and tire of faces before they are even aware of voices. So the same good voices are used over and over again, forming a select group of voice-over professionals who do very well financially and who enjoy a measure of job security.

Because he is used repeatedly, a voice pro can build working relationships with his clients and become the voice for a certain account for a period of time. A professional is also able to turn out a large number of spots in a small amount of recording time. One pro in Chicago did 13 television commercials and 15 radio spots for Pizza Hut — two years worth of advertising — in one four-hour session.

Your look and your abilities may dictate what you can do in the business, but also consider your inclinations.

Being Realistic About Yourself and Your Opportunities

Now that you know a bit more about what it takes to do certain jobs, it is time to zero in on what is right for you. You are going to have to be realistic about yourself, the physical changes it may be necessary to make before you are right for certain areas, what skills you can actually learn, and whether you do have the talent to develop. You will also have to be realistic about what job opportunities are available in your hometown.

There is work for models and talent in towns and cities across the nation. There is work for models in every town with a department store that has informal or fashion show presentations. There is work for talent in every city with television and radio stations that air advertisements for local businesses. While it is true that the greatest volume of work in this industry is done in Chicago, Los Angeles and New York, the city you live in probably has some professional activity to offer you.

As you can see, how you define success and how many and what kinds of jobs you get are largely going to be dictated by the city in which you work and the extent of your ambition. Doing a local commercial or two, several photo jobs and a few trade shows

each year might make you a busy pro in Cleveland, Ohio, and it might provide ego gratification and a supplement to your income. But it would hardly shine your shoes in New York City. You must have a realistic idea of what you can do and how much you can develop in the city in which you're trying to find work.

Few cities have the kinds of work or the volume of work to support full-time professionals. This means that most of you will be working on a part-time basis, competing for whatever work is available, and regarding your income from this business as a supplement to other earnings. The big money in fashion is in New York, where most of the nation's clothing catalogs are photographed, where the designer houses are, and where the fashion and glamour magazines are published. The big money in commercials is in the national and network advertisements, and most of them are produced in Los Angeles and New York. "Let's not kid ourselves," says one Boston agent. "They come here for one reason. They're not coming here for our production facilities or our talent, and we do have some good talent. They're coming here for the surrounding historical sites. That's it. This says Boston. That's the only time we get them big, when they have to come here for a reason."

Much of the fashion and advertising photography you see in your local newspaper advertisements and Sunday magazines is not done in your city, no matter where you live. If you live in Cincinnati and are aware that Proctor and Gamble is headquartered there, don't assume that Proctor and Gamble's national commercials are done in Cincinnati. Many large companies are centered in the Midwest, but it is quite likely that their commercials are produced by ad agencies in New York or Los Angeles.

It is somewhat ironic that the creative grasses seem to be greener in some other city — which may, in truth, offer better production facilities or a larger talent pool. Advertising agencies are often unaware of what their own cities have to offer, because they are accustomed to traveling elsewhere for their creative endeavors. Advertisers in a city the size of Charleston, West Virginia, may go to Cleveland to produce their ads, Cleveland may go to Chicago, and Chicago may go to New York without ever looking into the talent that Chicago has to offer. It would be hard to find a group of people more nervous about their jobs and covering their tails than the folks you'll find in advertising.

You must remember to be realistic when seeking information about the business. Someone who promises that you can become a professional model in a small town — or earn your living — is leading you astray. The people who actually are in positions to offer sufficient amounts of well-paying work don't offer job guarantees. Even people who have signed with the big agencies in New York are let go if they just aren't working out. You may be given your chance at the big time, working in New York or Los Angeles, and still strike out. It happens all the time. So be realistic about what you can expect in your hometown and about your chances of making it big.

You have got to be realistic about your appearance. While your look is going to make you right for a lot of work, it is going to limit you from a lot of work. You can't have it all ways. "A lot of talent don't realize how they are perceived by others," comments one agent. "They just aren't seeing in the mirror what we see here in the office." It is hard to be objective about yourself, but it is crucial in this business.

You are going to be "typed" or categorized according to your appearance. You may find that your type is at variance with what you see or how you would like to be seen. I have worked with a lot of people who would like to think of themselves as fashion types when they are actually commercial types. They want to be photographed in furs or bikinis when I know they'd have more of a chance trying to sell coffee.

An actor in Chicago says "I have trouble viewing myself in a particular mold because I get called for totally different categories, different types. I was put in a nurd category one day, and the next day as a nice-looking guy. I know I have always been put in a young category, which means I am reaching when I play a young father, which is chronologically what I'm right for. But I look in the mirror one day and see the nurd type — which I'm not real pleased with — and then another day I'll see a straight announcer or straight on-camera presenter. So I just don't know." Once you have been put into a category, you may not be called for anything else, no matter how gifted an actor you are or how much you protest.

It is important that you be willing to make the changes — reasonable changes — that an agent might suggest. You may be asked to lose weight, have your hair re-styled, your makeup redone, your eyebrows re-shaped, to shave off facial hair, have unsightly teeth capped — whatever improvements have to be made in order for the agent to get you work. You will have to be ready and able to hear this kind of criticism, and willing to go to the expense or effort of making these changes. "We've had people who were

here at our door two or three times and never came in because they were afraid we wouldn't like them, afraid we would tell them there was something wrong. They didn't want to be criticized," says one agent. You may be fine, but you may still have to make some changes.

But the changes must be reasonable. There have been people all too willing to have plastic surgery performed on their noses, legs, bottoms and faces, convinced that this one physical change was going to open the doors of the industry to them.

"I know people in the business who are very indiscriminate about telling people to have all their wisdom teeth pulled because it will do something for their bone structure," says a spokesperson for Wilhelmina's agency in New York. "I just don't like to play God with people's lives. We are very careful about that. There is no guarantee that the change will be worth it." He has recommended one nose job in 27 years in the business, and the girl was accepted into the agency following the operation. But there are no guarantees that major surgery is going to increase your chances of finding an agent or getting work. If you're already an established professional, surgery can prolong your career for a few years, but surgery is a very "iffy" supposition for a beginner.

Some things you can change and some you cannot. You have a basic look. You can learn to do corrective makeup, you can slim down, you can do your hair differently, but there is still a certain basic you that is not going to be altered drastically. No matter how hard you try, how positively you approach it, you may not be right for some jobs. An agent in New York says that he's "had people totally wrong for the business come in for interviews. With one girl, I was curious, because I'd never seen anybody who was more wrong for this business. She was unattractive and wrong in every respect. I asked her why she was so determined to be a model, and she finally told me it was because her analyst told her she could do anything she wanted to do. *That's not true.* This is a narrow, totally visual business. If somebody doesn't fit into a specific physical pattern, there is nowhere for her to go." Even if your mother, your best friend, your hairdresser, your modeling school teacher, or your analyst tells you you have what it takes to be a model, it may not be so. It could be that you can work in the business, but not as a fashion model. Follow your dream, but know when to separate your dream from your reality.

You may find, under certain circumstances, that a department store will accept a girl who is 5'3" for runway work. Occasionally a photographer will use a

A young father . . .

. . . a businessman-narrator . . .

. . . or your average klutz.

girl who is six feet tall. But these are the exceptions, not the rule. "No matter how gorgeous you are, if you are 5'2", I can't get you work. The same applies if you are too tall. If you are 6' — I'm talking about women, of course — I can't do much for you," says an agent in Washington D.C. So end the dreams of every tall girl's mother. Accept who you are; there is not much you can actually do to change.

One model who lives in Indianapolis and who works out of several cities confides that "I am a girl who cannot work in New York. I'm 5'5". I could lie and say I'm 5'7", but this is what these young girls out there don't know — you can't lie to anybody in this business. I can walk in, and they can look at me and say 'you are 5'5'.' I might have six-inch heels on, but they know. They have an eye. They know how much I weigh. I can fudge only by a pound or two. You're dealing with experienced people. I can't work in New York in modeling. In the Midwest, I can do everything, and I have been. I have been making an incredible living in the Midwest since I was 19 years old, and I just hit 31. It's marvelous, because here I can cover every facet of the business."

The beginner in this business is usually overly concerned with details. Slight imperfections and unkind fate will generally be blamed for holding back the beginner's career. The seasoned professional, whether model or talent, accepts his or her look, is comfortable with it, and alters it as necessary to keep up with or anticipate changes in the industry. The professional is confident in his or her continuing marketability, and that confidence is what makes all the difference. Accept yourself. Be realistic about the job opportunities available to your type and about what is available to you in your hometown.

A Special Message to Actors and College Theater Majors

Why do you people rate a special message? It's because so many of you have such conflicting feelings about getting work in commercials and modeling. Some of you say that you'd rather starve than prostitute your craft by going commercial, and others say that they'd do anything for money. Certainly a well-informed, resourceful actor or actress fresh out of college should consider the potential of his or her theatrical abilities.

While you're waiting for your big break in films or on Broadway, how are you going to support yourself? It's grand if you have doting parents, a supportive spouse or a generous patron, but even these sources run dry at some point. Many actors and actresses end up as waiters, waitresses and bartenders to make ends meet while waiting to hit the big time. Is this less of a prostitution than working in commercials? If you're willing to expand your craft and develop different techniques, if you're able to communicate effectively in an environment quite unlike the stage, your talents and abilities can provide a comfortable living, creative and challenging work, contacts in a business that can carry you to New York and Hollywood, and a lifestyle that will allow you to support your theater habit.

If you're still feeling conflicted when you enter an agent's office to register, don't let it show. Many of you turn the agents off. I was surprised, during the course of my agent interviews, to find how strongly some of the agents feel about you new people. A lot of you bother them. You're too pushy, you're unrealistic, you're uninformed, you're unprepared, defensive, or too sensitive to their professional assessments. Many of them said that a lot of you aren't seeing in the mirror what they're seeing in their offices.

If your attitude about this work is that it's beneath you, if you feel that you'll condescend to grace the agency with your registration until the big break comes, don't bother. The agents are busy as it is with hopefuls who are willing to do whatever is necessary to work in this business, people filled with enthusiasm, energy and determination. Most agents are not interested in working with and developing a talent who intends to leave them and who makes that intention obvious.

It's a shame that hundreds of colleges and universities are turning out theater graduates who know nothing about marketing the skills they have been taught. It's unfortunate that many of your professors and instructors are people who are as blind as you are to the procedures of getting theatrical as well as commercial work, who can't tell you how or where to go to find work, who don't know themselves what a professional actor's photograph or resume should look like. It's not your fault, but many of you are not of any interest to the agents simply because you know nothing about the business and go to them totally unprepared. One agent in Boston says, "I'm not interested in theater majors. I can't sell theater majors. They just don't adapt, without any experience, to cold script reading and to being in front of that tube. That tube will wipe out a Shakespearian actor!"

The following statements are made by former theater majors who now are in some way connected to this business.

A professor, theater department of Northwestern University — "There used to be the old ethic that, if you were an actor, having a family and a house and all the other increments of our civilization were somehow never to be had by you. The actor was some sort of an outcast. That's left over from the 16th century. It's time we got rid of that. You are either a starving artist or you live in a mansion in Beverly Hills — never the twain shall meet. That's ridiculous, now, because there are so many areas in which an actor's craft, skills or talent can be utilized for incredible money which can, in effect, support his theater habit. I don't know any successful actor in the theater who does not, in some form or another, involve himself in commercial work at some level. The only people who don't are people who are consistently and continually employed at the highest salaries within the theater. But the number of those against the number of people registered in the (actors') unions is miniscule.

"Any students who don't explore the full potential that their craft allows them to are idiots."

A New York theatrical and commercial agent — "I'm not interested in anybody who does not have theatrical training. Those are the people I object to, people who just happen to have a good look and lucked out in commercials and now want to be film stars. I guess because I trained in theater for a long time and most of my important clients have a heavy theatrical background, those are the kind of people that this agency is looking for.

"Be prepared in terms of training and experience. Those are the two most important things, I think. I do think that agents in New York are more accessible than agents in California, that they are more in-terested in and more willing to see new people, young people, talented people. We get over 100 pictures a week, and we select out of that 100 pictures at least 20 people to be seen, so we are available and accessible to new talent.

"Knowing the way the business works in New York, I also find it unfortunate that more college situations don't teach or prepare people for the New York situation . . . if they are talented actors, the easiest way to make money quickly in New York is to do either modeling or commercials if, in fact, you have the right look. And for those people, and other people as well, talented people, I think it is unfortunate that they don't teach a commercial reading course so that the kids would come to New York prepared to win commercials. They don't tell them the right kind of resume to have, the right kind of picture — I mean that kids come to New York, talented kids who have had four years of theatrical training at a good college situation, who don't know about pictures, who don't know about resumes, who have to be told all this by someone."

A New York voice-over talent, who makes over $100,000 annually, on the occasion of leaving college — "Well, I know what I want to be doing next year, but I know how big the abyss is between where I am now and where I would like to be. And there is no way to jump across it. That leap is too far. All you can do is just dive right in and say 'How's the water, what's going on?'"

Modeling, commercials, radio work, photo work, industrial films, trade shows, soaps — they can all supply an actor with enough money so that he can lead a comfortable and secure financial life and still have the freedom to explore and gratify his artistic needs. Let your talents and skills work for you, theater people. Investigate the possibilities of finding work in commercials and modeling. There is something right for you!

3

What It Takes to Develop a Successful Career

Now that you are aware of the kinds of work opportunities that exist in this business and have zeroed in on what is most interesting or available to you, there is more you should consider before you actually make an investment, financial or emotional, in starting your career. The business does have a lot to offer but it also demands a great deal.

The amount of time, energy, faith, commitment — and luck — it takes to develop a successful career is enormous. It is for this reason that many agents, particularly those in big cities, only want to see people for whom this business is *the only choice,* the only kind of work from which they would derive satisfaction. Because it can be difficult and trying, these agents look for people who want to be involved so much that nothing else matters, people who would be miserable unless they were involved, people who intend to make this a career. They advise you to do something else if you have a choice. If you are intent on breaking into the Big Time or if you are just trying to get an occasional job in your hometown, the business is going to make demands of you. This section will familiarize you with the conditions you accept and the risks you take in pursuing this kind of work.

Working Conditions

Unless you knew something about the business before you started reading this book or you are just naturally realistic, chances are that you're going to discover that modeling and working in commercials is not what you'd thought it was going to be. You may have been harboring secret hopes of being discovered, thinking that it was necessary to go to school and spend money to "learn" to model or that the actual jobs would be lots of fun and excitement. You may have been attracted to the business because it offers good money — you've heard models make $50, $75 and even more than $100 per hour. Chances are good that your expectations will not be met. The business is just that, a business, and while its facade indicates glamour and big bucks, insiders know it to be fickle and demanding. Devastating, even. You're aware of the few who do wind up on the covers of *Vogue* and *Seventeen* or on the Kellogg's cereal boxes. You don't know about the hundreds who were not selected. If you have a flair for it, the right look, the right skills, the right attitude, you will probably not find the actual work too difficult. But getting into the business and staying in it is hard work.

Whether you intend to make this a full-time profession or you just want to get what jobs you can in addition to your regular job, you must be available for auditions and actual jobs. If you are ambitious, much of your time will be spent promoting yourself. You need to consider the demands of the work itself, what is necessary to get that work and whether the reality of the business is close enough to your fantasy to make your efforts worthwhile.

What It Means To Be Self-Employed

Models and the people who work in commercials are self-employed. You will not find regular employment in one company, with one boss, earning a weekly or monthly salary, as a model or commercial talent. You are not looking for "a" job in modeling; you will be distributing photos, auditioning and interviewing to land as many jobs as possible. A job may be a one-hour photo session, a style show, a commercial that takes a full day or two to shoot, or a trade show lasting for two weeks.

You may get some of your jobs through an agent, you may get some of your jobs on your own. You may work a lot one month and not at all for the next two months. You may do one three-hour commercial session and earn thousands of dollars for those three hours of work. Times will be busy; times will be slow. There's not much prediction or control concerning when you'll be working and when you'll be in a slump.

Few of you will be busy constantly. You will not know when a job will be coming in nor are your jobs likely to be conveniently bunched together. "The thing about this business that aggravates me," comments a New York model, "is its ups and downs. It runs hot and cold. You're going to have weeks that are really busy, and then you're going to have weeks that aren't busy at all. It's annoying. I like to work and keep busy. Or you may have a booking first thing in the morning and one late in the afternoon and you've got the whole day between the two with nothing to do. It's a small thing, but if it happens every day you don't know whether to go home or whether to stay in town. You have to be prepared to take the rough with the smooth."

It is particularly important that you are aware of the sporadic nature of the business if you live in a smaller city where it is likely that weeks or even months may pass in between calls. Agents in small cities say that it is difficult to motivate their people, to keep their models and talent enthusiastic and professional when there are so few calls to send them on.

In spite of the lack of predictability, no matter where you live, you are expected to be available when the call finally does come in. Part of being professional is being available, whether you have another job or not. One voice-over talent in New York says that "sometimes they call me at 10:30 in the morning and say 'Can you be at J. Walter Thompson in an hour for an audition?' I have to be available, I have to make myself available Monday through Friday, 9 a.m. to 5 p.m. That's part of my job. But all of my work amounts to — if you added it up and put it all together into eight-hour days, five-day weeks — at the most, four weeks a year, including auditions. If I could fix it so that all of my work was back to back, and I did six hours a day for those four weeks — I'd take the rest of the year off!" This fellow puts in those hours and makes a six-figure annual income.

The pace of the business will be determined by the city in which you work, but be aware that you will be needed during regular business hours for most modeling and commercial jobs. Rarely will the jobs be dictated by your availability. Do not assume that you will be able to work modeling into your spare time; very little is done in the evenings or on weekends. Many agents will not list you if you live at too great a distance from the city where the work is going on, as you may be called in the morning to be at an audition early that afternoon. Many agents will not list you if you mention how difficult it will be for you to get away from your regular job. You must be available for interviews and jobs during regular business hours.

If you do have a job, it is essential that your employer know that you are trying to get work in modeling and commercials and that there will be times when you will have to be absent from work. And therein lies one hang-up. Few employers are willing to spare you the time you will need for auditions, jobs and rounds (if it is essential that you make rounds). If you are self-employed, a sales rep, or able to name your own hours, you're in good shape. For this reason, many would-be models and talent take jobs tending bar or waiting on tables in the evenings so that their days are free to pursue their real interests. If your schedule is not flexible, if you say no to an agent or a client once too often, you'll find yourself out of work. The call won't come again.

There is no guarantee of work, not even when you're signed with an agent. The more effort and time you put into generating interest in you as a professional, the more jobs you are likely to get. It is largely up to you to advertise, promote and present a more appealing product than anyone else has to offer, and, if freelancing, to negotiate the deal and collect the fee. As a self-employed person, you will have to keep your own records and see to it that your taxes are prepared. You will be in business for yourself, and only those of you who treat this as a business will meet success in it.

Financial Considerations

If you're thinking of entering the business in order to get rich quick, forget it! With those reports of models making $100 an hour and money constantly pouring in from commercial residuals, many people think they're going to strike it rich in this industry. There is a fantasy multiplication that implies that with an eight-hour work day, at $100 or even $50 an hour, you'll be able to retire after a few months' work!

Nothing could be further from the truth. No one in this business works a 40-hour week consistently. Even in the big cities, seasoned professionals may go for weeks without a call for an interview or job. In a small city, where the volume of work just isn't that great and the likelihood of a good talent or model quickly becoming overexposed is high, you may go for months between calls. And even when you are called, it might be for a one-hour photo booking. For most of you, modeling will be part-time and the money you make will supplement your regular income. Given the way the business operates, you may not even see your extra income for 90 days or more.

Your potential costs to enter the business include:

- Photographs

- Duplications or printed composites

- Typing and printing of resume

- Voicetape (demo or jingle tape)

- Duplications and packaging of tape

- Wardrobe and accessories

- Hair and makeup styling

- Makeup

- Portfolio

- Answering service

All or some of these expenses will apply to you.

Note: In most cases, there will be no charge for registering with a reputable agency. You may be assessed a nominal sum to cover the cost of printing your photo on the agency headsheet or the cost of mailing out your promotional material.

There is no guarantee that you will make back even the money you spend on these initial necessities. You'll have to view this money as an investment, almost as if you are playing the stock market, in that you won't see any return for some period of time. But here you have more control over your investment. Your own persistence and ambition can get your investment dollars working for you.

There are some hidden costs as well. Whether you're looking around for an agent, going to an interview, making rounds, or traveling to a job, you're going to spend money. You will have to be mobile, and you will have to know how to get around in your city. If you don't have a car, you will have to know how to use public transportation and you will spend money to ride the bus, subway, el, cable car, trolley, taxi, train or whatever you take. If you own a car, you will be spending money on gas, tolls, parking and the inevitable tickets you will get when the job goes overtime. How the industry is spread out in your city will determine your methods of transportation. You could spend a whole day walking and not see everyone connected with the industry in a five-block stretch in downtown Chicago, but you would need a car to merely see several agents in Los Angeles or Atlanta.

Don't forget to include the costs of eating downtown, which you'll probably have to do on occasion, and making phone calls to confirm appointments, touching base with the agency, and checking with your spouse. You could spend over $1, not including a tip, for a cup of coffee down the street from Eileen Ford's agency in New York; and you could spend a minimum of 25 cents each time you make a call in the Miami area. Depending on where you live, these costs can spiral.

You may decide at some point to take a class or get private coaching from a professional in order to increase your marketability and develop different skills. These lessons aren't free. You will spend money to keep up with changes in the industry, purchasing new shades of makeup and new styles as needed. If you send out mailings to promote yourself, the material itself and the postage will be an expense. You may need to hire an accountant to do your taxes for you. Even as you become successful, you will continue to invest money in your career.

Asked what information is most important to new people just entering the business, an agent in Boston advises "Be prepared — you must invest in the tools of the trade before you can expect to be regarded at all — you must spend money to make money." When deciding on this as a career, keep in mind that you will need to make those initial expenditures, an investment on which there is no guaranteed return.

"People who approach this business with the idea of making a living are kidding themselves. There may be a few who can honestly say they are making a living. But your Twiggies are temporary people, your Cybil Sheppards and Farrah Fawcetts . . . they've made a lot of money but how long it is going to last is debatable. A secretary can type, she's got a job that's steady. But the model — here today, gone tomorrow. Today they love her, tomorrow they don't even like her.''

That sentiment comes from an agent of many years in Pittsburgh, but it is echoed by a male fashion model in his 20s who is currently very much in demand in New York. "I do make what I consider to be quite a good living at it. It is a business that you have to make good money in, and save some of it while you are still in the business because it doesn't last forever. You'd have to be pretty damn silly to think that you can keep on doing this!''

Still another professional, a commercial spokeswoman in Chicago, adds that "the older you get the fewer auditions you are right for, are called on, and so your work load is cut down. You can't look forward to as much money or count on earning "X" amount of money per year. Unless you get into voice work or something where the wrinkles don't matter, you have to face the possibility of getting into some other field. You can't model forever.''

One agent says that models seem to last about five years in the business. The first two years are spent breaking in and getting experience, two years really working, and that last year is spent easing out of the business. Few, she adds, have much money saved or invested when they leave modeling, no matter how successful their careers have been. Because of the sporadic nature of the business, and because it is fickle, you cannot count on regular income and you cannot assume that your look or skill will be marketable forever. Make hay while the sun shines and invest it wisely or develop new skills and other interests.

Dealing with Rejection, Moving Toward Success

Just as much as you'll have to be in a position to make a financial investment, be prepared for a few emotional upheavals as well. Your decision to try your hand at this business may affect those around you, and you, yourself, may experience doubts, insecurities and feelings with which you've never before had to deal.

Just remember that it is a business, that decisions are ultimately being made for economic reasons — no one is out to get you personally — and are out of your control at any rate. It is your business to understand the business, to accept it for better or worse, to know that there will be punches, and to learn how to roll with them.

For example, if you're shooting on location and there is no other option, you may be asked to change clothing behind a bush, in a van, or in the privacy created by an open car door. If facilities are crowded in a dressing room, and they often are, you will have no time and no space in which to be modest. Time is money, and your priority will have to be how quickly and how carefully you can change outfits.

You may also meet people whose sexuality differs from your own. If you are straight, chances are very good that you'll come into contact with some people in the industry who are gay. If that fact bothers you, reconsider your decision to try the business. If you are gay, many of the people you come in contact with will be straight. A lot of clients will also be very straight-laced. Be whatever you want to be, but be aware, warns a Midwestern agent, "that if your sexual preferences are obviously offensive to the client or potentially distracting to the purpose of the job, you won't be booked.''

You will have to be resilient in handling the many rejections that are a predictable part of this business. You're simply not going to be right for every job; and if you're going to beat yourself each time you hear the word "no," you're in for a rough time. You may not be the right size or the right coloring; you may not have the right look or the right voice; you may not match the man they've already selected to play the husband in the floor wax commercial. Rejection is an undeniable aspect of this business.

One model/actress says, "Mistake number one was going through the period where I took rejections as being personal. I would cry and say 'I know that the girl who got it has darker hair. Maybe I should do my hair darker. I know the girl who got it was taller. Okay, I can't make myself taller, but I think I'll go on a crash diet to make myself skinny.' Well, I have a certain body structure. I can lose 10 pounds, and I'm still going to be this wide at my shoulders and this wide at my hips, and then I'll just look gaunt. That's not going to do me any good. So I'd say, 'She's flatter-chested. Maybe I'll make myself flatter-chested.' Going through all that personal comparison instead of having the experience, the maturity and the knowledge of the business to know that it had nothing to do with it. They liked me! I was good! I just wasn't what they were looking for.''

Sometimes, when you're not what they're looking for, they're going to be blunt. The critical comments are often harsh. You're likely to hear that you look too old, your legs are too short, your eyes are too wide, your accent is awful, your voice is all wrong, and that you're not whatever they're looking for. You're still a fine person, you're just not what they want. If you interpret every phone message that is not returned as a personal affront, a lack of interest in you, just another in a long line of rejections, then you're going to be a pretty sad, dejected person. You're still fine, your party just didn't have time to return the call! Place your call again!

You must know that you will, and then be able to, fail. If you cannot handle failure, go no further. The ratio between the average number of auditions you do and the jobs you get may be 11 to one. That applies to the pros, too. You may fail 10 times for every time you succeed. If the success doesn't outweigh the failure for you, financially and emotionally, you're in serious trouble.

You will need the ability to make decisions and be satisfied with them. Indecision, procrastination and beating yourself for past mistakes are all unproductive pastimes that can drain you of the energy you need to get out and get work. You will have to make choices between paths that will bring immediate gratification and paths that will insure future success. You're going to hear conflicting opinions about any direction you take; one agent will commend your choice and another will condemn it. One client will want one thing from you; another will want something else. This industry is full of people who are full of opinions, and you are going to have to learn to be selective about which suggestions you act on. You will have to take the path with which you're most comfortable, and sometimes you may be wrong. You just want to be right a lot more often than you're wrong.

You're going to need commitment, drive and self-discipline to get you past the tough times. And there will be tough times. You will need the energy to continue, even when you're feeling defeated, inadequate and frustrated because you can't see the results of what you're doing. You're going to have to live and eat well enough to stay healthy; you're going to have to sleep enough to be alert and look fresh throughout the day; you're going to have to support yourself well enough to enable you to dress well and equip yourself with the tools of the trade. This all takes commitment.

Your Life Outside the Business

As if it's not enough that you have to handle the tensions of competition and the unavoidable failures, you will also have to deal with criticism from professionals, your friends, family and you, yourself. Not regarding sound professional advice could cost you jobs. In a field so bitterly competitive, however, don't be surprised to discover your friends in the business undermining your confidence, telling you you're wrong for commercial work, you're not pretty enough to be a model, you've got the wrong complexion, that the coach with whom you've been working for the past 14 months is no good. You're going to have to learn to distinguish bad advice from good advice.

At a time when you most need support and understanding, you may find that your interest in this business is being met at home with jealousy and contention. ''People in this business have a higher marriage wipe-out rate than other industries,'' comments one commercial photographer in Cleveland, who cites the long hours, odd hours, estrangement and dedication to the work as explanations for the statistic. ''When you're doing your work, nothing else gets involved. That's it. It's very hard for husbands, wives, lovers, children, dogs and cats to understand that. It's an exclusive kind of thing, and it causes resentment.''

Even if you have a partner or family who is supportive of your efforts, you may find yourself dealing with a load of guilt. Men who have been raised to believe that they should be fulfilling the provider role may have to deal with the fact that their partners are going to be making ends meet until they have established themselves in the business. And that's a gamble, for they may not ever get to that point.

Moms and dads who work are going to have to deal with the fact that there will be some weeks when they may not see their children very much, and that there are others to take into consideration when planning to make rounds and go to interviews and jobs.

One working mother says: ''Having a child gives me more responsibility, definitely. I have a lot more factors to think about every time I take a job. Can I get somebody to take her to school, who's going to pick her up, what about the babysitter, what if she's not available — there are so many more things to consider. But no, I don't feel hindered by her, it just takes more time and planning. No, that's wrong — I do feel hindered. I'll tell you where I'm hindered — I have to take less work. I choose to take less work because I am a mother. I have to turn down jobs in order to be with my husband and my child, and I have to keep a check and balance. There are weeks when things get out of proportion and I'm gone the whole week, but when that happens I take off the whole week following. As long as I keep things in check and balance, it works very smoothly. I have chaotic days like anybody who works; nonetheless, as long as I give my family time, they give me what I need.''

Many successful professionals admit that they owe a great deal of their success to their partners. After doing battle and being rejected time and time again downtown, there's nothing like going home to a friend who is supportive of your efforts, who will soothe you and rebuild your confidence to face the lions once again. Someone who understands the business, is not jealous of the time you give to it, and who enjoys or can tolerate occasional solitude is going to be a real source of strength for you.

You may find the pursuit of work, success and acceptance somewhat unbalancing. There are workaholics in this field, as elsewhere, but here all the energy is directed toward yourself. It is very easy to — almost difficult not to — become an overwhelming, egocentric bore. You've got to have other things going on in your life. At the same time you're pursuing your career, have other diversions to keep you going. It is very easy and very destructive to totally immerse yourself in this business. There is a life beyond your work, and there are other people with other concerns just as valid and interesting to them as yours are to you; don't forget it.

You're taking chances when you enter this business. Whether you measure your success by doing a few jobs each year or by becoming a full-time professional, the process of becoming a working model or commercial talent is going to put you through some changes.

Farewell to Fantasy

There are no overnight successes. If you want to work as a model or commercial talent, you will have to pursue this work. You will not be discovered in a convention, pageant, school or drugstore. If you are fortunate enough to be approached by a legitimate agent or photographer, the motivation or drive to become a working professional will still have to be sustained by you. You will have to appreciate and utilize salesmanship when you first approach an agent, audition for a job, and then do the job. There will be much to learn and you — not a sponsor — will have to accept the demands and conditions of the business. No one can do it for you.

In addition to having the right look and the right skills, it's your duty to be a business person, to know how to sell, how to support yourself, and how to manage money. You must keep your agent or agents and, most importantly, your clients happy and excited about your work. One photographer comments that "the people who get into this business, more than any other business, are dilettantes to begin with and that's why you see such short tenure at all the (modeling and talent) agencies. Nothing succeeds like hard work!''

If you think that each job is going to be champagne and beautiful music, curious people standing around watching, everyone acting as if it is one big party, you're in for a surprise. You will be expected to stay alert and remain cool and fresh-looking under hot lights, holding positions but making them look casual and natural, pinned or taped into the garments you must make look good. You will wait, relaxing but on your toes, while a commercial set is arranged, lighted, dressed and wired for sound. Then you may be expected to do take after take, repeating the same words, gestures, timing, trying to give a perfect reading for a director who may not know what he wants. You'll be on your feet all day at a trade show, and if it's one open to the general public, you may be coughed on, leered at, and regarded as an object by all sorts of humanity. Whether you're advertising camping equipment or swimwear, you may be shooting next summer's photo in October or March, and that's going to demand some acting to hide those goosebumps!

The professionals with whom you're going to work may be temperamental, difficult or demanding. They may know exactly what they want, and you'll have to strive for precisely that, or they may not know what they're doing and provide you with no direction. Their reputations and the accounts they're working on are always on the line. You may bear the brunt of the pressure they feel.

Hours are totally unpredictable. An agent in Detroit says that "with car advertisements, for instance, so much of what is shot is done on location. Due to getting a nice soft light and not shooting in the heat of noon with glaring sun, much of it is shot at dawn and at dusk. You may have to go out on location somewhere and be there at 5:30 in the morning, and you may have to be somewhere else at 6:30 or 7:00 that night until it gets dark. The glamour soon wears thin. I think that people who really stay with it find other aspects that are fulfilling to them.''

You may be asked to advertise a product you don't believe in, or to do something you think is just plain silly. One model/actress confides that "there are times when I really am not proud of all the things I have to say about a product or the way we have to hype things that really aren't that good — it makes me feel uncomfortable about the work." If they're paying you, they're not asking for your opinion of their product or the way in which they're merchandising it. You'll be expected to carry it off professionally.

You won't be discovered. Statistics indicate that only a small percentage of the people involved in these businesses earn enough to make a living. Rejection is inevitable and often presented harshly. You are a commodity; your look may be marketable one season and passé the next. Even if you are 5'9" with classic cheekbones or you have a wonderful announcer's voice, you won't make it in the business if you don't have the right personality and drive. It takes hard work and time to get established as a professional. It takes investment and faith. If you don't enjoy the pressure of competition and performance, there's no sense in going much further. If you can't live with the knowledge that the business is fickle, that one day they may no longer have use for you, spare yourself. Don't get involved. If, on the other hand, you can accept all of this, knowing that it's a risk but still determined to get involved, read on!

One Last Word of Caution — The Con Games

There are a few more things you should know about the business. For every legitimate agent, reputable photographer and newsletter, magazine or seminar that truly offers useful information, there are dozens of frauds, swindlers and cheats. If you're just getting started, chances are that you'll have difficulty telling a line of bull from a genuine job offer, that you won't know which people carrying cameras are professional photographers and which are just trying to con you. That's exactly what these con artists are counting on. Your lack of knowledge, your lack of experience, your willingness to hear and believe that you're pretty enough to be a model, or that your child is perfect for television commercials, or that there is some easy way or kind person to help you break into the business — these things make you vulnerable. These swindlers know it, and they're going to try to cash in on that vulnerability. Don't doubt for a moment that there are unscrupulous peo-

ple in your own town willing and ready to take advantage of your curiosity about modeling and commercial work.

You may be approached by mail. You may receive a letter stating that you have been recommended for modeling by so-and-so, that classes are being offered at a discount for a limited time only, or that your child was seen at school or in a local play and shows real potential. Your name, most often, has been purchased. There are businesses that sell computerized lists of names and addresses in any category imaginable. You may have been selected by neighborhood, income bracket, elementary school, by hospital and date of birth of your child — you name it. Often these companies will offer to "manage" the careers of your children for you, which means that you will pay an additional percentage above and beyond what you will have to pay an agent. A manager or management association does not get work for you. You can't really expect a business located hundreds or even thousands of miles away from you to represent you as a model or commercial talent. This business just isn't run through the mails. You will have to decide if you need this management or if what you really need is to find out for yourself how to go about getting work in your area.

You may be approached in person. While walking down a street, sitting in a restaurant or shopping in a store, someone may walk up to you and ask if you're a professional model. Blushing with pleasure you reply that no, you're not, but you had thought about it from time to time . . . and the con game is on. He's a photographer, he's a magazine publisher, he runs a modeling agency, he works in advertising and knows of a job you'd be just right for, or his brother-in-law runs an agency or photographs models for Playboy, and on it goes. I say he, but there are shes who can con, too.

You may read advertisements for these management companies, photographers, schools, seminars, and newsletters in newspapers and magazines. They may be posted in supermarkets and restaurants. You may even see such advertisements on the walls of agency and union offices. Before making any calls, ask someone in the office if he or she is familiar with the work of the individuals offering the services or if such services are recommended. Quite often you'll find that classes and private consultations are being offered by "professionals" no one in the business knows or has ever seen.

Quite frequently the newspaper ads will go something like this: "Female photography models wanted, no experience necessary, 19 to 35, attractive with good figure. Excellent pay. Send photo, detailed information, and phone number to . . . ." Forget it. Why do you suppose they are looking for people with no experience? If you were experienced, you'd know this setup was fishy. You'd know that this is not how professional models go about getting work. The real work goes through established businesses. Established businesses who really have work for professional models and talent do not often advertise in newspapers.

A lot of the people who have been conned say that "it looked like the real thing. He had all the equipment, there were pictures on the walls, all the lighting and stuff . . ." If you are just beginning, how do you know what to expect in a photographer's studio anyway? Anyone with enough money can buy a Nikon camera and lighting equipment. Anyone with enough money can have business cards printed. Anyone with enough money can rent an office, advertise for models, take your money and close up shop within a matter of months. Anyone can drop a name, promising you connections with well-known New York and Hollywood agencies, or tell you he is photographing the Hanes Pantyhose ads and ask you to please take off your clothes.

The legitimate people in the business resent it. Some agents and photographers do scout new faces and new talent 24 hours a day. However, they won't ask for your number. A professional will express interest, indicating his or her opinion that you have potential, and give you a card. The rest will be up to you. It will be for you to decide if you want to pursue the lead and call during regular business hours for further information. You, of course, are encouraged to investigate the reputation and motivations of anyone encouraging you to enter the business. No professional will push you into a contract, a job or even registering for work in a field in which you have no curiosity or inclination.

Any agencies that you have questions about should be checked out with the Better Business Bureau. Unfortunately, the bureau is often unaware of unscrupulous practices and consumer complaints until it is too late. By the time the bureau has a record of complaints, these businesses often have already closed up shop, disconnected the phone, and skipped town. If the city is large enough, the same dishonest people have been known to open — and close — agency after agency, changing their names and the names of their businesses each time. They will try to sell you services and products that are totally unnecessary. Many of them require fat fees for registra-

tion, money that you won't get back when the agency bankrupts. Some of them will high-pressure you into using the services of a photographer connected with the agency — the agent's boyfriend, brother or, sometimes, the agent himself — for exorbitant prices. The photography is often twice the price of that charged by legitimate photographers in the field, and the services for which you will be paying these con artists are free from legitimate agencies.

Do not be pulled in by lavish promises and catchy phrases. If you were to believe all that you read in the school advertisements, you would be assured glamour, sophistication, popularity, more friends, better times, fun, better jobs, better pay, a new you, a better personality, world or nationwide travel, world or nationwide job placement — all this in 10 easy lessons. Don't fall for name or place droppers — Sally Schmoe, direct from Hollywood, or Susie Bigtime, straight from the runways of New York City. Anyone can drop a name or make a call to agencies in the big cities. Anyone, even you.

Much ado about nothing could describe what goes on in most of the schools, but you'd never know it from the way they present themselves. There are "colleges" and "academies" as well as "schools" and "institutes." You will be enrolled in a "curriculum" — Makeup I, Makeup II, Makeup III, Advanced Makeup, Runway Walks, Runway Turns, Runway Pivots, and upon completion of these courses and all the others, you will probably be awarded a "diploma." This, of course, comes only after you have purchased their makeup, their hair care products, their books or pamphlets and photographs done by their photographers, usually at a cost above and beyond what you've already paid in tuition!

In some cities there are agencies that specialize in trade show work. Be wary, though, of agencies that are more interested in supplying companions or female escorts than professional sales-oriented models. Hostessing means greeting clients, serving cocktails and assisting your employer to entertain personnel and clients in some cities; it means a lot more than that with these other agencies. If you are uncertain of an agency's reputation, ask them exactly what you would be expected to do on the job and ask other agents and models if they have heard anything about the agency. If the word "swinger" or "playmate" appears in the name of the agency, chances are you wouldn't be working trade shows.

Often people are conned into thinking they need to attend modeling school before they can get work as models. According to most of the agents interviewed for this book, these schools can actually harm your chances of becoming a professional model. The schools are in business to make money; those who have tuition in hand are accepted, regardless of potential, and are frequently taught by teachers who have little or no professional experience. The schools flourish in small cities, where a less sophisticated clientele is more easily taken in by big promises and the illusion of glamour. There is no school that can turn out a professional model or commercial talent; you become a professional when you work and are paid for what you do.

Here are some comments from professionals across the country:

New York, a spokesperson for the Wilhelmina agency — *"A lot of the schools, unfortunately, are run by people who are no closer to the mainstream of what is going on than what happened in 1938. With operations like that, I just feel sorry for the people who waste their money on them.*

"If a school sells hot, and indicates to everybody they accept that they'll do well in modeling, and indicates that they've got a contact with Eileen Ford or Wilhelmina, then I think they're selling hot and misrepresenting . . . there is not a school in the country that cannot call Eileen Ford, that cannot call Wilhelmina, or Zoli, and say I'd like you to see somebody, who would get turned down.

"There may be any number of people who operate agencies and schools all over the country, even all over the world, who can truthfully say to somebody I can arrange an introduction with Wilhelmina. But by the same token, any girl in New York who walks into our office between 10:00 and 10:30, four days out of the week, will be seen by someone here who is in a position to make a decision. It does not take an Act of Congress to be introduced to the agency. What I'm saying is that people don't need a contact. Anybody can come in and will be seen."

Washington, D.C. — *"My only argument with the modeling schools is their saying that they turn out models. They may do a great deal of good, in terms of poise and self-assurance, just a knowledge of how to care for yourself and make yourself look your best. But to tell someone that she's going to be a model as a result of all this . . . it's not truth in advertising."*

Los Angeles — *"99 percent of the schools are terrible. I don't think I have ever represented anyone who went to a modeling school. As soon as I see that diploma I won't even look at them, because I know they won't work out."*

Atlanta — *"I don't recommend modeling schools, and I don't even like to see someone who's been to one. They put a lot of false hopes in their heads and direct them in a lot of wrong directions. As far as I'm concerned, most of the modeling schools are just there to take money away from people, and they can't really do a thing for them. They get a lot of girls from small towns who see their advertisements and who think this is the way they should go about it. Then their folks end up spending all kinds of money for no reason at all. Then they find out that most agents are not even interested in seeing anyone who has been through modeling school."*

Chicago — *"Many of the students have an attitude that says 'I've spent money — wherever it may be — and because I've spent my money, I am automatically a professional. I should be able now to move into this business and make lots of money . . .' and it isn't that simple. Most of the modeling school students try to put everything they've learned and every bit of their makeup on their faces at one time. All on the same day and at one time. They're so surprised when they walk in and I say, 'Oh, you've been to modeling school,' 'How did you know?' 'I know because you're wearing too much makeup!' "*

New York, a spokesperson for the Eileen Ford agency — *"For personal grooming, I think it's excellent. But for the promise of them all being successful New York models, no. Sometimes they've learned habits in front of the camera that are not right for New York or are old-fashioned — it's hard for them to break those bad habits. Knowing nothing could be better."*

Knowing nothing could be better. And it will cost you lots less money. If you are in the market for poise, self improvement, charm or whatever they call it, then enroll yourself in one of the schools. But chances are you will not learn in a school what you need to know about getting work in professional modeling or commercials.

If you do respond to a letter, advertisement or suggestion of an encouraging person you met on the street, proceed with caution. Some of these outfits will send representatives to your home to talk with you. Do not be pressured into anything about which you have misgivings, whether you are in your home, an office or a studio.

Following is a list of suggestions to help you safeguard yourself.

1. Don't sign a blank contract. Read carefully and be sure you understand any contract before you sign it. Once you have signed it, you are bound to what the contract states. The sales representative is also bound to what is stated in the contract, not what he tells you in conversation. Consult a lawyer if you have doubts or questions.

2. Don't be rushed into signing anything by talk of a "great opportunity" or implications that you only have a few days in which to make up your mind before you lose out on a good thing. If the business or service is legitimate, they will still be in business when you are ready to sign with them.

3. Have assurances or promises put in writing. Few guarantees can be made in this industry, even by legitimate agents.

4. Don't hesitate to investigate the business reputation of the individual expressing interest in you or your child's modeling and commercial-making potential. Professionals encourage you to examine the many opportunities that will present themselves during the course of your career in this field.

Just be careful. Getting into the business is difficult enough without being the victim of fraud.

4

Getting Started

Now you're well informed about the business in general and interested in finding out more. You're anxious to begin work. Where to start? In your hometown, of course, which most likely has some kind of modeling or commercial work to offer. There is the possibility of work in any city that has a department store, specialty clothing shops, a newspaper or local magazine, commercial photography studios, film production facilities, or a television or radio station. Professionals in New York, Los Angeles and Chicago encourage would-be models and performers to find out about the business and get experience in their hometowns before heading for "the Big Time."

What do you do first? Gather as much information about the business as you can. The best sources are friends, relatives, neighbors and even friends of friends who work locally in modeling or commercials. Anyone connected with related industries, such as advertising, retail fashion, merchandising, publishing, television and radio may know where to go and who to see. If you see models in department stores or at fashion shows, talk with them. If you see people on the street or in malls distributing promotional material, approach them and ask how they got their jobs. Be aggressive in getting information and following up the suggestions.

At some point you will probably have to make a choice to find out more about the business and actually get work by associating yourself with an agency or school/agency or by launching an intensive freelance effort. Particularly as you are learning the ropes, your best choice is association with a reputable modeling and talent agency in your hometown.

Agencies and Agents

There are two words to take note of in that last sentence, *reputable* and *agency*. Why an agency? It is an agency's function to get employment for you, steer your career in the right direction and send you to the auditions right for you. For those efforts, it will take a percentage of your earnings. The agency does not make money unless, and until, you do.

Why reputable? Be warned again that this business is loaded with swindlers, frauds and cheats who run their businesses just two steps ahead of the law. Many of them talk quite knowledgeably about the business, but their knowledge does not make them reputable.

You can find these agencies listed under "Modeling and Talent Agencies" in the yellow pages of the phone directory. The ones you're interested in often print "An Agency for Professionals — Not a School" right in their yellow pages listings. If they indicate that they're franchised with Screen Actors Guild (SAG) and American Federation of Television and Radio Artists (AFTRA), which are the unions connected with the industry, that, too, denotes a reputable business.

The vast majority of reputable agencies charge absolutely no fee for their services. Those who do charge for registration collect a nominal sum of $5 to $20 which is used to prepare the mailings and agency headsheets needed to promote models and talent. Legitimate agencies are in business to make money, but they only do so when you do.

Do not be surprised to find that, outside of New York and Los Angeles, most of the agents and agency staff are women. Many of them are former models or talent who have had firsthand experience. Others may have learned the business through their association with advertising agencies, photo studios, union offices or production houses. Some may appear glamorous to you, and some may come on as supportive Moms. Some may be straightforward businesswomen interested in making a living. Because most of you will be dealing with agents who are women, the following references to agents and agencies will be in the feminine gender.

What an Agent Does for You

What does an agent do for you?

Theoretically, this is how it works: After you have seen each other and discussed your career goals and work availability, and if both of you are interested in joining forces, you'll register with the agency. You will, in a reasonable amount of time, supply the agent with photographs and resumes, for she cannot get much work for you without having these tools. The agent will then send out these photo-resumes to the various photographers, production houses, advertising agencies and others likely to be interested in using you. When a client does show interest in seeing you in person, or when an actual job comes up, your agent will call you and set up an appointment.

Then you're on your own. It will be your job to sell yourself to the client. If the client is interested in using you, if you do win the audition or interview, he will get in touch with your agent, who will then negotiate your fee for the job. Your agent will contact you with the information about the job, you will do the job, and some time later, you will collect your

earnings from the agent. For her efforts on your behalf, the agent will take a percentage from your gross earnings before you receive them. There are variations of this system, but the above basically describes the talent-agent relationship.

Once you begin to make money, your agent will deduct a commission from your earnings. For work that falls under union jurisdiction, the percentage an agent is permitted is fixed. For photo bookings, fashion shows, trade and industrial shows and some other kinds of work, the percentage taken varies from agent to agent. It may be as low as 10 percent or as high as 30 percent. Some states regulate the amount an agent can deduct from your earnings.

What are an agent's obligations to you? That depends on how the agencies in your state are licensed and what has been spelled out in the registration forms or contracts you sign. Some agencies are licensed as employment firms, and their obligation may be limited to finding employment for you should you meet their requirements. Other agencies are licensed as management; they may be obliged to offer you assistance with your business and financial affairs and to consult with you regarding your dress, manner of presentation or career plans. Agencies that are union franchised are regulated by union agreements. Under any kind of agreement, the agency is obligated to deal in the utmost good faith with their models and talent, and cannot secretly profit from any dealings regarding the people they represent.

The terms agent and agency are often used interchangeably. There are agents who handle only a handful of clients, and there are huge agencies that have many agents working for them. Two of the latter are ICM (International Creative Management) and William Morris, both of whom have offices in New York and Los Angeles.

In most other cities, however, you will list with an agency. Being signed with an agency often means that you have joined the hundreds or sometimes thousands of other registered models and talent who are interested in getting work in your city. It's not that signing is not a big deal, for you will fare better, professionally, with an agent. But you are not likely to get the kind of career guidance and management from an agent in Atlanta or Chicago that you will get from an agent in New York or Los Angeles. Many of these agencies act as booking agencies, which means that a certain number of jobs are going to go to a certain number of models and talent, and the agency will collect a commission no matter who gets the job.

Why an Agent, Not a Manager?

Do not confuse an agent with a manager. A manager endeavors to take care of your financial and personal matters and advises you on career choices. In return for this, he, too, receives a percentage of your earnings. You'll still need, work with and pay a percentage to an agent, as a manager does not negotiate contracts or send you on interviews and auditions.

It is true that the big-name models and commercial talent often employ managers. At this stage in your career, though, you don't need a manager.

Until you are working in New York or Los Angeles and pulling down a six figure income annually, don't worry about having a manager and don't be taken in by bogus offers of career management.

What To Look For in an Agent

What are you looking for in an agent? You want someone who can get you work and with whom your dealings will be professional and pleasant. You want someone with a sharp eye who knows how best to market you and who has the clients who use your kind of look or your kind of talent. If that client pool extends to other cities, so much the better.

You want someone who will advise you on important career decisions. An agent should supply clients with good information regarding the advisability of calling on certain photographers and clients. An agent with business connections in other cities can open doors for you, should you decide or be forced to move, by providing a letter of recommendation or by paving the way with an introductory phone call. Many agents have understandings with agents in other cities. It is particularly recommended that you have strong introduction into New York and Los Angeles, cities in which the agents are largely inaccessible to nonprofessionals or even working pros who are unknown to them.

You're also looking for an agent who can make these business transactions as enjoyable as possible. The honeymoon will soon be over with an agent who makes it a policy to call you with important information at midnight prior to the job, who burdens you with the details of personal and professional problems, or who deliberately or unconsciously undermines your confidence immediately before an audition or job. You want an agent who treats you kindly while still getting the job done. One actor in the process of registering with agents reports that "the worst I've run into so far is indifference — indifference at a time when acceptance is really important."

Some agents advance funds to models and talent whom they feel are worth the risk. Other agents throw parties for their groups. One agent in Boston puts out an agency newsletter, reporting whose composites have been depleted, which models in the agency have had babies recently, changes of address and phone numbers for photographers and clients on rounds lists, makeup tips, bargain charter flights available for those listed, the names of models recently listed, and other current items. One voice-over talent in New York who is thoroughly satisfied with his agent says that "they look out for me. I don't have to do anything. All I have to do is wait for the phone to ring. I don't have to make rounds, I don't have to go knock on doors, I don't have to carry my tapes around with me and try to get in to see people . . . my life is completely my own. My agent calls me and tells me when I have a job and when I have an audition, and I go. It's terrific and very professional. There's nothing wrong with my agent at all." These are the things you're looking for in an agent!

At some point you may want to increase your work potential by taking an acting class or developing your vocal skills. Your agent can direct you to theaters, local universities, improvisation companies, commercial acting schools and other groups that offer instruction that will be worth your while and the cost of the classes. While you're developing your talents you'll also be developing friendships with the professionals who are teaching and the other people taking the classes, who will be eager to trade industry information and gossip with you. You may hear about interviews, jobs and new agencies you would otherwise have missed.

Your agent can also supply the names of people in the business who are willing to meet with you privately for individual coaching.

These individuals often have waiting lists for their services and are expensive, but they're worth it. The instruction, tips and introductions a professional working in the business can provide you with are invaluable. They know what is important and who is important. They may also be called, on occasion, by casting people or agents who are looking for new talent. No one can work miracles, but these professionals can do a great deal to bring out whatever talent you have to develop.

Most important, your agent should be someone you can trust and who has work to offer you.

Approaching an Agent

The approach, indeed, is very important. You'd hate to turn an agent off, through ignorance or a lack of preparation, before you've even been given a chance to show your stuff.

The best and the most immediate way to find out how an agent wants to be approached is to make a telephone call. Think through your conversation before you pick up the receiver. Make a list of the questions you want to ask. Some agents say they are turned off to new talent merely by the way they conduct themselves in this first phone conversation. If you are unprepared, unintelligible, ask inane questions or in any way seem tiresome, you will probably be told that the agency isn't interested in seeing anyone new at this time.

You could also send a letter, but you might not receive the response you're looking for. If you're at so great a distance as to necessitate using the mail instead of the phone, the agents reason, how can you possibly make yourself available for the interviews and jobs you're hoping to get? In fact, some agencies require that you live within so many minutes of the city to be readily available to go out on assignments for which they call you. They won't be wild about making long distance calls to hear you say you can't make it. Initially, at least, it is advisable to make your inquiries by phone.

(Note: If you are considering moving to New York, Los Angeles or Chicago, you are encouraged to write prior to your move. See the chapters on New York, Los Angeles and Chicago.)

The Need for Photos

You are likely to be told that the agency is interested in seeing photos of you prior to seeing you in person. Be certain to ask what kind of photographs are necessary. Most agents will be satisfied with seeing a few good snapshots of you — that is a few (between two and six) — good (which means in focus) pictures of you (not Mount Rushmore and you, or your pet collie and you, but you), preferably a close-up and a full-length shot. Some agents may ask to see professional stills or proof sheets, but they do not usually demand them from beginners. Be certain that you have as many copies of these pictures as you'll need to send, retaining the originals for yourself, for it is not likely that the photos will be returned to you.

Believe it or not, that request will cut short the careers of about half of you who want to break into the business. Many people simply won't carry through on the request for photos. "I must get at least 100 calls every two weeks from people that want to be an actress or a model," says an agent in Cincinnati. "I see no one unless I see a picture first. I want to see mostly Polaroids and snapshots — and you would be surprised what that cuts down in the mail. Most people, after they make a telephone call, do not have the initiative to do it. They'll come out and see you but they won't go to the trouble of taking snapshots. Therefore, that cuts down my time tremendously." If an agent asks you for photos, send them.

Snapshots by friends will probably be sufficient to get you started.

Best Foot Forward

Many agencies set aside a regular time on a weekly basis to talk with beginners, answer your questions and consider your potential for modeling and performing in commercials. You may be asked to bring photographs to this meeting. Other agencies will set up an appointment time specifically for you.

Prepare yourself for this first encounter. As previously discussed, take some snapshots so that the agent can get an idea of how you photograph. Have enough copies made so that you can leave one with each agency you're seeing. Do not take your high school graduation pictures, your wedding album or prom shots. The agents do not wish to review your family scrapbook, they just want to see a few good shots of you.

If you are a student of drama or if you have had professional or community acting experience, you may want to prepare a scene suitable for presentation in an agent's office. It's not likely that you will be requested to do so, but it could happen and you would want to be ready. You may be asked to do a reading. In any event, be sure to mention any theater experience you have had. If you haven't actually written up your resume, be prepared to list whatever you have done.

It seems obvious, in wanting to enter an industry so concerned with appearances, that you would take care to present your most well-groomed, attractive self to the agents. Not so, apparently. "Every now and then you get people who come in and look like they just cleaned their basements," mentions a Detroit agent. "You wonder what possessed them to come in looking like that, especially when they're looking for modeling work!" I've seen people sitting in agency reception rooms cleaning their nails, picking at their hair, wearing pants so long that they sweep the floor with every step or suits and dresses with food stains, rips and missing buttons. This is an industry that tolerates, even encourages, individual flair in dressing. But whether you're wearing jeans, an original '20s dress or the height of today's fashion, take care that your over-all appearance is well-groomed and presentable. Clean your hair, your nails and your skin before you leave home, look over the clothing you're going to wear before you put it on, and have it all together before you walk into the agent's office.

One more piece of advice on business etiquette: Be on time for your appointment. Be on time for any appointment but particularly this first one. If a genuine conflict arises in your schedule and you will be unable to keep your appointment, let the agents know as soon as possible. Don't for a moment think that they're going to buy the one about your car not starting or the babysitter getting sick — they've heard them, and others, many times before. There's no way to hide the fact that you're chickening out, and if you're leaving them in the lurch this time, they may not trust that you'll be dependable for audition and job appointments. In this industry, time is money. Don't waste yours and that of the agent.

The time has arrived and you're at the address of the agency. What will you find? Very often agency offices are in typical office buildings, set up in suites consisting of a reception room and one or several inner rooms. Often the walls will be covered with pictures of people in the agency, beautiful models and funny characters. But don't be surprised if the address you're approaching is that of someone's home. It isn't the usual practice, and in some states it isn't legal, but some legitimate agents do run their businesses from their homes. Large auditions will be held in clients' offices or rented hotel space, but daily business is carried out in their homes.

Take a deep breath and walk right in or ring that bell. Your interview begins the moment you walk into the office. Not officially, of course, for you may have to wait a while before the agent is free. But the person who sits behind the reception desk is watching you and making notes that will be passed on to the agent. Those comments may be passed on even before you get into the office. In some agencies this person may also be responsible for booking you into jobs. So do not offend the reception person or comment on how long the agent is keeping you waiting. Be friendly, don't play with your hair or clothing, and sit down and read the book or magazine you've so thoughtfully brought with you.

What the Agent Will Look For in You

What is the agent looking for during this initial interview? First, your presence or style will be noted. Be as much at ease as possible. The agent will be watching to see if you're withdrawn, nervous, fidgety, too chatty or not chatty enough, able to converse, to present yourself in a positive, intelligent and likable way. If you can't handle this interview, you're not likely to be trusted in an audition or job situation. The agent will ask you the questions she needs to have answered, drawing you out and helping you to offer any information you feel is interesting or important. Comment freely and answer questions

Nervous . . .

. . . chatty . . .

. . . overdone . . .

. . . or just right.

truthfully. This is your opportunity to mention any prior experience you have had in the field, any theater or commercial training. You might also mention that you know it will take work and time to succeed in the business but that you are committed and willing to give it everything you have. The agent is looking for your ability and your confidence in that ability.

Second, the agent is going to be judging your appearance, determining if your look is compatible with "the look" of the city in which you're trying to get work. If you have a very gaunt, high cheek-boned New York fashion model look, you probably won't work much if you live in Des Moines or Indianapolis. If you have a moustache and long sideburns, you might be able to work in New York or Chicago, but you won't in Atlanta.

The agents do know what looks will and will not sell in their cities. A Boston agent says, "In most cases, when a man walks in here, I know immediately whether he's going to make it in Boston or not. With a woman, I can tell once I start working with her. A man must have a middle-of-the-road, conservative, strong, masculine look — and I say masculine over being too good-looking, or too handsome, too pretty. Pretty boys don't sell in Boston. Some moustaches, yes, a limited number. Beards — very difficult. The females are bright, clean, scrubbed, shiny-haired and have bright faces, great smiles, good teeth, good skin, good bodies — definitely not your New York look." The agents who have been around a while, who know their talent and the demands of their clients will be able to tell you what the regional look is and if you have it.

If you have any questions, be certain to ask them. Agents expect questions. You might ask how the agent sees you, and what kinds of work you'll be likely to get. If the agent has pegged you as a middle-aged ordinary housewife type, and you think of yourself as a candidate for the cover of *Vogue,* chances are you'll not be happy with that agent. Chances are, too, that you'll have to face up to the realities presented you by your age and your physical appearance. But shop around, if the possibilities exist, to find an agent who thinks she can sell you the way you want to be sold.

Yes, the agents expect questions, but know when to stop asking. If you ask for any kind of a guarantee that you will work, even if you ask for a guarantee that you will make back at least the money you've invested in photos and resumes, you're asking for something the agent cannot give. Asking once shows your justifiable concern; asking twice reveals your unreasonable insecurity. An agent in Pittsburgh says that 800 people are listed with his agency, and that about 30 percent of them will do at least one job in a year's time. "However," he adds, "I would have to be able to walk on water to know which 30 percent are going to get work." No one can give you any kind of a guarantee that you will work in modeling and commercials. You can stack the deck in your favor by knowing what you are getting into and aligning yourself with responsible professionals.

What other things, in addition to requests for impossible guarantees, irk the agents in these initial interviews? Apparently many newcomers ask about how much money they're going to be raking in, with visions of yachts, fur coats and Mercedes dancing in their heads. Wrong. As stated previously, there is no guarantee they'll make a cent. Unless you live in Chicago, Los Angeles or New York, or are an extremely fortunate individual in one of the other large cities, what you make from modeling and appearing in commercials will provide merely an occasional bonus to other income.

Some agents find it irritating that new people will enter the business not expecting to put a penny into it. At the onset, and throughout your career, you will need clothes, new makeup, photographs, voice-tapes, resumes, money for carfare, voice lessons, drama classes, or whatever is necessary to get work.

Your attitude can have a negative impact on agents. Perhaps you come on too strong, speak too loudly, brag too often, reassure anyone who cares to listen that you feel real good, real positive, about getting into this business. The agents know that your arrogance and cockiness are cover-ups for insecurity, albeit justifiable insecurity, but it hurts you anyway. They've heard it all before; most can tell an act from the genuine experience.

Another peeve several agents mention is the inability of both beginning and experienced talent to accept comment and criticism. If you can't take it at the start, when you really aren't aware of how you should look or what you should do to get work in the business, then perhaps this business with its harsh pronouncements and predictable rejections is not for you. You may be told that your contouring needs to be redone, that your hair needs to be restyled, that you ought to lose 20 pounds or have your eyebrows reshaped, that you have a slight speech impediment that will have to be worked out before you can do voice work, that your beard is going to limit your work potential, that your photos are out of date or not honest. The agents are not looking for debate when they make these suggestions or demands of you. They are merely stating what will be required of you before they can go about trying to get you work. If your beard or long hair is more important to you, so be it.

Be prepared to hear that the agent is not interested in handling you. If she feels that she would be unable to get work for you because your look won't sell, or there is someone like you already listed with the agency, or simply because she is not convinced of your potential, then make as dignified an exit as is possible and see all the agents in your city. One agent in Los Angeles says "I go by instinct. I have had many good people who want representation who just didn't hit me." One agent's poison is often another agent's cup of tea.

Don't burn your bridges behind you, shouting "You're a jerk!" as you slam the door. Many agents are impressed with persistence, particularly if you have made the suggested revisions and have something new to show each time you return. One New York agent revealed that he sometimes feels compelled to see people he has originally turned away because they are so clever and original in their persistence. He may still not be interested in handling them as clients, but he compliments a novel approach with an appointment.

An agent in Washington, D.C. is also impressed with hard work and persistence. "I had one model who just came back and came back. And every time this model came back, the pictures looked a little better and a little better. Finally, a month ago, I signed him exclusive. He put his heart and soul in it. He just kept on testing till he was good in front of a camera. He did it on his own, got his look together. Now I'm very proud of him. Someone who is constantly appearing at our door is really not a very welcome sight because it is interrupting activities that are keeping many people working. On the other hand, it worked out for this one guy and he is not the first of the persistent people that I've taken."

Registering with an Agency

If the agent is interested in taking you on, you will probably be asked to register with the agency. In some cities, this registration merely means filling out a card with your name, address, phone, statistics, experience, prior work experience, and an indication of the kinds of work for which you're available. There is nothing legally binding about such a registration. In other cities, signing with an agency means that you'll be exclusively represented by that agency for a set amount of time. This is a contract. Read it carefully. Make sure you understand what you're signing . . . before you sign. If you want time to think about it or wish to discuss it with your lawyer, any reputable agent would urge you to do so. If you feel that you are being rushed into something in the office, take even more time to make your decision. Legitimate agents don't push.

When filling out the registration card, be honest. If you are disinclined to state your real age, then give what you think your age range is. For instance, if you're actually 29 but you think you look somewhere between 25 and 31, then state 25-31 inside of a parenthesis. Often the agents will want to know your age simply to make certain that you are old enough, legally, to represent certain products. Don't be coy and don't lie. Most agents will know what you weigh — knowing is their business — no matter what you have written on your card.

Many agencies have a trial period, during which you prove yourself, following your registration and prior to signing you exclusively into the agency. You may be given a certain amount of time in which to change your makeup or hair, have professional photos done, and have the photos copied and in the files of the agency. An agent in Boston says that she signs one out of every 20 interested people and that half of those signed will actually work out. "They have a deadline the day I list them. They have two months in which to complete their portfolios, distribute their composites and make their rounds. To me, if they cannot accomplish that in two months, they're not going to accomplish it at all." She sends out a form letter two weeks prior to the deadline to warn them that portfolios, composites and beginning rounds must be completed or they will be dropped from the agency.

Most of the time, at the conclusion of this initial interview, the agent will merely ask you to fill out registration cards or suggest changes you will have to make before she will represent you. If it has been suggested that you have your hair restyled or that you learn how to apply makeup, be sure to find out where the agent suggests you have these services done. There are usually certain professional hair and makeup stylists whose work the agencies recommend and these professionals will consult with you, for a fee, about your individual look and needs. Have these changes made and be adept at recreating them yourself before you have your photographs done.

It is not unusual for beginning models and talent to feel somewhat let down when leaving an agent's office, even when the interview has been positive. Perhaps that is natural, for this is only the first step toward actually getting work.

Signing with an Agency

If you sign with one agency and one agency only, you are "signed" or "exclusive" with that agency. Very often a contract is involved, usually for 90 days or a year. Depending on the city in which you live, these contracts may or may not be binding. In Chicago, when a model wants out of a contract, the agent generally is agreeable, figuring that it isn't smart to invest time and effort in someone who isn't happy with the situation. In some cities, however, contracts are not so easily broken.

If you register with many agencies, you are "multiple-listed" or "cross-registered" in that city. If a client specifically requests you or a job arises for which you are perfect, there will be a flurry of activity among the agents to get in touch with you first. Whoever wins the race receives the commission. If, however, you are not in demand, your agents really have very little incentive to push you or to advance your career. Some agencies have thousands of people listed with them. That's great for a client who calls in looking for a 30-year-old woman, blonde, with two front teeth missing who can ride a unicycle, but it won't do much for you and the hundreds of others like you who are hoping to make a career in this field.

The problem with the nonexclusive agent relationship is that the agent pretty much deals with every performer on the same basis. An agent who has a "stable" of performers will limit her endeavor to those six, eight, 20 or 100 performers and very definitely try to push them. With models and talent who are not listed exclusively, the agent, in a sense, doesn't really care which registered performer gets the job. Models and talent often feel as if they are being neglected or shuffled about.

Many agents, including some who work in multiple-listed cities, are as unhappy as the talent about the nonexclusive relationship. One agent in Atlanta welcomes the switch to exclusive listings.

"In my own case, I am interested in the long-rangeness of people as talent. It is difficult to be interested on a long-range basis if they're working this job through you and that job through someone else and another job through someone else. There isn't any honest opportunity for rapport and common

'looking ahead' together. As an agent, I could look at it as booking only. I don't. I look at it as a career for myself and for the talent I represent. Therefore it must be much more long-range than day-to-day booking. There must be a strong commitment by both parties, so I encourage exclusive contracts. I think more and more agents are beginning to do that. I think all of us are a bit tired of the crossing over, and wondering who got who first."

Depending on the city in which you live, you may have to sign exclusively with one agency or you may be able to register with all of the agencies. An exclusive contract may be offered to you by one of these agencies after you've both had an opportunity to test each other out. You are free to discuss the success of your contract with your agent at any time. If the situation is not working out to your benefit, you should consider looking for another agent.

Freelancing

It may be, by choice or by necessity, that you freelance in order to get work modeling and making commercials. This means that you work without representation, promoting yourself, finding your own work and negotiating your own deals. Some seasoned professionals in cities offering agency representation freelance by choice. Even in Chicago, some very successful voice-over professionals prefer to work on their own. This discussion, however, is directed at those who must freelance out of necessity, who live in cities and towns where there are no well-established, reputable agencies.

No matter what size city you live in and even if there are agencies that can offer you representation, you should approach department stores and specialty shops if you are interested in modeling in fashion shows. Outside of New York, there simply isn't enough money in informal and runway modeling to make representing runway models worth the while of an agent. You will be looking for the fashion co-ordinator or the person in charge of producing style shows.

If you are interested in doing commercials, contact the local television and radio stations. Ask for the person who deals with talent. Very often the local commercials done in small cities are produced by television stations in their own studios. The pay will not be much, and they are likely to use their own television personnel, but you have nothing to lose by asking and you might gain some experience. The stations may also direct you to the advertising agencies or production companies that make — and therefore cast — the commercials.

If you live in a town that supports a major industry (perhaps the building of trash compactors), contact the advertising department of the trash compactor company to find out who does the photography for their sales literature. You may be directed to a local commercial photographer or to a local advertising agency, in which case you should call, express your interest, and make an appointment.

If photographs are used in the local newspaper to advertise clothing, products or the services of a bank or insurance company, call the paper or the companies direct to see where the photographs are being done. Look through the yellow pages for listings under commercial photographers or television production companies or film production companies, and call them to see if they use local talent. Also call advertising agencies and ask if they see new models and talent who are interested in getting work.

Do whatever you can to get work for yourself. If somebody knows somebody who can help you out, ask that somebody to introduce you by letter, phone call or in person. Particularly in small towns, you're going to have to hustle and use your own ingenuity to get whatever work you can find.

Of course, the same rules of business etiquette apply to seeing television and radio station representatives, advertising agency people, newspaper people, department store fashion co-ordinators, photographers and production crews that apply to meeting with agents. Arrive on time, look good, and be sharp. Have photos and resumes to leave with them, if requested, because many producers keep files of local people who have shown interest in working with them.

If it is necessary for you to freelance, be certain to familiarize yourself thoroughly with Chapter 9, *How to Get the Work.* Pay particular attention to the sections on Promotion and Making Rounds. As someone in business for yourself and representing yourself, you need to know the protocol.

There's got to be a catch, you say. Yes, there are some disadvantages to the practice of freelancing. Very often you don't know what you're getting into and for whom you're going to be working. After you have been at it a while and have experienced good and bad situations, you will be able to differentiate the real jobs from the lines of baloney. But until that

time, realize that you're going to make some mistakes while you're learning. Cut your losses and enjoy your successes.

While freelancing, the only jobs you get will be the jobs you've looked for, courted, or for which you've been recommended by a pleased former client. You will be doing all your own footwork. You will not have the advantage of the large client pool a well-established agent can offer. You will not be likely to get work outside of your immediate vicinity unless you go looking for it. You will miss calls unless you have a reliable phone answering service.

The freelance model or talent is in a very vulnerable position financially. You will have no one to negotiate a deal or a fee for you. Most of your clients, nice guys though they may be, will know that you're not likely to demand $75 for a job for which they're offering to pay $50, even if you've been paid $75 for the same job at some other time. They know that it will be difficult for you to refuse what they offer, particularly if jobs in your area come few and far between. The client can name his price when working with freelance talent in a small city.

Once the fee has been determined and the job done, it may be difficult for the freelancer to collect his or her earnings. If the client refuses to pay, you will have very little recourse. You have no protection, no clout, when you're representing yourself professionally.

The advantage to freelancing is that, when and assuming you are paid, you pay no 10, 15 or 30 percent commission to anyone. You save the agent's fee.

If you find yourself in the position where you must freelance, then set some rules for yourself and your clients. If you sense something funny in the way a client or prospective client is treating you, don't put up with it. If you do accept a job, be certain that your fee has been established and is acceptable before you do the job. It will help you establish your fee if you know how the job is going to be used — you'd ask less for a one-shot newspaper advertisement photo session than you would for a local television commercial shown twice nightly for 13 weeks. You will want to know how much and when you will be paid for each job, and if you can get the quotes in writing, do so. You may find, particularly if working for a department store, that your profit will be greater if you take your fee in discounted merchandise.

Freelancing can be profitable and enjoyable, provided you understand what is involved with every job you accept, and establish pay rates and schedules prior to doing the job.

Modeling Schools

You may find, in many small cities and towns, that your only choice is a combination school and agency. The catch usually is that you must attend their courses before you can list with their agency. If this is the case, you will want to see what they have to offer you in terms of job placement. Ask to see the vouchers of jobs done, noting the clients' names, models' names, and what was paid. You might even ask to see the stubs of checks written to the models and talent. What you're looking for is proof that this school/agency actually can offer you work, and work for which you will be paid. Remember, the objective in reading this book and signing up with an agency is to get work and make money, not to spend money on courses you don't really need. If the school/agency is the only opportunity in town, and often it is, you have the choice of playing the game or working freelance.

Most modeling schools, however, offer only classes. They will "teach" you what their particular idea of modeling is, but they will not get you work. In fact, according to agents across the nation, what you "learn" may actually hinder your chances of getting work. Many agents say that what it takes to be a top model or commercial performer can't be taught. You either have it — and careful management and experience present the opportunities to develop it — or you don't.

The schools are in business to make money. They do this by enrolling students — most often anyone who has the tuition in hand. They will not turn down money, which means they will not turn down anyone who can afford their classes. If what you're seeking is a course in self-improvement, and if what you're promised is a course in self-improvement, fine. If you are interested in learning how to groom yourself, or carry yourself with poise and present yourself in a confident way, and if this is what you're promised, fine. But if you are promised that you will be a professional model upon completion of so many classes for however much money, the promise is empty and you are foolish to believe it.

Many of the teachers are qualified to teach by the fact that they themselves recently graduated from the school. If you are investigating a school, ask to see your teacher's portfolio and find out what his or her professional experience is. Someone who has worked locally for a period of years would be most likely to have the tips you'll want to know to get work.

Sadly, you may be taught things that can actually harm you, things you will have to "un-learn." You may be taught makeup that is right for the teacher but totally wrong for you, or if your teacher actually did work in modeling 10 years ago, the makeup you learn today may be what worked 10 years ago. If you are taught runway walks and turns, and think that these unnatural gestures are going to help you out in fashion photography, you're in for a real surprise during your first real photo session.

Even sadder is the fact that the cost of this schooling can sometimes go into the thousands of dollars. The contract you sign when accepted into the school can bind you to tuition payments, even if you don't attend the classes. Be very careful. Know what you're getting into when you sign any papers.

5

Photographs: Your Most Valuable Sales Tool

Because photographs are your most valuable sales tool — your professional calling card — and because you will need good photographs throughout your career, it is important for you to have a grasp of photography as it applies to you as a model or commercial talent. This section does not explain film speeds or wide-angle lenses. You will find out, instead, how to choose the right photographer for you, what to take to a photo session, what body angles work best with a camera, what kinds of lighting are used, how to work with another model, what casting directors are looking for in photographs, what quality you should expect in your prints and reproductions, how to develop a portfolio, and much more.

It is essential that you have these photos taken, duplicated and in the hands of your agent or in your portfolio and ready for distribution as soon as possible. You are a nonentity without your photographs; you may be lucky enough to be sent on a first interview or two without them, but an agent cannot really do much for you if there are no photos. One Midwest agent says, "I can't represent them without sales tools. The photography is a must. Without it, I will forget them, and the client will never know them." If your photos are not in the agents' files, you're hurting yourself.

How much work is booked directly from photographs? "Quite a bit," states an Atlanta agent, "especially out-of-state work. We have clients from out-of-state who request pictures and many times that is how they decide who they want to see on an interview when they're in town." An agent in Boston estimates that about 70 percent of her print work is booked directly from composites and headshots. It is extremely important to keep your agent supplied with good, current photos and to check on that supply from time to time.

Determining Your Photographic Needs

Now there are some decisions ahead of you. Before you actually call photographers to find out about prices, number of prints, sizes of prints and other details, it is going to be necessary for you to know what your photographic needs are. Your agent, the custom of the city, your inclination, your time, and your budget will dictate whether you opt for a headshot or a full composite to represent you.

A headshot is simply a photograph that shows head or head and shoulders. It's usually printed on 8" x 10" paper and often referred to as a glossy or an 8" x 10". An agent in Chicago says that "the headshot is supposed to show your features and your face, your skin tone, bone structure, teeth, eyes, makeup skills and hair appearance. A distraction, be it a bold pattern on your shirt, a sparkly diamond necklace and earring set, a turtleneck that is too large — interferes with the idea of the photograph, which is to show what your face looks like." A commercial headshot, unlike a formal portrait, is unretouched. It should show you as you really are, at your best.

A good composite . . .

PHOTOS BY CECILY HUNT

BARBARA GUARINO

Size — 9-11	Bust — 35
Height — 5' 7"	Waist — 25
Weight — 120	Hips — 35
Hair — Brown	Shoe — 7-8
Eyes — Hazel	Pix date — July, 1979

S.S. No. 149-56-2383
ACTRESS / SINGER / DANCER

PRINTED BY WOELLER, INC. – CHICAGO

. . . reveals your talent and your many faces.

A headshot reveals warmth . . .   *. . . character . . .*   *. . . or sophistication.*

The headshot is traditionally the actor's professional calling card, while the composite is widely used by the model and commercial talent. Some actors have both a headshot and a commercial composite. A composite is a grouping of photographs showing you in a variety of poses, locations and outfits, relating to products, props, clothing, other people and particular situations. A composite shooting obviously is more encompassing and longer than the sitting for a headshot, and demands more preparation and planning.

In addition to determining whether you will need a headshot or a composite, you'll also have to consider the wardrobe you'll take to the photo session, whether you want your shots done in a studio or on location, whether they should be done in color or black and white. All of this will depend on what direction you want to take and what you want your photos to do for you.

Depending on where you live, you may have little control over these decisions. If your choice is limited to a school or combination school/agency, you may find that your photography session is included in the curriculum, and it may or may not be built into the cost of the schooling. If you do not care for the work of the school's photographer, there may be little you can do. Photographs you obtain from outside of the school will certainly cost you an addi-

tional photo fee and they may not conform to the specifications established by the school.

If you are in a city where you must sign exclusively with one agency, you may be asked to have your photographs done by the agency's photographer. Some agencies like to establish a certain agency "look" by using one photographer and having all their people represented in that one style. The photographer may have a studio set up within the agency offices.

You may be asked to see a makeup or hair stylist. An agent in Atlanta says that if a new person comes in with the potential for print work, the agency will set up a consultation with their makeup artist. "There is no point wasting your time in photographing pre-makeup, pre-hair, pre-everything, because the shots won't look like anything. More than likely, it will discourage the girl before she ever begins." Most agents, however, will supply a list of photographers, hair stylists and makeup consultants, usually professionals with whom they have been acquainted for a period of time and whose work they can recommend.

You may hear about certain photographers or makeup people or even printers being connected with certain agents in kick-back setups. These setups do exist, but if the services rendered or products offered are top quality, it really makes very little difference.

Publicity stills
often are headshots.

Many agents and professional photographers, though, are quick to assure you that they are not "in cahoots" with a particular agency or photographer. An agent in Cincinnati mentions that she supplies her people with a selection of photographers, taking no percentage on photography or printing. "And," she adds, "there is money in that."

Thus, you should definitely consult first with an agency before you have photographs done. One pro suggests that "if you possibly get friendly enough with one of the agencies before you have your first shooting done, ask for permission to just leaf through some of their composites of successful people. See what is marketable. See what clothing, hairstyles, expressions, lighting and makeup are being used."

An agent also can keep you away from photographers who have established reputations for hassling women or men, who are too expensive, not consistent in delivering quality work on time, or do not take the kinds of photographs necessary to sell models and actors.

"Testing" and Test Photographs

Your agent may also mention photographers who are willing to "test" new models and talent. A testing session is not an examination; it is more like an experiment in which something new — the photographer's new equipment, new lighting, different chemical process, different approach, or you the beginner — is being tried. A photographer who is trying to expand a portfolio, particularly a beginning photographer, may be interested in testing.

What makes this different from a job photo booking, where you are paid, and a composite or headshot photo session, where you are paying, is that the testing session is usually free. In return for his or her time, the model receives a print or some transparencies. In most cities no money is exchanged, only time for prints, but there are places where it is the custom for a photographer to charge, on a per print basis, for testing. Make sure you both know the terms when you go in for tests.

What's the hitch? You may not be able to find photographers interested in testing with you, at least within the time limit you and your agent establish. You may not be able to exercise as much control over the entire shoot as you would like. The test may not be successful. You may not be able to select which prints or slides you'll receive, and you may have difficulty collecting what you're due from busy or forgetful photographers. You may find that the old saying — you get what you pay for — has never been more true. In some cases, that's nothing.

Testing may provide you with enough good photographs that you can bypass the photo session for which you'll have to pay and move right into getting your reproductions made.

Selecting the Right Photographer

A newcomer may want to have a professional portfolio full of professional pictures to present to an agent right away. When you've made the decision to enter the business, it is quite understandable that you would want to present yourself as a ready-to-go professional. And perhaps some agents won't see you if you don't have photographs.

There are some risks. It is true that professional photographs will best show what you can do, and the fact that you have them indicates your serious intention to enter the business. But if you are new, and don't really know what is expected from you in a photo session and what kinds of photos will actually work in selling you or getting you into an agency, you're ripe to be taken. You may be posing for and purchasing photos that are inadequate, wrong for you or downright embarrassing when shown to industry professionals. One girl went to a suburban portrait studio, told them she needed a good head-shot and a body shot, and ended up with a high school graduation-type portrait and a cheesecake pose. Supposing this to be exactly what she needed, she took these photos to the nearest printing outfit and had 500 copies made. Imagine her surprise when each agent she visited told her that the composites were totally unusable. She had to go through the entire process and expense one more time. This could have been avoided had she consulted the agencies in the first place and been directed to photographers right for her.

Some photographers who merit investigation are:

1. Photographers of portraits or "Say, didn't I do your wedding pictures last year?" One agent in Detroit sums it up pretty well. "For this business the photo should show animation and the ability to move, whereas a portrait photographer only likes to take a good portrait." Portrait photographers tend to pose the fledgling models or actors as if they were posing brides and graduates — very formally. The stiffness and posed quality of a formal portrait is all wrong for you. You want photos that sell your personality, your best look, your animation and individuality — that sell you. Your photos should not be retouched, and you want a photographer who is aware of the trends in the advertising industry. Be careful, for portrait photographers often advertise "Composite shootings" in their ads in the yellow pages.

2. Photographers with reputations or "Say, I have a groovy pad. Let's go back there and you can see the collection of nudes I've done for Playboy." A lot of women particularly seek out female photographers because they have been bothered by male photographers. They don't want hassles, particularly on shoots for which they are paying. One girl says she was locked into a photographers's studio and escaped only after picking up one of his cameras and threatening to throw it against the wall unless he opened the door. Agents or other talent know which photographers are inclined to make sexual advances or suggest nude photos to naive models. Especially on a first shoot, you want a photographer with whom you feel comfortable.

3. Photographers who advertise in local papers or "Beautiful girls wanted. Portfolio photography for modeling. Cheapest rates in town." Sometimes amateurs who are trying to build up their portfolios will indeed provide their services very cheaply. Usually, those who are sincere about providing such services will approach the legitimate talent and modeling agencies, show their work, leave their cards, and hope that the agents will give a new photographer a break. And it often happens. Those who avoid the ordinary channels may have something else in mind, like trying to palm off rotten photography for exorbitant prices. You won't know that it is rotten work or too expensive because you know nothing about the business. Do not be impressed by lots of shiny photographic equipment. Anybody can buy a camera and some lights.

Some folks who think they are going to save money use an unestablished photographer who is cheap. They are displeased with the quality of his work and so go to another cheap photographer, and there is no guarantee they won't be displeased again. After all the time and money are spent, it would be more economical, and your career would get an earlier start, to go originally to the experienced and slightly more expensive photographer. In most cases, the established photographer isn't even that much more expensive. In fact, he or she may be cheaper than the fast talker who prey on uninformed people who are interested in modeling.

Advises one photographer in a production company working out of Charleston, West Virginia,

"Beware of anything that sounds cheap or free. We charge people our low-end commercial rate for shooting a portfolio. When somebody wants to get into modeling or acting, the portfolio is the main sales tool. It would be like the first brochure for a new company. You're going to end up establishing your image, establishing your range, and positioning yourself in the market. So spend just a little more money than what you feel you can afford and get the best photographer you can find to do it."

4. Photographers who approach you on the street or "Say, you're pretty — you should be a model." One agent in Chicago says that amateur photographers are her worst enemies. "Many times photographers will pick up young ladies off the street and tell them how beautiful they are and that they should be models. And they take pictures of them. And the girls come in here feeling very high because someone told them that they are beautiful and that they ought to be professional models. I have to say to them how sorry I am, but they will have to improve their skin or their teeth or their makeup. There are so many factors in putting a person together. Many times people will have the advantage of getting that kind of help at home, but often they don't, and I think these are the people who are duped by the people on the street. They are the ones who need to be told they're beautiful, and, more often than not, they're the ones who come in with the photographs and are people we really can't use at all. If I had one word of advice it would be that if somebody tells you you're pretty and that you should be in the modeling business and they would like to take your phone number and call you, tell them thank you very much and ask them instead for their phone number. Then call the nearest modeling and talent agency and ask the agent his opinion of your particular look. Then find out if the photographer on the street is really in business."

5. Photographers who are amateurs and are your friends or relatives or "Look, I've got the same camera the pros use — I'll save you a lot of money." Sometimes this does work out. You may have a friend who does know something about photography and with whom you feel comfortable. But do not — repeat, do not — use photos that are technically lacking in any way for professional purposes simply to avoid hurting your friend's or your dad's feelings. An agent can help you determine if the pictures will work. Do not be defensive if they aren't what you need. You pay a professional to work with you, to capture you at your best, to deliver high quality work in a reasonable amount of time, and to know what the trends are in this profession. Your friend many not be able to meet these conditions.

Asking Questions

When calling photographers for information, think of what you're going to ask before you call. You want to know if the photographer does this kind of work, what is the fee, what do you get out of the shooting, how long does it take (the shooting itself and the time between the actual shoot and when you can pick up your prints), and when the next available appointment time is. You are not obligated to make any kind of commitment when calling for information. Be sure to ask all the questions you have. Don't be shy. Even if your question seems stupid, ask it if it's about something that really concerns you. You have to get information somewhere. When someone sounds good to you, for a concrete reason or just a "feeling," make an appointment to go to the studio to see samples of his or her work.

A word of warning about photographers' studios, or at least about some studios. You may be surprised to see where some commercial photo studios are located. Commercial studios are often found in what some folks might call "rough neighborhoods." If this really distresses you, it's good to know about it now, because many of your potential photo bookings — the jobs you want — will take place in these very places.

Since you are comparison shopping, it is quite natural for you to ask to see the work of the photographer. Some studios have photographs displayed, some don't. I have artwork hanging in my studio and a full portfolio to show clients who come to see my work. I have stacks of printed composites that my clients have sent to me, and since most printers include "Photos by Cecily Hunt" somewhere on the composite, there is no question that it is my work. Sad to say, I have heard stories about models and talent asking aspiring photographers to see samples of their work, and being shown a portfolio of work that was not the photographer's own. There really is no way to tell about these things, especially when you are not well-versed in the differing styles of various local photographers. It is an awkward situation at best to just come out and ask a photographer if what he is showing you is his work, and chances are the reply would be untruthful anyway if you're dealing with the kind of person who would try to pass off the work of someone else as his own. People have asked me if the pile of prints and composites we were going through was my work, and I have always found it an odd question. But it is a fair question, and if you are wondering, go ahead and ask.

During this interview you should be sensing the kind of rapport you feel with the photographer. If he is not very communicative, makes you feel uptight, does not respond to your questions, seems temperamental or is sending out innuendoes that make you uncomfortable, don't forget that you're just shopping around at this point and that you may be putting out hard-earned cash for this person's services.

When you feel that you've found the right photographer, it is imperative that you reach an understanding prior to the shoot about what is going to happen during that day, what you're expected to bring, what you're expected to pay and when, where you're going to go, and any other questions you may feel are important. Do not assume anything. You are new to this field and you may totally overlook some important things.

I would suggest that you ask these questions:

1. How are you going to be marketed? You discussed this once, I hope, with your agent, but discuss it now with your photographer. If you think you need shots of you scrubbing kitchen floors and he wants to oil you up and photograph you in a bikini, you're both going to be surprised and disappointed the day of the shoot. Discuss your "type", the image you're trying to create and your photographic needs.

You can get ideas for your photographs just by studying magazines, newspaper ads, catalogs and television commercials. Keep current by watching current advertising and fashion trends.

You do want to present yourself in a variety of looks or roles, but these stretches should be believable. For instance, a 30-year-old woman wearing pigtails and cutely licking a popsicle is not an appropriate stretch. That hair style might be appropriate for that woman if she were involved in some sort of sports activity where she wanted to keep her hair off her face, but acting the child is not appropriate. It is extremely doubtful that she would ever be considered for such a young look. The stretch should make sense.

The stereotypes you include may also be dictated by the city in which you are working. For instance, there is a great deal of pharmaceutical advertising done in Chicago. For this reason, a lot of people portray nurses, technicians, doctors or pharmacists in their composites or portfolios. Think about the products that are manufactured or marketed in your area and that may give you an idea for a photograph.

You want to include photographs that will get you work in the areas you prefer. A woman interested in

A good way to do a body shot.

trade show or convention work might want to include a shot that is cute and sexy, maybe in shorts, riding a bicycle, or one that is sophisticated and glamorous in a jumpsuit or gown.

2. How does the photographer expect to be paid? I would recommend that you agree to pay a deposit, half or whatever is agreed upon, the day of the shoot and the balance due when you receive the prints. This way you are protected in the event that none of the proofs are acceptable to you or your agent and a reshoot agreement can't be or is not worked out.

3. Will the photos be black-and-white or color? The purpose of your first photo session is to get photographs you can have reproduced quickly and inexpensively in order to get your career started. Ninety-nine percent — or more — of the composites and glossies in professional use are black-and-white. "Color composites are simply a waste of money," says one agent in Atlanta. "The expense of printing would be just astronomical!" says another in In-

Present yourself in roles that are marketable.

dianapolis. Most agents agree that, while it is nice to include a few color prints or transparencies in your portfolio, the composite and headshot should be black-and-white.

4. How many prints will you receive, what size will they be, and will they be chosen by you? Some photographers overrule the print orders given by models and talent and print what they think are the best shots. Make sure you know what you're getting when you're paying for the session.

5. Who will keep the negatives, and who controls the rights to the images? This may be an important question for both you and your photographer. Some photographers are interested in retaining negatives as a matter of artistic control. Much of the art of photography is done in the darkroom. No two people print in exactly the same way; an amateur and a professional would produce two very different prints from the same negative. The photographer may simply want to insure that no one else will be printing from his or her negatives. If you have some burning desire to obtain your negatives, make sure your photographer knows this before the day of the shoot.

You might want to ascertain who has control of the images and the way they will be used. What we're actually talking about here is who legally controls the photographs. If you hire somebody to take your

photographs and you want to make sure that you control the way in which the images are used, you need to have an agreement with that photographer that the photographs are being taken as works for hire and that the photographer is technically an employee of you. The photographer must assign all rights to those photographs over to you, even though he may retain the negatives. This agreement has to be in writing.

Under no circumstances should you sign a release on photographs for which you are paying. Moreover, you should consult with an agent before you sign any release. If your photographer asks you to sign a release in any composite or testing situation, make certain you know exactly what the photo will be used for and what you will receive in return. Get that in writing, too.

6. Is the appointment time yours exclusively? Some photographers alternate their time between two or three people who may be sharing a dressing room and taking turns to be photographed. Such traffic would disrupt my concentration, and I think it would unnerve my client. Not all photographers run their businesses the same way. If you want your time all to yourself, make sure you mention it now. Otherwise you may find your shoot being disrupted by other people.

Ask if a stylist or photographer's assistant will be present. The stylist or assistant often helps the photographer by adjusting lights, pinning or taping clothes, adjusting hair and powdering faces.

You might want to ask if you will be permitted to bring a friend or relative along with you to the shoot. I do not encourage the presence of others during a photographic session. Very often they are distracting, even if they don't make a peep, because you are focusing your attention toward them, wondering if they're watching you or laughing at you or thinking you're foolish when you should be focusing your attention on what you're doing. One woman asked me if she could bring the man who had directed her through hundreds of Polaroids in preparation for her entrance into the business. "I'm accustomed to working with him," she said. "He knows just how to make me laugh and what my best angles are and how to direct me." She and I did not end up working together. Her friend would not be permitted to coach her in job situations and it was unrealistic to depend on him during a professional photo session.

I am also inclined to separate mothers from their children, particularly when the child is 16 or 17 years old. At this point, a mother running interference during a photo session is inappropriate and downright annoying. It may also distract the child. An agent in Atlanta says that she once interviewed a 17-year-old girl who had great potential for fashion photography.

They arranged a test shoot, but the agent was surprised to find that the proofs from it were dull and unexciting. They arranged another testing and this time the girl's mother was asked to stay in the dressing room. "Those second shots were dynamite! That girl was a fox!" The agent's suspicions were confirmed, the problem corrected, and the new model signed to the agency. Don't limit your chances for success by asking a friend to hold your hand through your first photo session. It's not professional.

7. Who will provide the wardrobe? You will provide your own wardrobe in photo sessions for which you pay. Clothing is provided on job shoots where the product being sold is the clothing or a special uniform or outfit has been rented or purchased specifically for that particular shot.

8. Who will provide the makeup? Most often, you will provide your own makeup. As a working professional model, you should know what makeup is appropriate for you, how to apply it, and what changes to make for different kinds of photography. A makeup artist will be present on some jobs to achieve a particular look, but you can't count on this happening. Find out if your photographer is going to give you any makeup tips and if he or she wants you to arrive makeup-ready.

9. Who will provide the props? Often you will find interesting and photographable items in a photographer's studio. If you want to include one particular prop, however, such as your rare jade chess set, then of course you will have to take it with you to the shoot. If you are expecting to use any products in any of your shots, find out now whether you will have to provide them. I like to include a product shot in my composite shoots, if it is appropriate to do so, because it shows my client's ability to relate to products. Some clients have mentioned that advertising people, producers and others who thumb through their portfolios have asked them if the product shots we set up were actual job shots, and that's what you're after. You want to look like you've done it, and can do it.

10. Will you be going on location? This is an important question. It means leaving the studio and all its controls and going outdoors or to indoor locations, such as grocery stores, banks and offices. Some photographers may not be willing to do this. One photographer told a client that he did not want to use locations, because the backgrounds were too busy and detracted focus from the subject. He liked to work in the studio, because "If you can sell it there, you can sell it anywhere." I tend to disagree. I think location shots, properly exposed, add interest. The

The product types this actress as a "Mom".

Putting him in a library makes the bookworm more believable.

appropriate setting helps put actors or models at ease. What better place to photograph a business man than a bank or office? What better place to shoot a commuter than on the train platform or at the bus stop? What more logical place to find a waitress than in a restaurant?

One agent in Chicago says, "I encourage all new models who come in here to do as much location work as possible. Putting the person in the setting makes it more believable and that's that whole idea. The models should portray themselves as they want to be sold or as they want the clients to see them." Another says that "outdoor and location shots do more good than just all studio shots, for the all-around model. Maybe a high fashion model can get away with and may need all studio shots with different clothes and different poses. The all-around model who is trying to get started needs more."

Many clothing catalogs use locations these days. Christmas catalogs and print jobs are shot frequently in beautiful homes. Product advertising, too, is reflecting a trend toward natural-looking photos shot on location.

One model says he was surprised at the agents' reaction to his first set of photographs taken for him by a friend. "I just thought they wanted different kinds of looks and didn't care about the backgrounds, but the whole thing is important. They weren't bad-looking pictures, but they said you just don't do jeans in front of a backdrop." You should be in a setting that complements or explains the outfit you're wearing.

11. Will the photographer provide direction? I am often asked, especially by new people, if I will tell them what to do. Some have had experiences with photographers saying "Okay, you want to be a model, you know what models do, go ahead and make the moves," and they have felt foolish, ignorant and inadequate. If someone requires direction or asks for it, I am glad to provide it. It often is necessary for brand new people. Experienced people are certainly easier to work with, as their experience has given them confidence, flair, and the security to experiment with new things. I understand also that new people have to start somewhere.

In job situations, some photographers will give direction and some will not. Ask for it now if you need it, and be sure you can follow directions whenever you're asked to do so.

12. Can you include your children or pets? If you want to present yourself as a mom or a dad, or a grandma or grandpa, you may need children for your shoot. Or if you have an unusual pet or want to emphasize your warmth by cuddling a kitten or puppy, you may want to bring along your dog or cat. It is ad-

Perhaps your comp will win jobs for the family pet.

visable to check out in advance with your photographer how he or she feels about this and what special provisions may have to be made. You may want to include your children in a composite for yourself, printing their names underneath their pictures so that producers and agents will know they are available for work. If your children are over 10 or 12, however, and you are trying to look younger than you are, they will age you. Borrow some younger kids from a friend or arrange a shot with your own children in such a way that their sizes are not revealed.

Something to remember, in the event that you use your kids or your pets, is that you will have to make provisions for them following their part in the shoot. With kids, someone should be there to take them home or a babysitter should come with you to attend to them during the rest of the shoot. This is a time when you most certainly need to concentrate on yourself, and just on yourself. I remember photographing a fellow who had a regular job and, therefore, had to shoot on a Saturday. Unfortunately, this fellow was divorced and saw his kids only during the weekends, so he brought them along with him. I sympathized with him, but it was tough for him to concentrate on relaxing and getting just the right expression when his kids were quarreling within earshot. In this case, he should have left his kids with a sitter. They distracted him.

13. Are you expected to do nudes? If this is a question that genuinely concerns you, go ahead and get things clear now. Nudes are really up to you. Outside of a handful represented in New York and European composites, nude shots are not included in composites. I would not suggest a nude shot for someone interested in modeling or commercial work. That does not mean that I have not done a fair number of nude shots, it simply means that I would not be very likely to suggest them. In Chicago, one must be very careful about the way in which a nude or even a bathing suit shot is presented. A printer here who has watched composite trends for years states that "Most agents do not want women that are showing too much bosom or are in provocative poses. Nudes or bathing suit shots should be jazzed up with water or oil rather than look just nude. One top agent has made it clear to us that she does not like a lot of cleavage and a lot of skin. She's not a prude — she's strictly interested in what's going to sell. It's business."

Many of the nudes I wind up shooting are done once the client understands that the commercial usefulness of such a picture is quite limited — perhaps the model knew this from the start — but wants the photo anyway for a gift. I've found that a lot of nude shots are intended to be gifts, not professional tools.

Setting Up an Appointment

Now that you've had all your questions answered to your satisfaction, it is time to set up an appointment at a time mutually convenient. Some folks set their date for a month in advance, hoping to lose extra pounds by the time the shoot arrives. Many experienced actresses and female models check their calendars before making the appointment to see what time of the month will be best for them. Menstrual periods often are accompanied by complexion changes and a feeling of being bloated, so naturally this would be something to consider.

The vacation you're planning is something to consider also. Peeling or sunburned skin presents problems. A dark tan will distort black and white skin tones, causing you to photograph much darker than you really are. A tanned look, if desired, sometimes is created with a bronzing makeup. Excessive sun worshipping tends to dry your skin and cause you to wrinkle, so limit your time in the sun. One girl showed up for her shoot, having just spent several weeks at tennis camp, with white rings around her eyes and very red cheeks. She was burned and had the look of a raccoon. I suggested that we wait

until the rings were less noticeable and the tan evened out. Even though she was impatient to get started, she waited for the right time.

Preparing for the Photo Session

Until the big day arrives, you should be preparing yourself for the shoot. Watch the pros on television and study the ads in newspapers, magazines and catalogs.

Use your full-length mirror to see what movements look best with the clothes you're planning to take to the shoot. Use the poses you've clipped from magazines. Practice facial expressions in the mirror when you brush your teeth, shave, or put on lipstick. Set aside time to use the mirror for no other purpose than to study yourself.

One model who is now an agent suggests that you "put on the garment, get in front of the mirror and learn to see where the natural wrinkles fall, where the ugly wrinkles fall, what does your elbow look like in this full sleeve, do your hose look all right with these shoes. Move in front of the mirror, a practice session without the camera, so that you know if there is anything obtrusive you want to avoid. For in-

*Practice with a mirror before
you pose for a camera.*

stance, if a skirt is full and you have a fairly full hip and you look heavy in the hipline, then you make a mental note to keep your hips at a three-quarter angle and work within that frame. If it is an expensive dress, there may be strange wrinkles you'll have to watch and after a while you learn where they are. If you're trying to learn how to model you need to get the feel of it. The way to get the feel is to take an ad of a good professional model from a magazine, perhaps an editorial photo instead of an advertisement, and tape it on the mirror and duplicate that pose. Mentally ask where your weight is, on your left foot or your right foot, is it distributed, where are your hipbones, your shoulders. Take another photo out of the magazine. You'll find there will be a consistency in where the body weight is and you'll get a feel for it. Then, when you get in front of a camera, it will feel familiar, it will feel right, it will feel successful.'' Models who have followed this advice have been pleasures to work with, even during their first sessions in front of a camera. Practice pays off.

A few days before the shoot, you ought to be getting yourself together. That means looking over your wardrobe, accessories, hair, makeup and props you want to include, making provisions for babysitters, and taking care of details. Here again you are going to have to make decisions. Which clothes, which hairstyles, which accessories, what props? You must do your thinking now so that you arrive at the studio prepared, calm and confident. Don't be like the woman who showed up a half hour late, hair in curlers, asking "How do you want my makeup?" Think of your first shoot as your first professional experience.

Your Wardrobe and Accessories

You've decided on your marketing strategy and you want to take the appropriate clothing. You would not be whipping up a Pillsbury cake in a long gown, you might not want to show yourself in a tennis outfit unless you really have the body for it, and you would need a dirty jacket and jeans if you want to portray a car mechanic at the local gas station. Watch ads and commercials for current advertising trends. Include several selections for each category you want to represent so that your photographer can make a choice.

If you are interested in fashion work take along clothes that move well. Fashion fads, while fun to wear and photograph, tend to date your composite, particularly if that look comes and goes in one season. The clothing should fit you, although taping and pinning can provide the finishing touches.

Don't take clothes you haven't worn or don't like. Take the things you think you look best in and in which you feel good. I ask people not to buy clothes specifically for the shoot unless they need those particular items anyway to round out their wardrobes. Borrow clothes or uniforms if you need more variety. Some people rent outfits and props. A practice that is not uncommon but not heartily endorsed is buying clothes, concealing the tags during the actual shoot and returning them to the store after the shoot.

If you want to show your body without really showing your body, jumpsuits, short sets, swimsuits and athletic wear do the job. Jogging, running, roller skating, racquetball, tennis, bicycling or just tossing a frisbee are activities that display your full look and eliminate predictable cheesecake or beefcake poses.

Check your clothing for wrinkles, stains, tears and missing buttons before you leave for the studio. Unless you're trying to achieve a disheveled or "before" look, such oversights on your part will not reflect well on you and could cause your shoot to be postponed. While it is possible to conceal these problem areas, it means focusing attention on disguise rather than creating exciting photographs.

Action shots can be fun,
unique and revealing.

Too much of everything.

A simple neckline is much better.

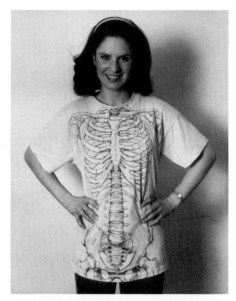

Avoid clothes with writing; you want people to look at you, not to read your clothes.

Many studios will supply irons and steamers for last minute touchups.

One experienced model and actress says, "I would recommend that whatever clothes you intend to buy not be too 'faddy' — in other words, that they be in good taste. Perhaps fewer things that are more expensive and more tasteful than more things that are a little on the frivolous side. I would recommend that you invest in solid colors in medium tones, because that's what you're going to be asked for, mostly, especially earth tones, which include the beiges, the greens and the soft colors. Muted colors photograph best."

Some photographers may ask you to avoid black or white clothing, as it is somewhat more difficult to retain highlights and detail in large areas of black or white. But if your favorite dress is black, be certain to include it.

Particularly on a head shot, plaids, paisleys, huge polka dots, big broad stripes and other bold patterns may be distracting. You want to wear the neckline that most flatters your face. An agent in Chicago says, "I don't think you should wear any neckline that overpowers your face, and if a turtleneck overpowers you, then it's the wrong neckline. I like a blouse that does show the collarbone and the length of the neck. It's prettier on a woman. For men, turtleneck and sport coat says

1967, and is too theatrical." You will no doubt hear many different opinions wherever you go, so once again, you alone have to make the decisions as to what is best for you.

Don't forget the hats, scarves, shoes, belts and jewelry that give the finishing touches to all these outfits. A lot of people, when packing at the last minute, forget to include shoes other than the ones they're wearing. One fellow who wanted to do a jogging shot brought the shorts, sweat band, sweat socks, and only the wing-tips in which he had arrived. Needless to say, he had to forget his jogging shot.

A lot of actors tend to change their hats to change their moods. Some models have a hat to go with every outfit. Hats are fun, but they do cover your hair. Just be sure that some of your pictures show your hair fully, and don't go overboard with the use of hats.

You should remember to include the right bras and slips for the clothing you will be wearing. Take along at least two extra pairs of nylons to any shoot you do. Snags do show up in a photograph, so you may be asked to change your nylons for this reason. Sandalfoot is the style generally recommended. Some men have worn bathing suits — the bikini variety — under their clothes during composite sessions so that they could change clothes quickly anywhere, even on sidewalks.

Your Hair

For the majority of your setups and certainly for your headshot, you will want your hair to look the way it does most of the time. That is providing, of course, that both you and your agency are pleased with the style and appearance of your hair. If not, make the proper corrections by seeing a good hair stylist — your agency will be able to recommend several to you — long enough before the shoot so that you are accustomed to the new style and able to work with it.

Hair that can be worn in various styles should be changed during the composite session. If you are planning to change styles, be sure to have experimented with the styles before you arrive at the studio. No miracles are going to happen the day of the shoot. You would be surprised at the number of people who want to achieve a certain effect with their hair who have never tried working with that style prior to the shoot!

This actress shows braids . . .

. . . a schoolgirl bun . . .

. . . and romantically long tresses.

You will be expected to be able to duplicate the looks you represent on your composite and to achieve a variety of looks on your own. It is part of being professional. That is why you should not go to a beauty salon to have your hair done specifically for this photo session. If it looks "set", you may be asked to comb it out to achieve a more natural look.

A hair style that is versatile is best. Generally that means collar or shoulder length hair. Many college women have hair that is very long, very straight, and very difficult to work with. I often recommend that they see an agent before we shoot, and many come back with new styles.

If your hair is inclined to fall, keep that in mind when you are deciding the order in which you are going to shoot your various sets. If you intend to wet down your hair, do it at the end of the shoot. Be sure to take along curling irons or hot rollers to make occasional touchups if you know your hair will need it.

Wigs are not currently much in use. Some women do use wigs that are flattering and natural looking to create a different look. You can also achieve a change by using scarves, hats and barrettes. A fresh flower or baby's breath adds a lovely touch.

Men should keep their hair neatly trimmed and on the conservative side. One black actor in Chicago says that he got more jobs as soon as he shaved off his goatee and reduced the size of his afro. The emphasis, with most agents, is on a clean-cut image.

Beards, sideburns and moustaches have probably caused more careers to come to abrupt ends than any other feature. The number of men who are emphatically attached to their facial hair is incredible. Unfortunately, the combination of a food product and a beard or moustache is not an appealing one to most advertisers. Moustaches, kept trim and neat, are acceptable in certain areas. Many men shave during their composite sessions to present both "before" and "after" looks. Some character actors show up with a few days' growth to add believability to their portrayals of down-and-out characters.

The third composite I shot, years ago, was with a recent theater school graduate who sported quite a moustache and set of lambchop sideburns. I mentioned to him, before the day of our shoot, that the agents would probably not take kindly to his facial hair and asked him to check it out with them. He replied, and he was not the last fellow to utter these words, "Either they'll take me with my moustache and 'burns, or they won't get me at all!" So we went ahead and shot an entire day. And that's what we actually did — we blew the entire day's work — because the agents told him he couldn't use any of the pictures. They told him they would not be able to provide any work for someone with that much facial hair. Find out what is right for the city in which you're trying to find work, and don't buck the system if working is important to you.

Your Makeup

You will discover your own individual needs in making up and your own individual style through instruction given you by an agent, professional makeup artist or experienced model. One model in Indianapolis says she learned most of what she knows about makeup from a commercial photographer in Chicago, 10 years after she had started to work. Different looks are needed for different jobs, and you will be expected to know those looks. Again, a stylist may be on hand to help you with your makeup, but don't count on it. Arrive at a shoot makeup-ready, and be sure to take your makeup to the shoot in case you are asked to make additions or changes.

For color work and most television commercials, the makeup is natural looking but applied a little more heavily than normal. Black-and-white photography, one Cleveland agent says, "is where you have to use all of your makeup, touch, glimmer, highlight and contouring. Contouring is probably the most important aspect of makeup. With contouring you can totally reform your face. A plump face can go high fashion."

One model reveals her secrets: "For black and white photography, I do change my street makeup. I may do almost nothing but contour and contrast. Of course, it depends on what look we're trying to get. If I'm trying to go real young, I'm not going to hollow myself out too much. I use a lot of brown and a very light pore-minimizing base and that's it. I use pancake only for television. For any type of photography, color or black-and-white, or for television, I set my makeup with a loose powder. For color television, I am closer to my street makeup, only with everything exaggerated. I use my most extreme makeup for black-and-white photography. This is for a fashion look, certainly not for the young mother. It all depends on what I'm doing. If it is for the mother look, I might go with just the light and dark, but not so severe. I'd keep the face a little plumper.

Of course, you have to learn your own face. You know there are certain things you have to do to your face regardless of what job you are doing. You may have to narrow your nose or shorten your chin. Your look is constantly changing, so you have to keep up with it by reading *Vogue* and *Cosmopolitan*. Check, with an experienced eye, the makeup job that is done on the cover of those magazines. Then, too, that look changes from New York to the Midwest to California. So you evaluate also the area in which you're living and what is selling in that area, because that is just what you're doing — you're selling a look!''

People who have done community, school or professional theater work sometimes think that the techniques and kinds of makeup they use on stage will be suitable for photography. Not so. What might look great from the last row in a theater is definitely not going to pass in front of a camera. Often character or acting shots are done without any makeup at all.

If you are living in an area where winter temperatures and winds can cause chapped lips and flaking skin, be certain several days prior to your shoot to moisturize these chap-prone areas. Peeling lips can present problems, and if you are not usually apt to wear makeup but intend to do so during your shoot, you may not be aware ahead of time that your lips will flake under the lipstick. Protect them during the days prior to the shoot and prevent the damage, rather than worrying later about how to cover it.

Even though false eyelashes are, as one model puts it, "just not being worn these days," many women still want to use them to accentuate their eyes. Often these women won't ever have worn lashes prior to the shoot, and they expect to be both beautiful and comfortable for their photo sessions in eyelashes they've never worn before. Become accustomed to whatever makeup or hair variations you're planning prior to the day of the shoot.

Learn to use a lipstick brush. It enables you to make a definite outline and gives you a lovelier lipline.

If you are a man and you are considering getting into modeling, the idea of putting makeup on had better not ruffle your feathers. You would be wise, in fact, to have a supply of basic makeup and know how to put it on if you are asked to do so. If you have a heavy beard, there is makeup available for the correction of that problem. One actor in Los Angeles who does a lot of work in television commercials and print has forceps scars on his cheek and routinely covers them with makeup. It may be that your coloring precludes the necessity for makeup. One fellow who does fashion in New York says, "I never was one for makeup. A man doesn't really need it unless he has a very dark beard and he needs to cover it. I never use a bronzer unless I'm sick. Sometimes, if

Photographing without makeup is risky . . .

. . . as is forgetting to powder.

A hat . . .

. . . a glass . . .

. . . an accessory . . .

*. . . all help to create a certain look,
a special feeling, a completeness.*

you've got a bad cold, you might look really terrible, very pale. Then you may want to use a bronzer. Sometimes they'll ask you to. Once I got a scratch down my face, and I had to cover it with makeup. But for the most part, no.'' While you may not be required to makeup for some job shots, you should know how to apply it if you are asked to do so.

It is important to have translucent powder to remove gloss and shine from your skin, no matter what tone your skin is. It gives you a matte finish without giving color or changing the makeup underneath. One black agent says that "black women need a matte finish just as white models do. I don't think a shiny face fits anywhere in this business. It gives the photographer a fit and makes the model look terrible. A dewy look is one thing, but a shiny, oily-looking complexion is another thing. Cosmetic companies don't educate their customers about what to do with makeup, and many cosmetics are bought on impulse. The dime store client often looks like she's left a dime store, and that's unfortunate.'' Perspiration and natural oils reflect the lights used in photography and the reflection seen in the photograph draws attention immediately to the shine. Powder down before you face the camera.

You may love him but he's just too big.

Other Things To Consider

Props often add the finishing touches to all your other preparations. In fashion shots, a pair of gloves, a necklace, an evening bag, sunglasses, a wineglass or any number of items will give your hands something to do or somewhere to go. Novices often comment that they just don't know what to do with their hands; holding something can be helpful.

You must be careful also that your props don't overshadow or overpower you. A child who is cuter and more animated than you, a horse whose size overwhelms you, or an instrument that is so large that it's difficult to work with can displace you as the center of focus. Whatever you choose to have with you in a picture, it must not remove the limelight from you. This is your composite.

A special tip: Many working models and actors take a kit loaded with whatever they have found necessary to achieve and maintain a polished appearance to every shoot.

This kit varies from individual to individual, but the basics are:

• Translucent powder

• Makeup

• Hair accessories — blow dryer, curling iron, hot rollers, hairspray, brush and comb

• Shaver

• Nylons (two pairs)

• Tissues, towel, safety pins, needle and thread

• Deodorant, dress shields

If you're not going to be able to keep your appointment — if you've lost your nerve, you haven't saved enough money or your mother is coming to visit you — be sure to call and let the photographer know. If you call and say that you are sick, have had an emergency, or have broken out in pimples, you increase your chances for rescheduling. No matter how sheepish you may be feeling about it, do give a call. It will be worth it. More than one pro has called to say that he has an audition or her skin has broken out the day before a shoot. Go ahead and call.

Now you've made your decisions about what to take with you to the shoot, and you've practiced whatever you felt you needed to practice. Go to sleep and get a good night's rest.

6

The Photo Session

Make certain you know where the studio is and have adequate directions for getting there. Give yourself plenty of time so that you don't arrive out of breath and feeling as if you've lost control. Treat this as if it were a job. Be professional and arrive on time.

Generally, I like to start out a composite session by sitting down with a cup of coffee and making a list of the shots the client and I are going to do. Once we've made that list, determining which clothes will be used in which locations, what hats, accessories and hair styles we want to include, then we order the list to make a schedule. This schedule makes it easier for both of us to operate. While we're shooting I don't have to be thinking about what's coming next; we're prepared with whatever props are necessary for the location shots, and we don't have to make two trips to the same general locale. The schedule is important because it answers a lot of questions before the shooting even begins.

Many people arrive with the oddest notions of what a photo session is going to be. If a 5'2", 180-pound woman arrives harboring a fantasy to do high fashion, I want to know about it before I pick up my camera. We'll have to discuss marketing and what the purpose of these pictures really is. If they are the fulfillment of a fantasy, that's one thing, but if they are intended to get work for the individual, that's another thing. I don't want us to work at cross purposes during a shoot for which the client is paying, and such a discussion seems to answer a lot of questions and dispel a lot of fears.

This approach is not what you will find with every photographer. It certainly is not the situation you will find on a job shoot, where time is money.

But when you're paying for pictures, you have every right to know what is going to happen and to ask questions freely. Do not let the newness of the situation intimidate you. By the same token, do not disregard the answers professionals offer.

The Studio

The studio itself is an interesting place full of equipment and gadgets. You will become better acquainted with these objects as your experience broadens, but right now you may feel a little uncomfortable around them and not quite sure what to do.

The following is a list of equipment commonly found in photography studios:

1. Cameras. There are several formats you are likely to find in a professional studio. Large view cameras, 2¼ single lens reflex, and 35mm cameras are what you will probably encounter. Polaroids are often used to check the lighting, set or composition before a job is actually shot with one of the cameras just mentioned. Polaroids might also be used to take a quickie of you during an audition or interview or while you are making rounds. Photographers sometimes like to file their own Polaroid along with your composite or glossy. Nikons, Canons and Leicas are among the brand names you will see if a photographer prefers the 35mm format. Hasselblad, Bronica and Mamiya are a few in the 2¼ single lens reflex format; Sinar, Toyo and Deadroff may be what you will find if a view camera is used. All have advantages and disadvantages.

The lens is a part of the camera. During a shoot your photographer may remove one lens and replace it with another. There are lenses made specifically for portraits or close-ups, and others that show an overall scene normally or with as little distortion as possible. These are the lenses with which you will probably be photographed most often. For your composite or glossy pictures, these are the lenses with which you should be photographed. Very interesting effects can be achieved by using a wide angle lens at close range. The distortion that results, however, makes the shot an interesting portfolio inclusion but definitely not appropriate for presentation to clients.

Film is exposed inside the camera when the shutter is opened and sufficient light hits the film to make an image. This latent image is later developed into negatives. If a view camera is being used, one sheet of film, usually 4'' x 5'' or 8'' x 10'', is placed inside the camera. Needless to say, much time and care will be spent in setting up for this one exposure. With the 35mm or 2¼ formats, however, exposure after exposure can be quickly made until the film runs out, after 12, 24 or 36 exposures. If your photographer is using a motor-driven camera, you will be astonished at how fast the session moves.

2. Tripod. The three-legged support on which any of these cameras may rest is a tripod. It provides a stationary support for the camera so that long exposures may be taken without risking image blur. A cable release may be attached to the camera so that the photographer can trigger the shutter from a distance.

3. Light meter. A light meter is an instrument used to measure the amount or intensity of light falling on or reflected by the subject, which in this case is you. Light meters are also called exposure meters, and some cameras have the meters built right into them. The photographer uses the information taken from a light reading to make the camera adjustments necessary for a proper exposure.

The photographer will probably get close to you with this little hand-held instrument to read your skin tone. Sometimes people react as if it is a dentist's drill and recoil in fear. Relax. Light meters won't hurt you.

Taking a light reading.

The wide angle lens . . . not the effect you want for your headshot or composite.

4. Lights. There are different kinds of lights used to create different kinds of artificial lighting. The term "lighting" sometimes refers to the lamps themselves and the way they are arranged, sometimes the actual process of adjusting those lamps to produce the desired effect, and sometimes the quality or feeling of the illumination as it is observed on the subject. At any rate, don't ever touch or disturb the arrangement of the lights or the lights themselves. The arrangement may represent time and careful placement that is not immediately apparent to you. The lights themselves are fragile. Be careful, too, that you don't trip over all the electrical wires. You'd be surprised how easy it is to do when you're nervous.

You will find different lighting setups in different studios. Each photographer has his or her own reasons for choosing a certain setup. Steady light is supplied by tungsten lamps, which are specifically designed to withstand high intensity heat for long periods of time. This is much like theatrical lighting in that the lighting will be set, turned on, and remain on the entire time you are shooting a particular set. Short bursts of light are provided by an electronic flash or "strobe" lighting setup. Unlike the flash cubes used with instamatics, electronic flash tubes are capable of repeated use. Blinders or barndoor attachments added to the lights will enable the photographer to control the distribution of light. You may be lit by a natural light source in the studio, such as the illumination from a window or skylight. These lights are usually set up on stands.

Connected with these lighting setups are various objects whose purpose it is to reflect the light back onto the subject. The floodlight, which holds the flashtube or the tungsten lamp, reflects the light. Special photographic umbrellas with white or aluminized interior surfaces are often added to the light stands to act as light reflectors. Portable panels or flats may be used as backgrounds or reflectors. These are sometimes referred to as "bounce boards," as they bounce or reflect the light back onto the subject. Walls and ceilings are used to bounce light. One photographer occasionally rigs a parachute to actually surround the entire set, using the white material reflecting overall to produce the most even lighting possible.

Pictures that are so dramatically or harshly lighted that the emphasis is no longer on you but on the dramatic effect are not the kind of photographs you need to get work. The purpose of these pictures is to sell you, not the ability of your photographer to create artistically notable or bizarre lighting setups. You need an honest and natural looking photograph.

5. Background paper. Long rolls of seamless paper, which may be 9 or 12 feet in width, provide a blank

Dramatic, but we don't know what she looks like.

background for many studio shots. These rolls of paper come in many colors, as well as black, white and shades of gray. Unless care is taken to avoid making footprints, each time you step onto the sweep you will leave some marks. If the shots are to be full-length, more paper may be rolled out whenever the area you are standing on is deemed too dirty to continue shooting. I have heard this material referred to as a sweep, a background, a seamless, a drop, paper, and various combinations of the five terms.

6. Wind machine. Also known as a fan, a wind machine may be used to cause a model's hair or the garment she is wearing to flow with the breeze.

You may find other fascinating items in a studio. Some photographers use background projectors, whereby a slide is projected onto a screen and you, the subject, are photographed in front of the screen with the projected image behind you. If the slide being projected is of a tennis court, it is intended to make you look like you are on location on a tennis court. You could be on a luxury yacht, a gondola, a riverboat, or at a horse race. This practice was mentioned by several Los Angeles agents who thought that the whole idea was rather silly and not very convincing.

76

One thing you may not find in a studio, at least outside of the dressing room, is a mirror. Novices occasionally ask if there will be mirrors available during the shoot so that they can see what they are doing. One model-turned-agent comments that "A mirror is a distraction. If you have a mirror behind a camera, then the model is so interested in looking at herself or himself that the rapport that makes for magical pictures is lost. And magical pictures are what all of us wish to attain, be it model or photographer. The use of a mirror is essential to a model, but not while the camera is being used."

It is an unreasonable request. You won't find it in a job situation. You simply must rely on the photographer's directions and the photographer's ability to make you look good. The photographer or assistant is there to tell you that your hair is in need of straightening or to straighten it for you, to see that your collar is right, to mention that your posture is sloppy, your pose too angular, or your nose too shiny. The shooting session is not unlike a theatrical performance. You have applied your makeup, fixed your hair, gotten into costume — and once you've made your entrance onstage and the photographer has picked up the camera, the process has begun. You are no longer preparing, you are doing.

Shooting on location provides a lovely background for this headshot.

Shooting on Location

You may leave the studio for some of your sets and go on location to get your pictures. This is sometimes referred to as doing "remotes." Going on location can mean going into a bank, office, grocery store, greasy spoon, fast food or elegant restaurant, library, classroom, kitchen, living room, bathroom, gas station, or just about anywhere. This may take some prearrangement or some fast talking. It also requires that the photographer be accustomed to working with existing light and that the light that is available is sufficient to make a good exposure. That factor is going to eliminate many places immediately. Other places will be eliminated because they will not give you permission to use their establishments as backgrounds.

What better place to photograph a model who is trying to establish a business image than in an office or bank? What is more reasonable than photographing a would-be housewife type in a kitchen or grocery store? Doesn't it make sense to place a character male slinging hash in a greasy spoon, pumping gas at a station or downing a beer in a pub?

The store sign links a face with a name . . . she's Lauren Baskin.

A pretty backlight . . .

. . . or cause for squinting eyes and harsh shadows.

If photographed properly, these locations add interest to rather than distract attention from you. Many individuals, particularly those who are new, enjoy getting away from the controlled atmosphere of the studio and actually going into the environs of the characters they are portraying. Gestures, clothing, props and expressions seem to fall into place and make sense.

Going on location can also mean going to forests, parks, jogging paths, bridle paths, beaches, city streets, campuses, ballparks, swimming pools, tennis courts, playgrounds and alleys. And, under most circumstances, you will have sufficient light to photograph anywhere you wish to go. There are, however, certain things you and your photographer must remember when shooting outdoors.

The bright sun can be a friend or an enemy, depending on how you use it. It can provide a most effective means to backlighting and adding fascinating highlights to your hair. If you're not accustomed to working with bright sunlight, however, it is quite easy to ruin potentially beautiful shots. If you feel sunlight hitting your face directly, you're likely to be in trouble. If you are asked to face the sun, with the sun at the photographer's back, the

most obvious and immediate problem is going to be that you're squinting. Squinting is not a very flattering facial gesture. It will be very difficult, if not downright impossible, for you to face the sun and have a relaxed and pleasant look on your face. Even if you avert your eyes and look in another direction, the sun is going to cause very harsh and unflattering shadows on certain areas of your face.

If you turn around and keep the sun at your back, it is possible that you still may run into problems. If your photographer does not know how to expose film under these conditions, you may wind up with a lot of photographs in which your face is underexposed and therefore appears much darker than it really is. The background will look fine, because that is what your photographer was exposing for, but because your skin tone is inaccurate, the picture will be of little professional use to you. To make matters worse, if you happen to have your head sufficiently tilted back, the sun will catch your nose and give you a condition I call "beaknose." Your nose, eyebrows and lips protrude from your face and whatever is protruding will be highlighted. The effect is rather clownlike, making the nose look like a ping-pong ball attached to a much darker face.

There is often beautiful light at dawn and dusk. It is a very soft, diffused kind of light. I also like a cloudy, bright day because I can photograph anywhere outdoors and not worry about shadows. If it is a cloudy, gloomy day, however, the light is flat and may not be sufficient to expose for photographs with contrast. Rain is often accompanied by this kind of dull light. There are times when a shoot will have to be postponed or rescheduled, if location shots are important to the model, due to poor light or inclement weather. Better that you suffer immediate disappointment and impatience than face a proof sheet of dull and inadequately exposed photographs.

Not much that is good can be said about rain as it pertains to location photography. The only times I feel that rain is an ally is when a woman wants a slicked-down dripping wet look for her hair, a look which is flattering only to a few women, or when we are doing a fashion look in rainwear. Rain might work to our advantage for a golfer stranded on the ninth tee, a businessman straggling home after a long day, or a mailman bravely carrying on. Generally speaking, however, rain ruins hairdos and spots clothing.

Snow, on the other hand, often adds a touch of softness and prettiness to a photograph. The light that accompanies snow is often diffuse, lush and very flattering. One head shot I did during snowfall captured the large flakes falling onto the actress' brunette hair. It couldn't have been prettier had we staged it.

Snow also provides a nice background for a shot in which you drape yourself with a fur coat. Be careful how you wear the fur, as it can make you appear fat and full if it isn't properly worn. If you look good in a turtleneck, add a scarf, some mittens and maybe a knit cap for a snowball fight or a walk through the woods with your dog. It's a perfect opportunity to do a winter group shot with the whole family included for sledding or skating.

Too much exposure outdoors during extreme cold is bad, however. The skin turns red, the nose starts to drip, and even the most determined or experienced models may have trouble controlling the appearance of goose bumps on exposed skin.

Getting Through the First Few Sessions

Whether you are shooting on location or in a studio, it is most important that you appear natural and relaxed. Even if you quaking inside, you must appear confident. One successful fashion model in New York comments that "as far as coming off on film, you get better and better. It becomes more natural. When you start modeling, you're very stiff and stilted and not really comfortable. After a time you become looser — you get to know what sort of positions to stand in. You get to know about the lights and how to make the garment look decent and wrinkle-free."

People who are uncomfortable often look it. It is written in the eyes, the way in which the body is turned, or in how the neck is being held. The stance is wooden and strained. Sometimes, however, the photographer may not pick up on your discomfort. It is then up to you to announce your feelings. Whether the discomfort you're feeling is mental or physical (you may be thinking that your neck is hurting or your arm feels awkward, or wondering how you could possibly look good when you feel so bad), you should mention your feelings. You may be told to get into a position that feels more comfortable for you, or you may be told to count on the photographer's assurance that the pose looks good. If a woman has long hair, is carrying extra weight, or has some physical characteristic that is hard to photograph, she may be given instructions that feel uncomfortable but are important to making the most flattering photograph possible.

The same applies to mental discomfort. Perhaps the photographer asks you directly or indirectly to do something you don't want to do. Maybe you feel that what is being asked goes against your image — you have a sultry look, and he is asking you to scrub kitchen floors. Or maybe he is suggesting nudes or something more suggestive than what you care to do. Be certain to say so.

In any type of job situation, you take directions. You may feel that the situation is open enough to add your own input by making suggestions, but very often you simply take directions and give the client and photographer what they want. On the job, you are paid for it. Here, you are paying for the photo session and you should make your feelings clear.

Each photo booking and test shot you go through will teach you something new. Each experienced model who tosses out a pointer or two or whom you feel you can approach with questions will help you get the feel of things. Each time you go through a set of proofs with an agent you will see something different. Experience and the good fortune of working with professionals who take the time to guide you will teach you many things and give you the confidence you may not feel at first.

Too far forward . . .

. . . just right.

. . . too far backward . . .

Following is a list of some tips that may help you through your first few shoots:

1. Posture. The camera takes pictures on one dimension. When doing a closeup, in particular, keep the plane of your face in line with the plane of the camera lens. There are many angles and variations possible within these limits, but if you bend your head forward too much, you will be emphasizing the top of your head, your forehead and your nose. A head bent too far backward will direct attention to the nostrils and chin and make you appear to be looking down your nose. Your head should be held in a natural way.

When sitting for a close-up, you want to appear relaxed. This does not mean slouched over. Try to get support from your lower back, leaving your upper torso free to move into relaxed and flattering positions. You do not want to hold yourself so tightly that the pose becomes one you would do for a high school graduation picture. The quality you're seeking is animation.

Sometimes, if you sit with your shoulders forward and face the camera directly, pictures can look like criminal mug shots. This particular stance can also broaden you. The angle from which the picture is being taken will determine whether or not this effect occurs.

One male fashion model working in New York suggests that you lift your shoulders and avoid bringing your arms around as this movement creates wrinkles in the garments. Lift your shoulders to keep from slouching.

Women should be careful not to press their upper arms and elbows into the sides of their bodies when wearing sleeveless garments. Your upper arm will spread out and appear much plumper than it actually is. Hold your arms lightly away from your body.

2. Gestures and expressions. These will be determined largely by whatever you're trying to say in the picture — "Buy this dress" or "Come to McDonald's." You don't want any expression that is so large it comes off as mugging, but you do want to exude personality and generate excitement in the product by facial expression and body movement.

If you're going to be kicking up your heels and swinging your arms in a happy, big, carefree gesture, then do it. Go the whole way. If you're going to go for a seductive look, put your whole body into it as well as conveying the message with your facial expression. Do the thing without apology. It's better to have made an investment in an idea and made a large gesture that just didn't work (you'll look at the proofs later and have a good laugh, learning while you're laughing) than to have a whole series of shots that are bland, unexciting, perhaps usable but not interesting. None may be a big mistake, but none may be the zinger you should be going for. Take a chance. Really get into whatever it is you're trying to convey.

3. Eyes. Many pictures are hits or misses simply because of the eyes. A person may be smiling with the lips and cheek muscles but if the eyes are dead, the picture fails. The eyes also tell if the subject is nervous; you can see right through them to fear and discomfort.

If you are asked to look away from the camera, be sure to focus on something in your mind or on something off in the distance. If you are feeling vacant, your eyes reflect that vacancy. If you are looking at nothing or thinking of nothing, your eyes will tell of that emptiness. Have some motivation for whatever expression is on your face.

In a headshot, particularly, it is common to make eye contact with the photographer's lens and therefore with anyone who views the shot. It is very much as if you were in a social situation — your picture is more likely to have a greater impact and to leave a longer lasting impression if you make eye contact with the viewer. Since you only have one chance with your headshot, don't waste it.

There is a technique called cheating which you ought to know, particularly if you intend to include

Don't just stand there . . .

. . . do something!

*Let's hope she's not as
dull as she looks.*

The wearers of contact lenses are concerned that the lenses are going to show up in the photographs, as they sometimes do — those red eyes — in instamatic color pictures. That won't happen in professional photographs. If the bright lights in the studio bother your eyes, then remove your contacts, but remember that you're having your pictures done in order to get more work having your picture taken. If the lights really present a problem, you might want to think twice about trying to get print work.

*Glasses can finish off
one look . . .*

products, pets or children in your photographs. In real life, you bend your head to read, look directly at a small child, or check out the cereal in your bowl. In pictures, if you bend your head as much as you do normally, much of your face is obscured from view. If you were to turn your head as you normally would to look at someone standing next to or slightly back of you, all you would present to a camera in front of both of you would be your profile. For these reasons, in order that more of your face be visible and on a plane with the lens, you may be asked to "cheat your eyes." You will actually be looking at one point while appearing to focus on another. You will get the hang of it after a few tries.

If you wear glasses in real life and you are likely to be wearing them for auditions, interviews and rounds, then wear them for your photographs. Even if your vanity protests, wear the glasses in at least some of your sets if you are shooting a composite. Many people who don't need corrective lenses wear fake glasses to change their looks or give them an air of authority and character. One fellow who was just another pretty face in New York watched his career take off when he put out a new set of pictures featuring him wearing glases. One actor in Chicago, whose wire-rim glasses were a part of his established character look, ordered new frames in a modern style and went back to the wire rims when his career started to wane. There are some professionals who have special glasses — frames without lenses — they use in order to eliminate reflections or glare. So if you wear glasses, use them. They could become your trademark.

*. . . and add character
to your photos.*

Another problem regarding eyes that some models occasionally encounter is infection. Some models apply so much makeup, so often, and sometimes incorrectly, that they infect their eyes. Remove your makeup when you sleep and see a doctor immediately if you notice any puffiness, redness or irritation of your eyes.

4. Lips Because people are often a little nervous when having pictures done, they ask if they can just go on talking and have the photographer click away while they are doing so. Yes and no. Talking very often helps to establish a character or a mood and lends much to the visual idea you're trying to capture. There are times, however, when you are not going to want to be photographed with your mouth open or a broad expression on your face. Sometimes, too, certain words tend to contort the lips in unflattering ways. An agent in Indianapolis tells her clients to use different vowels to get different facial expressions, or to try the word, "say." Practice at home in your mirror using different words and sounds. See what works best for you.

5. Hands. Hands seem to be a real problem to beginning models. They never know where to put their hands, how to place them, or how to make relaxed gestures. The touch should always be light. Whether you're fingering your collar, toying with a necklace, or resting your hand on your hip or your leg, the gesture should always be light and delicate, not sturdy and muscular or showing strain.

One agent suggested that, if no hand gesture feels natural at the beginning, you try placing the third and fourth fingers together. You can always hold an evening bag or other appropriate prop to give your hands something to do.

Men modeling clothing for photographs pose with one elbow slightly crooked, held gently away from the body so that the garment shows, and hold their fingers in a manner that almost suggest a fist. The other hand is often placed lightly on the belt or in the pocket, taking care not to wrinkle or pull the clothing. Never assume that shoving your hand in your pocket is going to look good. Place it lightly.

Again, studying good fashion ads and practicing hand gestures in a mirror will help you find what feels comfortable. If you're interested in getting commercial work, the numerous props and products you'll be using to add interest to your photos will supply you with something to hold in your hands. Of course, you should not use any prop that is so large that it obscures you, or hold a prop in such a way that it hides your face or causes your face to fall into shadow. People generally know how to handle Burger King "Whoppers" and cans of Coca-Cola and packages of Alka-Seltzer more readily than how to

flow a skirt or place a hand on a hip to show off a Dolman sleeve. All things come with practice and experience.

If you are using your hand as a support upon which to rest your chin or your check, the gesture should be light. If you really place the weight of your head heavily onto your hand, you will push up the skin of your cheek or chin. The result is quite unflattering.

6. Other models. If you are working with one or more other models, there are a few rules of etiquette. Do not disturb someone else's balance or sense of space. If you are supposed to look as if you are leaning on another model, merely rest your elbow, arm or hand on her or him. You will throw off her balance if you put your weight on her. You do not want to upstage another model either, unless the picture is being taken expressly for your composite. Otherwise, the photographer will probably group you in a manner that will best display the clothing or product.

Rest lightly.

You may not understand everything the photographer is doing. That's understandable. It may be helpful to know, however, why a few things are happening. If your photographer is taking three or more exposures of every shot you have set up, then it is likely that he is bracketing. This practice occurs when conditons make it impossible for the photographer to be absolutely sure that one exposure will be exactly correct, and so he insures the success of the shoot by taking several different exposures. This may not occur during a composite shoot, but if it does, you will be asked to go through the same pose, expression or movement several times.

You may also be asked to move in one direction or another, camera left or camera right, upstage or downstage. Camera left would mean that you are being asked to move to your right. If you are asked to move downstage, you should move closer to the camera. It is doubtful that you will run into these terms in your first few shoots.

If something is said that you do not understand, however, ask to have it clarified. The language of the business may seem perplexing at first. During the interviews I did for this book, some agents used terms I'd never heard before, some of which aren't in any dictionary. Simply ask for an explanation if you're confused about a word or a direction.

After the Shoot

You are going to need to know how to choose the best shots and make quality judgments about your prints and reproductions. It is not necessary that you understand darkroom technique or the reasons why certain pictures look as they do; you just need to know if the work you're receiving is acceptable for your professional needs. You do need to know a few basic terms and processes so that you can converse in the language other professionals use. You'll be making decisions at least three times: selecting from your proofs, accepting your prints and accepting your reproductions.

Proof Sheets

The proof sheet, or contact proof, is the first step. Proof sheets are generally about 8'' x 10'' in size, although they can be made on 11'' x 14'' or 16'' x 20'' paper. The 8'' x 10'' proof is made by placing the actual strips of negatives directly on photographic paper and exposing it to a light source,

Proof sheets:
(top) 2¼ inch - 12 exposures;
(bottom) 35 mm - 36 exposures.

so what you're seeing is the actual size of the negative. These proofs are unlike some that you might get from a portrait studio in that you may subject them to direct light as often as you wish. That's good, because you and your agents will be spending a great deal of time examining them.

Depending on the format of the camera used, (35mm, 2¼ or larger), your proof sheets may consist of 12, 24 or 36 different pictures, all given one general exposure. What this means is that some may show your skin tone as it really is, and some may be slightly lighter or slightly darker than you are. Unless your photographer was drastically off when taking the picture, he or she will be able to compensate when making the enlargements for the ones that are slightly off in tone. Don't overreact to proofs that show subtle variations in skin tone.

People react to proof sheets in various ways. The more experienced professionals find the outstanding shots in a quick glance and concentrate on those. The novice usually zeroes in on the ones where the eyes are closed, caught in a half blink, or the lips are frozen somewhere between a sneer and a smile. Failure! Well, even the pros occasionally have a failure where they are caught in between expressions, where the timing is off ever so slightly. It is true that fewer goofs appear on the proof sheets of more experienced photographic models and that that consistency is something the agent or client may look for. Sometimes a model will reproduce an entire proof sheet as her composite or part of her composite, to show that she is capable of 12, 24 or 36 consistently good and varied exposures.

With a head shot, you are looking for the one zinger that you are going to send out to represent you. If you are having difficulty seeing your successful shots, take a blank sheet of paper and cut out a hole the size of one of the negatives. Then view each photo on the proof, examining each one for its merits or disappointments and making mental notes as to what can be done differently in the next photo session. Usually this diminishes the feeling of being overwhelmed by 36 images of you staring back and helps you choose the one or two that will market you to your best advantage.

I strongly recommend that you use a magnifier to check expression on the proof sheets, particularly facial expressions on full-length shots. Magnifiers start at about $2.50, although you can spend more on ones with fancy attachments such as flashlights or grids. A 35mm magnifier is more useful to you than a magnifying glass, although a magnifying glass is more useful than nothing. You can purchase these

A magnifier really helps.

magnifiers, designed just for the purpose of looking at proofs, at your local camera store. Get one. It makes life much easier.

So now you've spent hours perusing each detail of each proof and you're thoroughly confused. That's par for the course. Now it's time to get a second opinion. A logical place to go is your agency. One agent says that a good way "to learn is to study the proof sheets. And you really study them. You see what works and what doesn't." Another agent in Washington, D.C., adds that "You can read millions of things in a contact sheet. You can see how models are doing their makeup, whether they are careful and meticulous. If their pictures show that they wear wrinkled clothing, what are they going to so with someone else's clothes? You can see from the first to the last frame whether they've loosened up or if they're still just as tense and whether it's positioning their arms or legs that's causing trouble. We look at these contact sheets with an eye to finding out what the problems are.'' The agents also know what is currently selling so they will be able to help you choose the best prints to market you. A grease pencil is often used to indicate choices and cropping, which are lines drawn to show what portion of the picture is to be enlarged.

Of course, another ideal person to go to for a second opinion is your photographer. You are not obligated to agree with any of the opinions you get. The comments from professionals in the business are, however, more valid than the ones from your best friend, neighbors and little brother. Think twice before letting your mom's comment of "Honey, you don't look happy enough in this one," dictate your professional decisions. You are the product being represented by your photographs, so you should be proud of and pleased with whatever material is distributed on your behalf.

If you have found photographs that you want to order — ones that are in focus, where there are no extraneous shadows, where the prop or product is not obscuring you, where the basketball you are shooting is not three times larger than you because it was closer to the camera, and where the composition and expression are pleasing — then go ahead. Make certain that the ones you are ordering represent a variety of expressions, cropping (full-length, three-quarter and close-up) and a few where you are not gazing directly at the camera. Your photographer has probably worked hard to represent you in a variety of ways. Be careful not to choose all smiles, all serious looks or all full-length shots.

On the other hand, it may be that, out of all those proofs, there is none you want to order. If it is a matter of the photographer's style or technical expertise, then all you've lost is your deposit. If there is something you want to change — your hairstyle, your neckline, your makeup or expression — then you may want to renegotiate with your photographer. He or she may be willing to re-shoot for the cost of the film and processing if you have some concrete ideas for changes you are going to make. It's probable that your deposit will not be refunded, as the photographer has spent time preparing you for the shoot, doing the shoot, developing the film, proofing the film, and mailing out the proofs.

Even if you do decide not to order any prints, the experience has been valuable for you in that you have a photo session under your belt. Pick yourself up and start over again.

Prints

When you are placing your order for prints with the photographer or his assistant, be certain to communicate your particular specifications. Be certain to establish what size prints you will be getting, and if they will be dried with a glossy or matte finish. These things are important to the printer. If you or your agent have any requests for cropping, mention them when you are ordering the prints.

The 11'' x 14'' print size is the standard size for portfolio photographs. One printer says that the model is better off to start with that size because the printer will return the photos, undamaged and unmarked, when the composite or glossy has been printed, and the pictures are then placed in the portfolio. "Quite a lot of experienced people come in with a small print, maybe not even an 8'' x 10'' size, and expect us to work from that." Even though the headshot or composite size is never 11'' x 14,'' it is best to order your composite prints that size. Head shots printed to a full 11'' x 14'' are larger than life and quite overwhelming. The 8'' x 10'' is appropriate for your headshots.

Can a headshot be cropped from a full length or three-quarter length shot? Not very successfully, and I wouldn't recommend it. Any time you greatly enlarge a shot or a portion of a picture, you run the risk of expanding the grain and reducing both the focus and the contrast — and, therefore, the effect — of a picture. A head taken from a body shot would most certainly not be sharp. It is best to order a head shot from close-ups taken specifically for that purpose. Sometimes I think people ask for such modification because they know the end product will be less clear and therefore less likely to reveal flaws they would rather be kept secret.

Prints are also called enlargements and blow-ups. When you go in to pick up your prints, there are certain qualities for which you should be looking. You want only top-quality photographs to represent you professionally.

Ask yourself these six questions about any photograph:

1. Is it in focus? If the camera moved, if you moved too much when the picture was taken, or if your photographer has problems in the darkroom, your picture could appear fuzzy or unsharp. Check your proof. If the picture is somewhat blurred in the proof and you ordered it, it's your problem. If it is crystal

Too light . . .

. . . just right.

sharp in the proof and the print is lacking definition, it's the photographer's problem.

Either way, you will have to decide if the softness bothers you. Many people include one print that is slightly fuzzy, perhaps because it is an action shot, in the combination of shots they choose to put on their composites. If this is your head shot, however, you might want to think twice before choosing a photo that is soft or lacking definition. A client might wonder what that softness is concealing.

2. Does it look like me? This can mean several things. Often actresses or older women will choose high fashion or glamour shots, with their cheekbones lit just so and their hair blowing. The shots do not represent them fairly. They may be boosts to the ego but the boosts are temporary. As one Los Angeles actor puts it, ''It'll only take once that you walk in and

don't look like your picture — they'll never see you again. Don't ever have pictures that don't look like you.''

A Midwest model adds that ''I don't want my photographs to represent me one way and then show up on a job and have them look at me and say, 'My God, I thought you were 25. You look like you're 35. I can't use you, honey. You're going to have to go home.' I have seen that happen, and I don't want it to happen to me.''

In the context of determining print quality, however, it means something slightly different. Does the skin tone look like your skin tone? It's that simple. It should not be too light or too dark.

One actress recalls that, on the basis of her head-shot, she was called in to a theater to read for a part for a black woman. Unfortunately, this actress was white. She had new pictures taken immediately. Many black people (and Hispanic) also have trouble

This photo will never reproduce well because it lacks contrast.

This is okay . . .

getting photographs that represent their skin tones accurately. Whatever your color, use photographs that really look like you.

3. Does it have contrast, or is it all gray? Again, you don't have to know why it looks the way it does, just that it is going to reproduce well and give you a professional look. A photograph that is washed out or too light is not going to do either. A good photograph has tones ranging from black to white, with good neutral or gray tones in between.

4. Is it actually what I asked for or what I like? One actress went to pick up some prints she had ordered from a composite photographer only to find that very few were ones she had ordered. Obviously you want to make certain that the prints are the size you asked for, dried the way you have requested and cropped to any specifications you may have indicated.

Many photographs are cropped by the photographer in surprising and often quite effective ways. Sometimes cropping can turn a mediocre photo into an exciting visual presentation. By the same token, if you have ordered a print from what you've seen on the proof, and if the cropping is so extreme when you go to pick up the prints that the picture is unrecognizable or unusable, you have every right to request that the print be reprinted with cropping as you ordered.

. . . but this is better.

You don't want prints
with specks . . .

. . . stains . . .

. . . or cracked surfaces.

5. Is it clean? We're not talking about prints that are "all-American" or non-pornographic in content. We're asking if there are any dust spots, scratches, stains or extraneous specks on the print, and if it smells. No joke — any print that has an odor to it is a print that is suspect, and I've had more than one novice model show me prints that smelled weeks after they had been purchased. The odor indicates sloppy darkroom practices and the stability — how long the print will look the way it does or be useful to you — is in doubt.

Also, stains or discolored areas also may indicate sloppy darkroom technique. Stained prints should be an immediate turn-off to you if you are interested in keeping photographs for more than a few weeks.

Dust spots, specks and scratches can be blended into the surrounding tones by using a fine brush and dye. This technique is called spotting, and your prints should be spotted before they are released to you.

6. Is the print in good shape? Photographs are fairly fragile items. The edges on your prints should not be dog-eared. If the photograph is bent or folded in any way, it will crack the emulsion and render the photograph useless, as it cannot be reproduced without showing the line of the crack. Occasionally your prints may be somewhat wrinkled due to the drying process, but these wrinkles will flatten out with time and will not affect the reproduction of the print into glossies or composites. Protect your prints with heavy cardboard or by putting them into a portfolio case as soon as possible.

If the work does not measure up to your specifications, do not accept it and do not pay for it. If you are in doubt, call your agent or take the work to the agency — with an understanding between you and your photographer that your check will be returned and another set of prints made should you request them after getting a second opinion. Most reputable photographers will be reasonable about valid complaints or mix-ups in orders. If you are displeased with either the product or the service, tell the agency. The information will be helpful to them in steering clear of certain photographers.

Composites

Now you have to decide which prints will be used and why, what to include in the written copy, how your prints are going to be laid out if you're going to have a composite made, how many duplicates to order, and whether to consult with your agent about these decisions. I would recommend, particularly if you are going to have composites printed, that you do spend time talking over these matters with your agent. Your agency may already have arrangements to have all their composites printed by one printer. Some agencies prefer or demand certain formats. A New York composite has a different look than one from Los Angeles, Boston or Louisville. Regional trends and photography styles will determine the look of your composite.

The purpose of the composite is to provide clients with a small sample of the work you are capable of doing. You don't want to limit your marketability or work potential by limiting the scope of your pictures, but neither do you want to make inappropriate stretches. One commercial photographer in Chicago comments that he likes to see a lot of variety and close-ups in a composite. He emphasizes that he appreciates honesty: photos that are true to the individual's appearance, not theatrically costumed, heavily made up, or mugged. A California casting director likes to see a composite that gives her a good idea of a person's range. The variety you show may be determined by the number and kind of excellent photos you have. If all your photos are usable, then you'll have to make choices as to which will best market you.

One talented man . . .

Two model/actresses comment about what they try to achieve in their composites:

"When I set up my composite I am interested in showing as many looks as I can possibly show without stretching. In other words, I could try to show the look of a 16-year-old cheerleader, put my hair in pigtails and do a short skirt act and look younger than I am, but I wouldn't quite be making it, obviously, at age 31. So I am not going to do that. Within the realm of validity, I try to show as many looks as I can. I am not going to put on a dark wig — wigs are out anyway — as I have blonde hair. I have always had blonde hair, I have blonde eyebrows. I would look hard, and I would look bad in a dark wig — so why show it? Within these guidelines I try to show several different hairstyles without being bizarre.

. . . five different faces.

"You should show your legs. They want to know if you have good or bad legs. I did a bathing suit shot that is not exactly cheesecake because they want to know about your figure. But at the same time I don't want them to think, by seeing a picture on my composite, that I do cheesecake. As a mother of a 5-year-old, I don't care to do that. And yet I'm not at all opposed to doing something for Catalina swimwear. In all of this I am trying to get across an image. And that's the image I have of myself and that I'm trying to portray to other people. And what I try to be at this point is a model who does classy things."

. . . and . . .

"I think that a common mistake people make when they get into this business is that they want to make a statement about themselves. I've seen a lot of people who either aren't particularly glamorous or who are a little older than they should be if they're competing for glamorous kinds of jobs, and they'll do pictures in bikinis or they'll try to do moody kind of 'Here I am, this absolutely raving beauty' picture when, in fact, they're not. In other words, they don't make true statements about themselves in the area in which they'll be able to compete.

"If, for instance, they can compete with a 22-year-old long-legged, raving beauty, all power to them. But if, in fact, a woman is 35 and has several children, then she should try to look as if she is a 35-year-old housewife with several children who still happens to look alive, healthy and pleasant. I've seen them do the sexy shots because it's fun, something for their egos, but I don't think it does that much for them professionally.

"The comp should be fairly uncluttered. Some photographers claim that you should have just a head shot and maybe one other thing on the comp. But I've seen it proved again and again that art directors are notoriously unimaginative. They want to cover their fannies, so to speak, and if you have a shot in a cowboy hat and they're trying to hire someone to ride a horse or appear on a fence with a horse in the background, then out of 17 composites they'll choose a model in a cowboy hat because they can see what she'd look like in their spot. If Rita Moreno auditioned as a gypsy and Farrah Fawcett appeared with one earring and a rose in her teeth, they'd probably hire Farrah Fawcett!

"What I am saying is that you almost have to spell it out. I think it should be as natural as possible and go after what you think your forte is. If you think that you are great for the housewife market, then show yourself in the kitchen or doing some kind of activity that says 'I am an attractive, wholesome housewife.'"

In establishing your image, your composite should show the advertising roles you fit into and the expressions and looks of which you are capable. If you are capable of a sophisticated and glamorous look as well as the expression that goes along with having an Excedrin headache, show both on your comp. Some models who have been working for years in both trade show/convention work and product printwork put out two composites from one photo session. One will appeal to clients interested in models for trade shows and conventions, and the other will appeal to clients in advertising. One agent, though, says that she would rather that money be put into a new comp every nine months or so than into two different comps released simultaneously.

It is probably a good idea to include some shots where your attention is not focused directly at the camera, although it is common for headshots to establish eye contact between the photographer's lens and the model. "I sure get sick of composites with lots and lots of poses that stare out at me," says one agent. "I really prefer to see at least one or two shots in a total composite consist of a more candid angle of the face."

Include at least one full-length shot in your composite, particularly if your appearance does not limit you to blatantly character roles. There most certainly should be at least one full-length shot — one that shows leg shape — in the portfolio if not in the composite.

You might include a few shots that show or imply action. Even though these will be set up, the effect is more candid and less posed than those that show you standing, sitting or leaning. Walking briskly, as the girl does in the Charlie television commercials, generally produces a good look for both men and women. You may have to walk through it many times before you and your photographer feel you've captured it, but the feeling of confidence and bounciness the photograph suggests is a positive image for a model to convey.

In your next composite you may want to include a job shot. A job shot is a photograph actually used in a print advertisement. The advantage of this is that it shows that you have worked professionally, and may link your name or face with a certain product or look. One model feels, however, that job shots generally are not satisfactory for inclusion in her

Action shots can be set up in series:
the line-up, the putt, the hole-in-one!

labs do this kind of work. You may receive three different prints, taken from the same negative, representing different values. Your printer will be able to select which will reproduce best. Generally speaking, color loses contrast and depth when translated into black-and-white negatives.

Limit the written copy you include with your photographs. On a headshot, it is common for a name only to be printed underneath the photo. Sometimes, however, the printing of the name is overlooked and this defeats one of the purposes of having a headshot, which is to link your name with your face after you've made rounds or auditioned. Some actors include union affiliations or their agent's name, if listed exclusively with one agent. This information, as well as other important data, is also listed on the resume, which is discussed a little later on. It is important to have your name printed on your headshot.

There is considerably more written copy included on a composite. Specifics vary from city to city and year to year, but the basic information printed is: Name, dress or suit size, height, weight, measurements (bust, waist, hips for women; waist, inseam and shirt sizes for men), hair color, eye color, shoe size, glove size, hat size, social security number, union affiliations and any special talents or features. Credits are often given to the photographer and the printing company. Composites may be printed with the date of printing included so that a client will know how recent the photos are. Agency exclusivity might also be included. Many models and talent who are multiple-listed have rubber stamps made which list all the agencies they're listed with, and a phone number where the model can be reached.

A printer who specializes in the printing of composites says, "One thing I have noticed, especially with the female models, is that they sure know certain measurements sound good, like bust 35, waist 24, hips 35, or whatever. And they use that. With a lot of them, it's quite obvious that they aren't those measurements. With men who have been around modeling or who have some friends in modeling, they'll put down 40 Regular because it is the size to be. Someone might ask me if I think they ought to put it down. I say, if you can't wear a 40 Regular, you better not put it on there. What if they call you in for a job and they hand you a 40 Regular suit!" It is common for men who are entering modeling not to know what their inseam length is, and some men don't even know what an inseam is. If you are seeking work modeling or advertising clothes, know your sizes before you go into the printer's office.

composites. The focus is most often on the product and not on the model, or the model may just appear as part of a group. In a composite shooting you have control over the locations, wardrobe, lighting and positioning of props.

You may want to include the work of several photographers even in your first comp. It shows you in different photographic styles and demonstrates that you are able to work with more than one professional. It indicates commitment and endeavor, for it takes a great deal of time and effort to go through the shoot-proof-print process with more than one photographer. To do this may cost a great deal of money if these shots aren't tests. Expediency and economy are the reasons many beginning models simply go through one composite session and use the work of one photographer.

If you want to include a color photograph in your composite, you will have to get a color- corrected black-and-white print made. Custom photo

A variation on the theme. Photo variety on the front . . .

Gunnar Lewis

Height: 6'   S.A.G. - A.F.T.R.A. - A.E.A.   Hair: Brown
Weight: 160   Eyes: Hazel

Theatrical Television

Blurred Visions..................Paul   Ile.................Captain Keeney
A Part of Me Too................Jack   Shy and the Lonely..............Paul
Drink to a Lonely Night.............Ed   Picture of Dorian Grey........Lord Henry

Theatre

Northland Playhouse

Detective Story w/Horace McMann................................Arthur Kindred
Mr. Roberts w/Horace McMann...Jack
Room Full of Roses w/James Coburn...............................Bill Hewett
Member of the Wedding w/Ethel Waters.................................Hal
Strictly Dishonorable w/Ceasar Romero............................Giovanni

Pheasant Run

Who Was That Lady w/Bob Crane..................................Robert Doyle
Up a Tree w/Janet Blair..Herb Howland

Rustic Barn

Marriage-Go-Round...Paul Delville

Forum

Forty Years On...Franklin

Vanguard

Purple Dust...Gilligan
Lady's Not For Burning...Thomas Mendip
Lower Depths..Vaszily

World Stage

Four Poster.....................He   Shadow of a Gunman...........Donald
Waiting for Godot.............Vladimir   Antigone....................Narrator
No Exit......................Gascon   The Immortalist.................Michel

Detroit Repertory Theatre

Tango...Stomil

Theatrical Film

Fury, 20th Century Fox...Topguy

Radio & TV Commercials

National, Dealer and Local Spots; **Voice Over,** oh yes, many! **On camera,** those too.
Industrial shows, a few. **Industrial Film,** more than I have fingers and toes.

Education

Formal and Informal, Experimental and Traditional, Experience and Theory.

TALENTPHONE for an over-the-phone
instant audition call©
(312) 664-9457
or
(312) 664-6160

. . . an actor's resume on the back.

You will also have to determine the layout of your pictures, and the format in which they will be printed. Find out if your agent has a preference.

The most common composite style contains two to eight different photos printed on paper that is about 8" x 11". It is printed on both the front and the back, usually with one shot on the front and three or four on the back. This is called a two-page composite and it can be printed on different kinds of stock, although offset and enamel embossed paper are typical. Four and six-page composites are available, but many agents feel that a two-page composite is all a beginner needs.

Another format is photo cards, which are approximately 5" x 7" in size and seem to have originated in Europe and filtered into New York. One agent in Boston prefers cards because they are easy to handle, inexpensive and can be changed frequently. She feels that glossies are cumbersome. However, a printer comments that "almost every agent in Chicago does not like them for a very good reason. Cards will be lost in the files — out of sight and out of reach." Many agencies don't care what format is used as long as they are supplied with pictures.

Keep the design of the composite simple. Years ago, some composites actually were collages of photographs cut up in stars, circles, and diamond shapes and pasted together. Another trend that an agent describes as "almost embarrassing" is the use of blue, pink, gold or colored paper, or sepia tone tints in the ink. You may think such additions show flair, but clients may find them distracting and unprofessional. Stick with a straightforward, simple arrangement. Your agent or a printer will be able to help you make the right decisions.

The photo you put on the front of the comp should arouse the interest of the client or the rest may never be seen. Some agents recommend that you put a head shot on the front, while others suggest that it be your best shot — whether it's a full length shot, action shot, product shot, character shot, or even a gimmick shot. The front of one of the most memorable composites I ever shot showed a fellow calling for his date at the door with flowers, tuxedo and a boutonniere. The problem was he had forgotten his pants. This composite stirred up a lot of attention.

Another man put three shots on the front and three shots on the back. He had been in public relations before he decided to try his hand at modeling and was aware that clients viewing composites tend to flip through them quickly, pausing over only the ones that catch their eyes or are the type for which they are looking. He didn't want to give them the chance to categorize him on the basis of one front shot, so he had a designer put three (a leisure fashion, a househusband character and a businessman) on the front, and three (a character businessman, a narrator type and a father) on the back.

Photo retouching is not recommended, but if you were tired the day of the shoot and want to have those dark circles airbrushed out, now is the time. Do not even consider having acne, scars, crow's feet, wrinkles, or other permanent features retouched. Your pictures must represent you just as you are.

Reproductions

You need to have your photographs duplicated in order to leave a supply with your agent or agencies, to have something to link your name and face at auditions and interviews, and to have something to leave with prospective clients when you make rounds.

Headshots, if printed in quantity on glossy paper, are often ordered at a custom photo lab that specializes in professional quality finishing. Your glossies are actually photographic prints printed from a negative that is made from the print you took in. Changes in tone or cropping can be made at this time. Because your duplicates are actually photos, it is important that you check them over, as you did with the original prints, before you leave the lab. Check for dust specks, extraneous shadows and chemical stains. The duplicates should match the original print. If you are not satisfied with the duplicates, ask to have them reprinted.

Composites are most often the product of an offset printing process, in which ink is applied to receptive paper, as opposed to a strictly photographic process. Because it is a lithographic process, composites may be called lithos in some cities. For this reason, once the printing plates are made, huge numbers of composites can be printed at relatively little cost. They are usually ordered in increments of 500. Order only as many as your agent recommends for your first composite. You will know so much more for your second effort, and you may want to make changes when your original supply runs out. If not, printers often keep the plates for a period of time and you may order a second set of duplications at much less cost than you originally paid.

If there are printers in your city who specialize in the printing of composites, as there are in Cleveland, Boston, Chicago, Los Angeles and New York, they will be glad to provide you, a prospective customer, with samples of their best work. Some will have entire books for your examination. These printers know how to lay out and design composites that will work for you.

Printers cannot, however, work miracles for you. They cannot produce professional-looking work from Polaroid photos, prints with coffee stains and dog teeth marks, or proofs. They cannot work from prints with absolutely no contrast. "We could never end up with a good-looking printed piece when the photograph is no good to start with. The worst thing is that most of the people will say 'I have to use them. I don't have the money to get different photographs.' We'll suggest that they check with their photographers to see if they could get a print with more contrast. Most of the time, they're either afraid to go back to the photographer or they'll say 'This is what I've got, this is what I'll use.' Even though we tell them it's not going to do them much good and it's going to make us look bad, they want to use the prints anyway." You must start with quality photographs.

Once again, check over your composites before you leave the printers and be certain you're satisfied with them. They are the result of all your effort. Are they too dark or too light? Is the written copy accurate? Printers have been known to misspell names. A reputable printer will recognize legitimate grievances and usually be amenable to making appropriate changes.

Portfolios

You can always identify a model walking down a city street by that special look and the book, or portfolio, that he or she is carrying. The portfolio is an album, usually leather or vinyl, designed to protect photographs and provide an efficient means for prospective clients to view the highlights of your professional accomplishments. Your book is a record of your most outstanding work.

The portfolio is generally 11" x 14" in size and resembles a large, zippered, 3-ring notebook. The pages are protected with plastic coverings under which you slide prints and other work. This way you can present your book to many people and still keep your photographs looking crisp and spotless. These portfolios may be purchased in art supply stores.

As a beginner, you will want to include all the prints ordered from your photo session, your composites, your proof sheets, resumes and agency

material, such as vouchers, that you may have. As your career gains momentum, you will want to add test shots, tearsheets, job prints, transparencies or slides, and any union materials you need to take to jobs. You do not include your wedding pictures, your high school graduation picture or your diploma from modeling school. One photographer says he likes to look at a well-organized book. "If they go over 30 prints, I'm lost. I can't remember that many images." The emphasis is on quality, not quantity.

Actors and actresses may want to include meaningful production stills and good reviews in their portfolios. They may also find that few casting directors or theatrical directors are interested in looking at portfolios. In some cities a portfolio or a composite is regarded as the tool of a model. An actor who carries a portfolio might not be taken seriously as an actor. One casting director who does take time to look at books feels that the portfolio, and not the headshot or commercial composite, should contain the pictures that demonstrate the age range and variety of looks an actor can achieve.

Your book provides an opportunity to show yourself in roles or poses that may not be appropriate to the image you are trying to create in your composite. One model who gets a lot of "pretty housewife" jobs likes to project a well-scrubbed country girl image in her composites. She once did a test shot, however, that showed her in a soft gown, an almost slip-like dress, reflected in a mirror. It was a beautiful mood shot, but she felt that it would not do much to sell her in her type. So it found a place in

The country girl image gets her work.

her portfolio rather than in her composite. It was a decision based on business, not ego flattery.

Your agent may occasionally ask you to leave your portfolio at the agency so that a client may view it. Be very careful where else you leave your book. At least three people have called to order a second set of prints because their portfolios had been stolen. The portfolio means nothing to a thief but it represents a lot of work to you, and parts of it are virtually ir-replaceable.

7

Making a Voicetape

If you intend to make yourself available for all phases of commercial work, you will, at some time, need a voicetape. The voicetape, also called the demo tape, is 2½ to 3 minutes in length and demonstrates the range and capabilities of your voice. It consists of a variety of short commercial spots, often borrowed from actual advertisements. If you are interested in singing on commercials the tape will consist of spots showing several distinct vocal styles. Such tapes are also referred to as jingle tapes.

The voicetape is always recorded on reel-to-reel tape, never cassette, and takes careful planning and professional guidance. It is not an inexpensive undertaking and will demand as much thought about the image you are trying to create as did your photographs. If you wish to get into the lucrative voice-over market, a well-produced voicetape is a necessity.

Three Methods to Consider

There are three ways you can go about producing a voicetape. The method you choose will be determined largely by the city in which you live, your prior experience in the field, what contacts you have or what voice-over professionals your agent directs you to, and the money you have available for this endeavor.

If you show interest, your agent may give you the names of several professionals who make their livings in the voice-over field. Such people, whose time is valuable, will charge whatever they think is reasonable for introducing you to the process, informing you about what the producers want to hear, and giving you tips for remaining comfortable during

a taping session. Some will work with you on speech, and some will coach you through the entire process.

One voice pro in Chicago, who has often been called upon to direct and assist friends who express interest in the business, feels that there is nothing better than having a friend's expertise and special interest in producing a first tape. "If you know somebody who is a practicing pro, that is by far the best way to go. If you've got a friend to get up and direct, to help you compile the material, to guide you in what is going to sell on that three minutes worth of tape — then you've got it all."

Another possibility is to approach a recording studio, buy some time and an engineer, and take a crack at producing it yourself. Some college students in Radio, TV and Film and some announcers in radio and television feel that they have the know-how to produce a professional-sounding tape themselves. Several agents say, however, that such efforts often sound amateurish and betray the fact that the individuals producing such tape are unaware of the requirements demanded by producers and agents. The sound is not "commercial", people make the mistake of introducing themselves at the beginning of the tape, include a lot of jingles, and in many cases simply don't know how or what to edit.

Three spots of 60 seconds each on a three-minute reel are going to make a deadly presentation, particularly when the tape should be grabbing attention and establishing your best style within the first 20 seconds. Unless you're experienced or ready to throw away several hundred dollars, don't attempt this major undertaking by yourself.

The most desirable method of producing a voicetape when you really know nothing about the field and have no voice-over friends to help you is to approach a recording studio that caters to beginners in this field. Your agent will probably be able to supply you with the names of these companies. If not, you can call recording studios and ask if they know of any studios or production houses that specialize in making first voicetapes.

Such setups provide the materials, the studio and engineer's time, and some guidance. They may help you with the selection and writing of copy suited to your voice and the direction in which you want to go, coach you before and during the recording session, supply necessary sound effects and background music, mix these elements, and edit them all into one master tape. These studios understand the anxiety and questions of the novice and are accustomed to working with nonprofessionals. The only drawback to such recording setups is that their approach is rather like that of an assembly line in a field where originality and creativity are honored. The end product, one agent says, is "adequate but nothing special." For your second tape you'll be an experienced pro, but for your first effort such studios might fill your needs and fit your budget.

Plan Carefully

Your tape must be well planned. The copy must be carefully selected and custom fitted to your voice and capabilities. Ask your agent if you may listen to the tapes of six or seven working pros, covering a range of talents and ages, including both sexes.

The studios catering to voice talent have good supplies of tapes for you to hear. They will familiarize you with the format and discuss the process of making a voicetape with you. As with photographs, you will have to have an honest and accurate self image in order to produce a tool that will be successful in selling your voice. A 55-year-old woman trying to sound like a breathless ingenue will not be convincing. You must value the opinions of respected professionals concerning what you can do well.

Where will you get your copy? You could write your own, but, as one pro puts it, "Most original material sounds like original material and not like what is currently on radio and television. You want a producer to think that all of it is real, all of it is running (on the air), and that you did it." Use real material. You may not be successful if you merely lift your material out of a magazine or newspaper ad — some writing is meant to be said, some meant to be read. Be sure that the copy transfers well to the spoken word.

The copy you choose should showcase your abilities. You might include something bright and breezy, something soft and sexy, something authoritative, something young and naive, or perhaps a voice registering the discomfort that only Alka-Seltzer can cure. If you have a funny voice, you might include a spot featuring your interpretation of the Hawaiian Punch character or the Keebler elves. In general, however, do not include too many strong character voices, accents or dialects. Show your voice in varying contexts rather than many different voices. Try a straight delivery, making the words sound natural and interesting. If you're being coached or directed, ask to have the copy well in advance of the recording session. Read it over with people whose opinion you respect. If you are preparing a jingle tape, include material that showcases your talent and covers more than one style of singing. Your tape might consist of some original material and some commercial jingles that have actually aired and are recognizable. Include spots that demonstrate your lyric sense, some that are languid and ballad-like, and some that are "up" and bright, that sound right for a soft drink or McDonald's ad. Show that you have a wide range, the ability to recreate the sounds of the Beach Boys and Barbara Streisand as well as a madrigal choir. One top pro encourages you to "show the various colors of your voice."

You can work on technique and style by practicing with a cassette or portable tape recorder, but don't be overly critical of what you hear. If you are not recording on sophisticated equipment, your tape will not have the quality of sound you are looking for. The practice in reading and timing your pace will prepare you for the day of your recording session.

The Recording Session

Prior to your session, avoid drinking or eating anything that might coat your throat. Milk and other dairy products, including the cream you add to your coffee, can create congestion and thicken the voice quality. Bubbly, carbonated drinks can cause a frothy sound. If you have a cold or sinus condition, try to reschedule your session, as breathing difficulties and nasal tones do register on the tape. One pro doesn't like to eat heavily prior to a taping session as he feels it weighs down his performance. He also refrains from having a glass of wine with lunch on the day of a taping, noting that the alcohol seems to take the edge off his performance.

If you are feeling nervous or tight, you may be able to relieve some of that tension by exercising prior to the session. Shallow half-breaths register almost as gasps when you're working as closely with the microphone as you will be, so use a breathing or yoga exercise to relax you. If your mouth feels tense, try rinsing it with water a few times. Stretching your mouth, as if yawning, also helps to reduce tension.

This may be your first time working with copy and a microphone in a soundproof booth. It is important that you understand you are communicating through the microphone, not to it. It is a tool, not an end. Imagine that you are talking to just one person, perhaps a child, your aunt in Des Moines, or your lover, or boss. You want to avoid sounding artificial or as if you are reading copy. Strive to achieve an intimate, one-on-one quality.

Try to create a mood solely with your voice. To do this, the voice must sound brighter, more up and livelier than usual. The timing and inflection are not those of the stage or real life. One engineer says that a common problem, particularly with theater people, is that they forget this is an audio performance. They make extravagant gestures, exaggerated facial reactions, and give a whole performance — in a recording booth. In taping, the acting is done with the voice.

It is not unusual for beginners to experience a sense of isolation. You will be able to watch the technicians as they work at the console and, unless they decide to tune you out, you will have constant voice contact with them. The technicians will give you feedback as you read through your copy. They may interrupt you, or allow you to read through an entire segment. You needn't worry about getting through the entire three minutes of copy perfectly in one reading.

The engineer will coach you, encouraging you to try different readings of the same material. Even though you will be asked to do multiple takes of the same material, try to avoid giving readings that sound tired and overworked. Use this opportunity to experiment. You have nothing to lose and an original tape to gain.

Expressing through the microphone.

The view from the control booth.

Singers should select commercial material that demonstrates style and range. Jingle singers must be able to blend with a group and sound good in solo performances. They sight read and transpose quickly and accurately. Beautiful, well-trained voices are not necessarily commercially successful. And with today's recording technology, you'll be surprised — and dismayed — to find out how few voices it takes to produce a sound as large as that of the Mormon Tabernacle Choir! Choose the spots you do include for brightness and versatility.

Once you have achieved what you and your technicians want, your part is diminished. Now it is up to the engineers to cut what is unusable, edit the best spots, and splice them together onto a single voice track. The appropriate music and sound effects will be added on additional tracks, and all the tracks will be mixed together. These many tracks will be recorded on a single track which becomes your master tape. It is the first generation of that particular piece of material.

Now you return to the studio and listen to what they have done for you. Some studios will encourage you to take this master tape to your agent to get a second opinion. Such studios may also try to prepare you for the confusion and conflicts in opinion you are certain to encounter.

Evaluating Your Tape

In many ways, the process of producing a voicetape is not unlike having your photographs made. You must be able to receive criticism, make appropriate and professional changes, and be pleased with the end product. If you have any doubts or suggestions for change, air them now.

As well as developing a sense of what you like, you must know what particular spots are repeatable and represent your talent most fairly. The first minute of the tape has got to be what you consider your most saleable style. If you're primarily a nice, easy sell — a mellow kind of person — and you think that is how you are most likely to work, then that's got to be the first spot on the tape.

The first spot represents your strongest facet because producers who are rushed often will hear only the beginning of the tape. One pro warns, "Don't put anything on a voicetape that you cannot instantly recreate. If it is on that voicetape, it says I do that, I do it well, and I do it swiftly." If you really had to work to create a certain sound or a certain character, you'd be well-advised to leave it off your tape.

A now-successful voice professional admits that "the first tape I put out was a disaster, an absolute disaster. I wrote the copy myself and went for what I enjoy doing the most, funny voices. But there was no way I would have competed with the people who are doing the funny voices. I just didn't have anything to go on. The second tape I put out was straight announcer, all straight announcer, pretending to be someone 45 years old. That was silly too, but at least I realized along the way what I couldn't do. The third tape started getting better, started being like me. Young kid — I knew that I could play a young kid, and that's when I started getting work."

Duplicating and Packaging the Tape

Once you've accepted the master tape, duplicate copies will have to be made. The studio that made the master may be able to do it, or you may have to go to another recording studio that has high-speed duplicating facilities. Consult with your agent as to the number of copies to order. Fifty should provide you with a good beginning. Often there will be a minimum order required, and the cost of the duplicates will decrease as the quantity increases.

Be certain that your duplicates are being made from your master tape, not the reel of outtakes you may be handed. One actress had been making rounds and leaving tapes for months when one engineer suggested that they listen to her tape. Imagine her surprise when she heard a series of bloopers and mistakes. The recording studio admitted their error and re-recorded her copies free of charge, but this actress vows that she'll check her material in the future. It's a good idea.

Now that you've put time and money into making a good tape, you will want professional packaging. The studios that make copies often put typed labels on the boxes they give you. Most voice pros indicate that such labeling is not sufficient. Many of them spend a great deal of money paying designers and printers to create distinctive packaging that is handsome and indicates commitment and investment. Your name must appear on the spine of the tapebox — in a bold type — as most agents and producers store rows of tapes on shelves. Some labels also include the phone number and photograph of the talent.

Your next voicetape will be much easier to produce. If you've been successful, you'll be able to lift the best actual job spots you've done. It will become an exercise in editing rather than a major effort in production.

Labels can utilize artwork or photography, or artwork and photography.

This box contains the tape of Dorothy Jordan, voice of Morris the Cat's owner . . .

. . . and this one reveals that this talent specializes in character voices.

8

Two Other Important Tools

At this point there are two more steps to take before you can consider yourself set up for business. A resume provides information about you that photos do not, and an answering service picks up the important calls you won't always be able to catch yourself.

Your Resume

A resume provides a lot of information you can not convey through your pictures. It is actually a list of your professional experiences and affiliations, educational experiences that would apply to this field, personal statistics, special or unusual abilities that might be useful in getting work, your singing range, the kinds of dance you do, and phone numbers — those of your agent, your service and, perhaps, yours.

The personal statistics you should include may repeat some of the information printed on your composite. That's okay. It is appropriate to list it in both places. Include your name, height, weight, eye color, hair color, age or age range — you may actually be 40 years old but look like you're 32 on certain days and 45 on other days, so your range would be 32-45 — and social security number.

Try to keep your resume current, updating it when and if you become affiliated with a union or a new agent. Certainly issue a new one when your work experiences merit a group of new listings.

Resumes are more important in getting work for actors than for models. As a model, your pictures and composite statistics tell the basic story. If you do have theatrical or film aspirations, or if you are interested in getting into television commercials, your resume is especially important.

As someone just starting out, you may not have a lot to put on your resume. It's better to have it look somewhat bare, however, than to fabricate productions you've been in or experiences you've had. Some people in the business say otherwise, but if you're caught in a professional lie, you could ruin your career. List any educational degrees and informal training — workshops and seminars — in this field, particularly if your instructor or coach is well known. Include any professional theater experience you might have. If you do not have these kinds of credentials at this point, list college, school or community shows you've done, and replace this data with professional credits as soon as you get them. Your summer stock experience with an Equity Theater means more than having the lead in 15 college productions.

Don't pad your resume. At this stage, experienced professionals can look at your credits and know immediately if any of them are significant. If they don't see many credits, it is hoped they will see potential.

If you're primarily interested in getting televion commercials, you should definitely include any comedy or improvisational experience you've had as it is excellent background for commercial work. Your resume should list other television commercials first so that the casting directors or clients will want you for their productions as well. There may be a problem, however, with listing the Coca-Cola spot you

104

A photo, your agent's stamp, or possibly the number of your answering service would go here

PROBABLY YOU

Height:	5'4"	Hair:	Brown
Weight:	120	Eyes:	Brown
Age range:	20-25	S.S.#	701-23-5412

SPECIFICATIONS

Measurements: 36-23-36	Dress size: 10	Glove size: 7
Brassiere: 34D	Shoe size: 7-8	Hat size: 7
Lovely hands		

EXPERIENCE

Informal modeling	Ward's Dept. Store	Cleveland, Ohio
Printwork	Allstate	
	National Trust Bank	
	Morgan's Furs	
Slide Film	Allstate/Sears	
Theatre	Once Upon a Mattress	Princess

SPECIAL TALENTS

Dance: jazz, tap
Most sports

TRAINING AND EDUCATION

B.A. University of Illinois
Dance: Lou Dano
Modeling: Wendy Ward, Take Two Workshops
Acting: Paul Glick Studios

Just starting out . . . you may not have a lot to put on a resume, so go ahead and list the show you were in during high school.

did last year if the people for 7-Up are interested in you. These are competitive products and the 7-Up people will think twice about using you. Many models and actors put "commercial credits upon request" on their resumes, indicating that the client can check with your agent to find out what you've done. Others avoid the issue by listing the production house or photographer or director, the ad agency and the year. This tells that you've done work for certain directors and agencies without mentioning the actual accounts.

The way you order your professional experiences and where you place each section on the resume is important. One agent says that "it's only logical that who you're trying to sell must be kept in mind . . . the order of the resume certainly has to do with what work you're trying to get. If you want to be open to all of them, put movies first, theater second, industrial films third and television commercials last."

If you are auditioning for theatrical film or television movies, the director is not likely to be very impressed by commercial work, which is why you would list it last, if at all. You would want to include any other television credits or feature film credits. "Never include 'extra' work on your resume — who cares?" advises one agent. List any equity shows you have done, the roles you played, who directed and at what theaters. "Certain directors and theaters are quite prestigious," says another agent, "and you would want to mention them." Equity showcase presentations should be mentioned also.

When you have worked a great deal in several performing areas, you might consider putting out several resumes. Many actors have two headshots, one smiling, animated look for commercial auditions and one serious, dramatic look for theatrical auditions. You might want to have several resumes listing the same credits in different ways for theatrical, film and commercial auditions.

You can pay a service to type your resume or you can do it yourself. Do not handwrite a resume; it does not instill confidence in your professionalism. If you do type it yourself, make certain that the ribbon is new enough that you make a bold, dark original. I watched a friend type his resume on erasable bond paper with an old ribbon. His original had no contrast at all and was too light to make good reproductions. Be certain that your original is neat and contains no typographical errors. The resume, like your photographs, is a professional tool and you want it to make a good presentation.

An Answering Service

Once you've gone to the effort and expense of getting the other things you need to enter the business, you'd hate to miss out on a job or interview simply because your agent or the client couldn't reach you. An answering service is a necessity in this business. You have to provide a number where messages can be left for you while you're out making rounds, taking classes, or at a job.

One way to do this is by attaching a phone answering machine to your phone. Depending on how you set it, your machine will pick up the call after so many rings. A recorded message — you will be the one to record it — will instruct the caller to leave his or her name, number, a brief message, and possibly the time of day when the call was made. The caller then has 30 seconds or so to leave information which you will play back off the machine when you return.

These machines are made by several companies, which offer a variety of models priced from $75 to $200. The most deluxe models offer an attachment whereby you may call in from anywhere and activate the machine to hear your messages. Needless to say, if you are downtown most of the day, it would be convenient to know that someone downtown wants to see you before you arrive home to hear the message.

The advantages of these machines are their convenience and the fact that they are a one-time cost. If you are not pleased with the performance of a machine, you can re-sell it. There is always a market for them.

One disadvantage of the machine is that it will need occasional maintenance. You will have to replace batteries and re-record your message from time to time. Another is that the machine will make some callers nervous, probably the same people who hang up if a service answers. Rest assured that people in the industry who need to get in touch with you will leave a message on a machine or with a service. Too, a phone machine can become the repository of your friends' bad jokes or occasional obscene calls. You never know what you're going to hear when you play back your messages.

Another way to avoid missing calls is to hire an answering service. This service will be electronically hooked into your line so that when a call comes in on your phone it rings the service also. After a few rings the service will pick up the call, whether you are near your phone or not, and answer with your name or

A photo, your agent's stamp, or possibly the number of your answering service would go here

PAUL ENOON
(AEA, SAG, AFTRA)

Height: 6'1"		Hair:	Brown
Weight: 160		Eyes:	Blue
Age range: 23-28		Vocal:	Bass

THEATRICAL EXPERIENCE

Tyco	**Tyco	Goodman Theatre, Chicago
Guys and Dolls (with Peggy Cass)	Dancer/singer	Pheasant Run, Chicago
King Lear	Fool	Goodman Theatre, Chicago
Shande and Ale	Phil Currant	Garden Theatre, New York
Vivan	Rhett Butler	Circle Theatre, New York
Georgie, Annie and Me	Chris	Miami University, Ohio
Prune Danish, Please	*Elmo Cllese	Miami University, Ohio
Cinderella	Mother	Miami University, Ohio

AWARDS
* Citation for Best Student Performance, 1978
** Nomination for Joseph Jefferson Award, 1980

COMMERCIALS AND FILMS
List available on request

ADDITIONAL PERFORMANCE EXPERIENCE
Chorus, San Francisco Opera, 1979 season
Member of Miami University Mime Troupe, 1977-78 (European tour)

SPECIAL TALENTS
Music: Sight reading ability, wide range of styles
Dialects: French, Cockney, Irish
Language: Fluency in Italian and German
Dance: Jazz, Modern, Ballet
Sports: Martial arts, polo, tennis
Other: Juggling, fencing

TRAINING AND EDUCATION
B.A. (Theatre) Miami University, Ohio
M.A. (Theatre) Northwestern University, Illinois
Dance: Phanto Studio, Lou Dano, Marion Mills
Voice: Trina Brinkle, Wayne Rogers
Improvisation: Second City Workshops, Bill Opene

One man, two resumes: one for theatre . . .

PAUL ENOON
(AEA, SAG, AFTRA)

Height: 6'1"   Hair: Brown
Weight: 160   Eyes: Blue
Age range: 23-28   Vocal: Bass

FEATURE FILM

Somewhere Is Now   Universal Studios
Savage Fury   MGM
Backwards Trot   MGM
Who Knows, Alas   SMB Productions

TELEVISION

The Dark of Night (CBS)   Paul
Hospital Action (CBS)   Gracie
One, Two, Three (ABC)   Phil

COMMERCIALS

List available on request
Voiceover for 7-Up, King Salami, Castle Onion Bits,
         Puppo Treats, Burger King

INDUSTRIAL FILMS

Century 21   Allstate/Sears
State Farm   Bell and Howell
RCA   Illinois Masonic
Kool-Aid   Crate and Cooks
Westbend   Cifani, Inc.

THEATRE

Tyco   Tyco   Goodman Theatre, Chicago
Guys and Dolls Singer/dancer Pheasant Run, Chicago
King Lear   Fool   Goodman Theatre, Chicago

SPECIALTIES

Sight reading ability, dialects, fluency in Italian
and German, jazz, modern and ballet dance ability,
martial arts, equestrian, tennis, juggling, fencing

TRAINING AND EDUCATION

B.A. (Theatre) Miami University, Ohio
M.A. (Theatre) Northwestern University, Illinois

. . . and one for film and television.

your number. The service will take the information the caller wishes to leave.

With some services you will be expected to call them to pick up your messages, or you can leave instructions for them to trace you if an important call comes in. This means that you must inform them of your schedule for the day and the phone numbers of the people with whom you have appointments. Some hard-core professionals carry electronic beepers with them so that they can be easily and quickly reached.

There is a third way to go. Some cities offer answering services that cater solely to people in this business. For a modest fee, in some cases as low as $5 per month, you can give the number of the service to your agent and clients and the service will take messages for you. They will not be hooked up to your phone; you don't even need to have a phone. You and hundreds of other models, actors and freelance professionals will give out the same number, and you will call in periodically to see if any messages have been left for you.

The advantage of a service is that the initial cost is not high and is payable on a monthly basis. The tracing service can prove most convenient if a job is down to the wire and a client needs you fast. Services don't break down so there will be no maintenance costs. A service is ideal for those professionals who travel from city to city in search of work; as long as they check in periodically, the service can provide long-distance traces. For those of you who resent the computer age, a service is more personal than a machine.

Ironically, that's one of the disadvantages of a service. How quickly your calls are picked up and how pleasantly the calls are answered is determined by the individual sitting at the board. Some operators are pleasant, some are nasty, and some are efficient. Another drawback is that if you use a service for a period of years, you will spend many times over the cost of a machine.

Don't let your spouse talk you into trying her or him out as your service. It will take just one missed phone call, when she was out grocery shopping or he was out washing the car, to point out the drawbacks of this arrangement. It's just not a professional set-up.

No matter how you work it out, it is essential that you have an answering service.

9

How to Get the Work

"Talent spend half the time — 90 percent of the time — trying to get the job."
That statement from one pro says it all. Once you have equipped yourself with the
necessary tools of the trade, you will spend most of your time looking for work.
Whether you are convincing your agent to send you to more interviews, promoting
yourself by making rounds, doing test shots, sending out mailings, or improving
your audition and interview skills, you will spend much time just trying to get work.

Getting Established with Your Agent

When you have your composites or photographs in hand, deliver them to your agent or agencies. You may be asked to stamp them with an agency stamp. Some agencies provide stickers to be attached to the photos. Others, if you are listed exclusively, may ask you to have the printer print their logo directly on the composite. This precludes the necessity to stamp or stick but, if you should move to another city or align yourself with a different agency, your pictures will automatically become useless. Be certain of your plans before you have agency information printed on any pictures or resumes.

Find out at this time what will be routinely expected of you during your association with the agency. Be certain you know what forms or agency releases, if any, you are expected to carry with you to jobs, and ask for a supply. Find out how often you are expected to check in. Some agencies suggest twice a week, some once a day, some ask that you not call at all, preferring to call you when they have an interview or a job. Some agencies encourage you to drop in occasionally, while others resent the interruption.

Agents appreciate models and talent who check their answering services frequently and call in promp-

tly to find out what's going on. When returning the agency calls, have pencil and paper handy so that you can readily take down information.

Most agencies expect you to contact them following an interview or job. They want to know if you have any problems, professional or otherwise, with people in the business. They want to hear from you if you're going to be leaving town and to know where they can reach you if an especially attractive job should come up. Giving them this information is sometimes called "booking out." Notify your agency of a change of address or phone number, even if you haven't worked through them for some time.

Indulge your agent and keep her happy, for her continued interest in you is essential to your being called for as many jobs as possible. Remember to express your gratitude when she has done some work for you or made a particularly helpful recommendation. Particularly at this point in your career, you need one another.

Promoting Yourself Through Contacts

Unless you are fortunate enough to find an agent who will assume total responsibility for promoting you, it will be up to you to advertise yourself. Promotion, in this business, is introducing yourself to and developing contacts. Promotion consists of the time, effort and expense you invest to generate work for yourself.

Who are contacts? They are people whom your friends, neighbors and relatives know who are connected to the fashion and advertising industries. They are people with whom you have studied who are professionally active, for whom you have interviewed or done a job; people who can introduce you to fashion coordinators, casting directors, photographers, producers, advertisers, agents and others who might have work for you.

Having a friend make a phone call or write a letter is only the first step, however. It will only get you through a door which might otherwise have been closed or which you might otherwise have disregarded. Many agents are glad to see models and talent introduced to them by other models and talent who are signed with the agency. They know that working models and talent won't jeopardize their professional reputations by introducing people who are totally wrong for the business. "But," one Chicago agent says, "if you don't have the qualities to make you a successful model anyway, having a friend make the phone call is not going to make it work."

A phone call or personal introduction is always better than a letter. If someone is really interested in helping you, ask him or her to make a phone call or arrange a meeting. It's much more immediate.

Some cities also have directories, usually sponsored by the advertising industry, in which are listed film studios, photographers, audio-video recording facilities, producers, other professional services (such as answering services, composite or glossy printers, designers), labor groups and talent and modeling agencies. There may also be a section where talent can advertise, listing name, experience, union or agency affiliations, photo and phone number.

Perhaps the most well-known directory is the Madison Avenue Handbook, which covers New York but also has small sections on Boston, Chicago, Detroit, Miami, Atlanta, Los Angeles, San Francisco, Montreal and Toronto. In Chicago, the CU Directory (Chicago Unlimited Directory) is a guide to advertising services. These kinds of directories are a great source for reliable, current information. Ask your agent or friends in the business if such handbooks are available in the city where you're working.

There are also monthly, weekly and daily papers and magazines that announce industry happenings. These most often include professional theater or major motion picture and television casting, but you may find some useful information regarding producers of television commercials.

One such publication is Ross Reports Television, a monthly statement on the casting and production occurring in the television industry, which includes a list of the New York producers of television commercials. It also lists talent agents, stating whether they see talent on a drop-in or appointment basis, accept photos and resumes through the mail, or receive phone calls. Your agent or friends already working in the field can direct you to the genuinely useful trade papers and publications.

Sending Out Mailings

In some cities, you will not be encouraged or even permitted to see or call the individuals in positions to give you work. You will have to promote yourself through the mail. A few cities offer services that will send out your photos and resumes to a certain number of casting people on a weekly or monthly basis. You will pay a fee for this service.

Most likely, however, you will have to build your own list of contacts and prepare your own mailings. Every ad agency that has a production department or talent contact and every department store that uses models for its fashion shows should receive your promotional material. Whether your agent provides a list or you comb the yellow pages, your mailing should go to anyone who could possibly have use for your talent now or in the future.

Keep an organized list of your contacts. A 3 x 5 file card system is ideal. Note your contact's name, company and position, business address and phone, the date of the last contact, and anything special you discussed — an upcoming project, friends in common, or nocturnal habits of anteaters. If your visit was in person, you may want to note the outfit you wore, particularly if you are interested in getting modeling work. If your contact is a photographer, note if he or she is interested in testing.

You could categorize your list alphabetically, but many models and talent categorize by date. That way, every four to six months, you will automatically know that is is time to renew your acquaintance. Repeat your visit and share the new tear sheets and test photos you have added to your portfolio. If you're just beginning, a second visit will let your contact know that you're still in the business. In six months time your contact may very well have new projects for which you will be right.

CHUCK ROWELL

Sending postcards or dropping off business cards is one way to keep in touch with your contacts.

What you include and when you send it out will depend on what is happening in your professional life at the time of the mailing. If you're beginning or things are going on as usual, send a photo or composite and resume. Be sure that your phone number or that of your agent is included. One actor who travels to different cities to hustle work in as many places as he can sends out postcards every three months to an ever-growing list of contacts. It's always the same card, with a photo of him printed on the front, and it mentions the commercials he's done that are currently running. It states when he plans to return to the city of the addressee and that he'll be stopping by.

If you're appearing in a local theater production, it gives you an ideal opportunity to invite your contacts to see your work. When you make the follow-up calls to your mailings, if someone expresses interest in seeing your show, offer to arrange for the tickets. In such a mailing you would also want to include exerpts from favorable reviews.

It had better be a strong production, however, with your performance an outstanding one. If your contact is merely likely to enjoy a free night at the theater and is not likely to be terribly critical, that's fine. One agent in Los Angeles says that any agent who has been in business for a while and who has seen hundreds if not thousands of showcase performances is not likely to be impressed by anything other than a brilliant performance. Be certain of your work before you invite industry people to judge it.

If you're appearing in a television program with a strong role on a certain night or if you know that a commercial in which you are principle and of which

you are proud is beginning to run, you might send out a mailing just prior to the set time. Include the date, the time, and the station on which your performance is being aired.

Some actors promote themselves by advertising in the trade papers when they are appearing in workshop productions or showcases. This may be effective in getting people to the performance, but unless someone contacts you, you will not know what the response has been. If you are concerned with promoting yourself to certain people, the best approach is sending out mailings or making rounds.

Making Rounds

In some cities it is the custom to call on contacts and potential contacts. Also known as "pounding the pavement," "wearing out shoe leather," "getting off your duff," and "hustling," making rounds is a way of building a client list and is an essential activity if you are freelancing.

Rounds, if encouraged in the city where you live, are vital to establishing yourself as an available model or talent. It is difficult for established professionals to make appointments and hustle work and it may be even tougher for a novice.

Knowing how to sell and continuing to do so even when you're riding a crest is an important part of this business. One Chicago actor who does very well in voice-over says that making rounds was "one of the most discouraging, disgusting, unhappy pieces of work I've ever done in my whole life. Basically because I couldn't see any results. It was terrible. I thought I'd never get work; I'd never make anything of myself. It was terribly important, however. Even though I couldn't see it, I was establishing myself and getting to know people. It's all a matter of confidence and waiting for things to click."

If rounds are encouraged by your agency, you will probably be supplied with a rounds list of their regular and potential clients. Or they may make the appointments for you, particularly with those clients they feel will especially be interested in seeing you. Often these appointments are referred to as "go-sees," as in "Go see Mr. So-and-so at J. Walter Thompson." Mr. So-and-so, however, may refer to the meeting as a "look-see." There will be times when Mr. So-and-so will offer you a job on the spot.

You can compile your own rounds list or expand the one given you by an agency by looking through the Yellow Pages under Advertising Agencies, Commercial Photographers and other production companies and calling such places to see if they use models or talent. There will often be a talent contact — the person who sees and talks with models and talent — in these places, but they go by many titles. You may be asking for a casting director or producer, the production coordinator or production assistant, the talent contact, the broadcast business manager or broadcast production manager, the radio and television director, a creative director, art director or a communications director. Just tell the person who answers the phone why you're calling and you will be connected with the right person.

When making rounds, call first for an appointment. Even if they prefer that you just drop in, call first to determine that. If you drop in and it happens to be a bad time, the person you're trying to see will be hassled. It's a no-win situation. Call first.

By calling first, you may also find out that some businesses do not see new models. One advertiser in Pittsburgh feels it is unprofessional for models and talent "to come walking in out of the blue. They are either new in town and don't know, or they are bold enough to go out and try it. It seems a little tacky." This is not the impression you want to make.

Once you have made the appointment, prepare as you did to approach the agents. Look good. Do what is appropriate for the city in which you're working. "I've never seen a model in New York in anything but jeans and boots and no makeup," advises one model turned agent. "And that's terrific if you're in New York. In Chicago, you better put your makeup on and make sure your blouse is very fashionable and your boots are decent looking."

Be on time for the appointment even though you may be kept waiting. Make sure that your portfolio is in good shape and that you've considered what you're going to say. If the day hasn't gone well for the person you're seeing, you may have to carry the conversation.

One model says that she hands her composite down side up to the person she is seeing at the beginning of their meeting. She always has a family shot printed on the back side of the comp, and she says it never fails to prompt a comment. This way the conversation has been started, and she lets it be known that her family is also available for work.

Most important, you should know when to leave. Don't tie up the time of the person with whom you're hoping to work.

One other word on professional conduct should be mentioned at this point. You probably will meet people in the ad agencies, photo studios and production houses with whom you hit it off. It is natural that friendships should develop between professionals who admire and respect each other's work. But do not — repeat, DO NOT — assume that an intimate relationship with any one individual is going to make or break your career. That fact is not going to prevent some folks from making the insinuation or blatantly offering to advance your career in return for your favors. But few professionals will stake an account, a portion of their income, or their professional reputations to repay you for your efforts. You'll have to be right for the job.

One agent admits that "this question comes up all the time. There is no one photographer or art director who is going to make or break you. You're either good, or you're not good. You're the person who makes you good, and I, the agent, am going to help you. You are it. I don't care if the photographer is one of the 10 top photographers in the country — you can still count on the other nine to bring in work if you're excellent. I particularly have this talk with my juniors who are going to New York — I emphasize this because the people who go to New York and make a success of it are usually in the 16 to 21 age range. Personally, I'm quite liberal — if you feel like sleeping with someone, go right ahead. But don't do it for a job. More often than not, it can hurt you. If you are associated with one photographer, the other photographers won't touch you with a 10-foot pole."

In New York, a top New York modeling agent states, "If you're good, you're good. You could sleep with the whole fashon industry and go nowhere!"

"Something to remind yourself of," comments a Chicago professional, is to "never compromise anything — any value, any moral value — for a job. There's no point in it. If you compromise enough by the time you get to the point where you don't have to compromise any more, there isn't too much left. You've drained the well." The choice is up to you. If you're attracted, consider it. But don't assume that sleeping with people in the business is necessarily going to get you anywhere, except into bed.

Finding Your Own Way: How To Get Work in a Fashion Show

Since most live fashion work — the style shows so many of you want to do — is not handled by the agencies, it will be up to you to investigate what work is available and how to get it. You will be both making rounds and promoting yourself to the department stores and specialty shops that hire models for live presentations.

Whether you are in a small town or a big city, if you want this kind of work you will have to contact the fashion office or the fashion coordinator of your local stores. If neither of these exist, ask to speak with the person in charge of hiring models for fashion shows. The most professional way to approach such people is to call, introduce yourself, explain what you're interested in, and set up an appointment. The fashion coordinator may be hard to reach because she often works with the display people as well and is likely to be in other areas of the store. Even if you have difficulty making contact with her, and even if the people you speak with say they are not seeing new models, keep trying.

You are probably aware that the stores are deluged by this kind of inquiry. In order to see the large number of interested people, many department stores in major cities will hold open auditions several times each year. Call the fashion office to find out when these auditions will be held and be ready for them. Practice your walk, your turns and pivots and prepare your resume and photographs. Don't be surprised if you walk in and see 200 to 400 other applicants. Just do the best you can. Even if you make a mistake, you will have had the experience of auditioning on a runway in front of a large group. There will always be other auditions.

Some stores set aside one morning or afternoon each week to interview applicants. Be certain that you know prior to this appointment what they expect from you. Many stores want only a good snapshot or two to attach to your application. If these are your favorite pictures, be certain you have sufficient copies to leave with all the stores at which you apply.

Some stores will require only a resume — please, not handwritten — claiming that they have no room to store the photographs. Stores in the larger cities may expect a more professional presentation, a resume and a composite. All your statistics should be included and they should be honest. These people will know if you fudge.

This interview is important. You may be observed as you sit in the reception room waiting your turn. Be sure to have made up, done your hair, and dressed the part of a model. "Someone who is in updated attire, not flamboyant though, will catch our eye more than someone who is wearing a polyester pant suit." One coordinator indicates that she is interested in previous experience and how personable the applicant is during the interview. A coded rating system is printed on the application form, and she rates the interviewee following their chat.

Another fashion coordinator says that prospective models are asked to walk, do turns, and are measured during the initial interview. She will ask a woman to try on some garments if there is real interest. She wants women who can achieve more than just one look by changes in hair style and makeup. She is interested in women who can appear sophisticated as well as young and kicky. A specialized, unique or extreme look can decrease your chances of finding work in such stores.

Use the interview to ask any questions you have regarding the store's setup. Find out if they have informal modeling, how many shows they do and at what time of the year, and what other work is available. Inquire about the modeling fees. Be pleasant and try to be relaxed.

Even though you felt you sparkled in your first interview, you may not hear from the store. If you are really intent on working as a model, keep calling back every two weeks or so.

Every time you go back, try something different with your makeup, hair or clothing. If you were wearing jeans and a blazer the first time, try a more fashionable dress the next time. Keep a file containing a card for each store and record who you saw, when you went, and what you were wearing. They will be aware of the changes, and your variations will illustrate your flexibility.

10

Winning the Job: The Selection Process

You will get some jobs solely from your composites, your voicetape, recommendation and exposure, or because you have previously worked with the people involved. Most often, however, clients and producers want to see you and talk with you before they make their casting decisions.

This is what you've been working for — an opportunity to strut your stuff. Auditions, interviews, readings and "go-sees" provide those moments when you finally come face to face with the people in positions to hire you. This is when you show them that what they want is exactly what you have to offer.

These moments may arrive every other month if you're working in a small city or several times daily if you're working in New York, Los Angeles or Chicago. Your years of training or your right look mean nothing if you don't present yourself well in an interview, so you've got to be ready.

For Printwork

Models used in fashion photography and advertising photography are frequently hired on the basis of their composites. That is why it is essential to keep your agent supplied with up-to-date pictures. Out-of-town clients and advertisers often use nothing but composites to make their decisions.

Other photographers and advertisers want to see the models in person before they make their decisions. The client whose product is being advertised may also want to be a part of the process, as he is concerned with the product image and the models used to create it. This job "go-see" may be as simple a procedure as having a Polaroid snapped in an of-

fice or photo studio, or dropping off your composite after those hiring have given you a brief look. You may be one of many under consideration or you may be the only model present.

Since they are interested mainly in how you photograph and if you have the look they want, it is not likely that an interview for printwork would be much more than a brief introduction and a few questions. They want to know that you can handle the job and that it will go smoothly. You must have the right look, the one that best suits the client's needs, but you increase your chances of being hired if you have a good interview style as well.

For Commercials and Other Live Work

Work in which movement, speech, timing or salesmanship are involved is a bit more complicated. If you have the right look but you also have a Brooklyn accent, chances are you will not be hired as a bank executive in a voice-over/on-camera commercial spot. If you have a lovely face, are 5'9" and a perfect size 7 but you can't walk five steps without stubbing your toe, chances are you won't be hired for a fashion show. If you're beautiful but shy, you won't be hired to work a trade show. Because more skills are involved in commercial work and other live performances, it is quite likely that you will be asked to interview for the job. Even if you do have the look they want and the skills needed to do the job, you have to present yourself so well during the interviewing process that you are remembered after all the faces have been seen and voices heard. Use this opportunity to show yourself at your best.

The words "audition" and "interview" are used interchangeably by some people in the business. Particularly in smaller cities where there may not be much professional theater, any meeting where you "try out" for a job may be called an audition.

Actually, however, auditions for commercial work are more like interviews than like typical theater auditions. While it is likely that you'll be asked to read some lines or "perform" a script, you probably won't ever find yourself on a stage, singled out in a spotlight, projecting undying sentiments about motor oil or crunchy flakes. Your audience will probably consist of a few business people sitting around a table trying to arrive at a decision about what talent they're going to hire to do the job.

While these meetings may not be auditions in a theatrical sense, they are also not interviews in a strict business sense. There will be no forms to fill out, no questions about your credit rating, family references or career goals. You will be performing and you will be judged from the moment you walk through the door.

The Interview: What To Expect

The whole process starts when you are informed that you have an audition or interview. You want to know where and when the interview will be, if there will be a casting director and who it is, if there is someone with whom you should sign in, what the product is, what the job is and when it will take place. If you have any schedule conflicts, mention them at this time.

If the interview is for a commercial, ask if the script is available. Many auditioners appreciate a prepared reading and the interest and professionalism that is indicated by preparation. Particularly with children, the agent is often forewarned not to send a child who can't handle the script. You want to know if a dialect is expected as you will want time to work on it. If the audition is for an industrial show, ask if you are expected to have a song prepared. Ask how you should dress.

An agent in Atlanta says that "many models will not listen to what I say. They are so vain, so egotistical, that they won't get away from looking like the cover of *Vogue* to read for the parts of mommies and housewives. I'm not saying look dowdy, I'm just saying don't look glamorous when reading for a housewife. Don't hurt your own chances." Some interviewers say they can envision you in the role they're trying to cast, while others appreciate the visual aid of appropriate attire.

If you aren't dressing for the part, be presentable. Show them that you're professional. One ex-Chicago talent who now works in Los Angeles says, "I spend a good deal of money on my haircuts. It is very important for me to look sharp at all times. I used to have a permanent press wardrobe. It was very nice and passable but small time. I now have one wardrobe that I only use for auditions. It includes shoes, slacks, shirts, ties, suits — one, two or three of everything that I could need from casual to executive. Now everything I go to audition in goes to the dry cleaners. For one thing I feel better. When you walk in crisp and well-pressed, and you look well-tailored, you feel better. I would definitely recommend a conservative wardrobe for commercials, because even though it's very hip out here, the people who have the final say on the commercials are from Dubuque and Peoria. My hair is a real plus for me because it is short; they love it, and they can identify with it. No matter what you wear anywhere else, you should have a few changes of clothing that are very conservative for auditions and jobs."

It's a good idea to carry your portfolio to an interview or audition. You will want to leave a resume and composite, and the interviewers may ask to see your book.

Most interviews will take place in offices. It may be an office in your agency, in a suite of rooms rented by your agent or the casting director, in the advertising agency or production house, or even in the office of the client. In Los Angeles, casting would never take place in an agent's office, but it frequently occurs in Chicago.

Before you enter the office, throw away your gum and check your appearance. Let this be your last check. Yes, they are interested in your looks and details are important, but if you start to be obsessed about details you won't have energy left for the important things. They're interested in *you*.

Waiting Your Turn: The "Cattle Calls"

"You may be entering a very quiet room or you may enter a scene somewhat like this: The phones are ringing, agents are there — of course, agents show up

She can look glamorous. . .

*. . . but she'd dress like this to read
for the part of a business executive.*

with people to auditions and callbacks because in a callback you're getting right down to the line — and the agents are hustling and bustling with 'Darling, you have too much blusher on,' and 'Ooh, take off that lipstick, put on more lipstick,' 'Do this, do that!'

"Maybe in one corner someone is concentrating on her lines and in another corner somebody is doing yoga, trying to psych up for this audition. Somebody is nearly at the brink of tears because she's so nervous her appointment was an hour and a half ago and she showed up an hour early, so she's been sitting here two and a half hours working up a state of nerves. Everybody is checking out the other person, thinking 'Oh, she's prettier than I am, she's skinnier, she's fatter, she's this, she's that.'

"Then there are conflicts going on between actor and agent. When you're nervous to begin with and a couple in the corner are having words, it's very nerve-wracking. You can cut the smoke with a knife. It's unbelievable — I never knew I could use a cliche

with such meaning. There is so much going on at an audition.''

Those auditions that resemble this scene described by a model/actress — which may involve 20, 30, 100 or even more people — are entitled, appropriately, "cattle calls." The unions, in recent years, have tried to reduce this pandemonium by requiring producers to schedule talent for specific time slots and by imposing fines on producers who keep talent waiting longer than an hour past their time slots.

Auditions in your city may not be regulated by unions. Even with the rules, waiting through a cattle call can be a frazzling experience. After you have added your name to a sign-in sheet, if one is available, you will have to do whatever is necessary to retain your composure and self-confidence.

Some professionals say a good way to pass this time is to study the copy, script or storyboard if these are available. The copy is only meant to fill 10, 20, 30 or 60-second time slots, and knowing the script will allow you to follow positioning marks, if there are any, and to hold the product, if it is handed to you, to its best advantage.

You might even disappear into a hallway, bathroom or broom closet for a few minutes to practice the gestures you intend to make as you read the copy. Some people take reading material, which is a good way to take your mind off the pressure and chaos around you. A lot of people in the business smoke, and waiting for interviews provides golden opportunities. Be aware of this, and if smoking bothers you, be prepared to cope with it.

Many people talk to pass this time. Some will talk to their agents, their friends, their rivals, even the walls just to hear themselves talk. It might be nervous, uncontrollable chatter, or it might be very purposeful communication. One agent warns, "A lot of times at interviews and auditions you'll find a lot of people trying to psych other people out, just to get them upset before the interview or audition, which gives them a lead, an advantage. And many times, they're able to get away with it. It works."

A model adds, "Intellectually, I know that it is a psych job when these people say, 'Oh yes, and when I did this movie last week with Paul Newman, Paul and I were discussing how to throw one's voice across the room and my speech coach said . . .' you know that's what they're doing and yet it works. It does work because you think 'Golly, I've never done a major motion picture, and I don't have a voice coach, and I don't know how to do such and such with my eyebrow' — you know it's a psych job but it works."

If you find yourself falling into the trap, walk away from it. Get up and take a little walk. Nobody is forcing you to listen, and if being subjected to a steady flow of bull is going to affect your state of mind, remove yourself from it.

You may look around and see that you're the only middle-aged brunette in a room full of teen-aged blondes. Don't panic. It won't be the first time that an agent has goofed and sent mostly wrong people to an audition. You may be just what they are looking for. Sometimes you'll be just who they hire even if they did request teen-aged blondes. Such are the whims of the business.

You're On!

You're being judged from the moment you open the door, so prepare an entrance. The best attitude you can enter an interview with, says an agent in Los Angeles, is that "they're going to cast somebody for this commercial and it might as well be me!" Think of a few conversational topics before you go in. Remember, these folks have probably been seeing models or talent for several hours. It's likely that they're tired of explaining their concept time after time and being forced to draw some life out of nervous, withdrawn people. "Try to remember," advises an agent in New York, "that the interviewer is as uptight as or more uptight than the person he's interviewing, because he has more at stake."

Help the interviewers. Offer information about yourself or the weather, and ask questions about their product, this commercial, or what is expected of you. Show them that you're genuinely interested in this job and capable of doing it well. Show them that you're confident enough of your own abilities and relaxed enough in this interview situation to be aware of their needs and goals.

You probably won't know who any of these people are, nor are they likely to introduce themselves to you. Your agent or the casting director or whoever has shown you into the room may introduce you. If not, be sure to introduce yourself. One professional feels that it is important to shake hands. "I will always try to touch somebody. It's a little inconvenient and sort of silly if there are more than five people there. If I do shake hands with all of them, I'll say 'This is like a wedding I went to last week,' like it's a receiving line or something. They are as nervous about this and as uptight as we are. I will always try to anticipate their nervousness."

This initial impression is most important. They want to hire someone whose bearing reassures them and inspires confidence. They want to know that you know you can do the job; they want to be assured by your assurance that they are making the right choice. They want to be able to work well with you.

If you have had an opportunity to look the copy over prior to the interview, you will be giving a prepared reading. If you walk in and read the copy for the first time, you will be giving a cold reading.

Some professionals prefer to give cold readings, making it known that this reading is their first one. "Then they can tell you what they want after your first reading," says one pro. "They'll hear things that are wrong, not the things that are right. I've learned that writers are very much more critical and much more narrow in what sort of interpretation they're looking for."

It allows them to give you some input. Others prefer cold readings because they come off fresher. A well-rehearsed line can lose its spark.

The following are tips from successful professionals and comments and suggestions from producers and advertisers who have listened to hundreds of readings.

These are suggestions, not rules. Try them out so that you can develop the interview style that works best for you.

1. *Go into the reading with no preconceived notions.* Do what comes naturally to you, and if there is no response, offer another approach or ask them what they're looking for. Sometimes they may like your first reading — love it even, and decide to use it — but caution and the rules of advertising dictate that they consider many choices.

2. *If you do ask for a second chance, a second reading, that's it.* Remember that each time you ask to try it a different way you're weakening your image. The more you go on, the more desperate you appear. And they want confidence, not desperation.

3. *If you are given a direction, react to it.* Make some change in your reading.

4. *If you've done it as you've been instructed to but don't feel that it's right, ask if you may try it your way.* They may not know just exactly what they want and actually be grateful for a pro's input. So give it your best shot.

5. *Don't read too fast.* The tendency in commercial readings is to rush. They're not going to cut you off, so don't speed on through.

6. *There are certain words, certain phrases you will want to emphasize in your reading.* Sometimes referred to as "buzz words," these words or phrases are emphasized in order to point out the differences of this product from its competitors. These words represent the difference in quality. They are important words in the ads and deserve added emphasis. They probably will not be marked in the script. Repetition, their position in the copy, and experience will help you to recognize these words.

7. *If you are taken off-guard by a request to read the copy with a certain dialect, do the best you can.* Tell them that you can do the dialect but that you need a little time to perfect it.

8. *You may be asked to make your reading more "conversational."* If so, listen to the speech of the person who is asking and try using his pattern of speech. A pro adds: "If I could strike one word from advertising, it would be conversational. Conversational is so dry. It gives me no direction at all. To me, it means stick in a few ums and ahs and hesitations. And that's rarely what they mean."

9. *Don't make derisive comments about the copy or the product.* Of the people sitting before you, one probably wrote it and another approved it. They're also the people who are going to hire you. If you want to point out a grammatical error, do it carefully.

10. *Be natural.* Don't act; show yourself. "Forget about the acting," advises an actor in Los Angeles. "I tried too hard in my first auditions. I was going in very serious, and taking the copy and studying it. Go in very low-key as an actor. They don't necessarily want to see actors. They want to see personalities."

11. *If there is an opportunity for humor, use it.* Many of these folks could use a good laugh by the seventh interview. If you improvise or make some bizarre comment or snappy witticism that's not in the script, they may remember you. Then, too, they might be irritated by it. Open yourself to the situation, read what's going on, and react to it.

12. *Be up, but not 'on,' not forced nor phony.* They can always ask you to tone down your reading, but they won't ask you to inject a little life into it. They'll merely assume you have no vitality or are too nervous to show it. Either way, you won't get the job.

13. *If you've been coupled with someone who gives a poor reading, don't be thrown by it.* Do the best you can do. The interviewers will see what is happening; if they're interested in you, they'll have you read with another partner.

14. *The interviewers may purposefully be rough on you in the interview situation to see how you withstand pressure.* One director says, "A lot of times we'll be really hard on them on purpose depending on who we're going to be working for. Some of our clients are real jerks — clients can jump fast sometimes. They want it over with in a hurry because it's costing them money. Talent had better be able to put up with that kind of pressure."

15. *Memorize at least the last line of the copy so you can lift your head and deliver that last line straight to camera, straight into their eyes.* Some pros refer to this as "giving eyes."

16. *Don't make excuses for your reading.* If you could have done better, you should have. Do the best you can while you're doing it.

On the other hand, you may not be dealing with anyone at all during your reading. Particularly for voice-over jobs, your audition may be as basic as walking into a storage room set up as a control room, giving a few readings, and leaving. In some cases, you will sign in with the person in charge, have your Polaroid snapped, read some copy to a tape recorder or a videotape recorder, and exit. Many talent express frustration about the lack of contact with the people making decisions during this kind of reading. "I hate that videotape machine," admits one Los Angeles actress. "There's no give and take." Even if you encounter this impersonal situation, the tips you've just read will be helpful to you in giving your best effort.

After your reading, make a businesslike exit. Thank them for their time. One pro says, "As I go out I say 'Good luck with your casting. I hope you find what you're looking for.' That brings a selflessness to it, and I am genuinely concerned about their need to come out with the right person for their job."

Make sure you haven't left anything behind. Going back to retrieve a sweater, jacket or portfolio weakens your final impression and may be disruptive to them.

If you feel hostile, defeated and angry with the world or yourself for giving a weak reading, it may mean that you repressed yourself during the interview. While it may seem difficult, particularly in the beginning, you'll have to learn to relax, to open up, and present what you have to offer during the interview. If you're so guarded against hurt and rejection, so nervous about how you look and how you're coming off, so resentful about feeling as if you're being put on the spot, you'll never relax enough to show them what you really have to offer and what they really want to see. Remember, they need to hire someone for the job, and that someone might as well be you.

Many advertisers and producers say that the talent they end up with is rarely what they envisioned at the outset. They have a creative vision, one on which they have spent time and money, a vision that has been sold to the client. Their egos, and quite possibly their jobs, are involved. So, good as you may be, you are rarely the vision they've created and probably expected.

There are two things that, in order to succeed in this business, you're going to have to accept. You have to accept yourself — your limitations, your strengths and weaknesses, and the way you look. You have to be confident in your own abilities (confi-dent that if you're not right for seven jobs, you will be right for the eighth) and able to convince other people of your appropriateness. Never will your self-acceptance be put more to the test than following an interview.

You also have to accept the business. You may audition brilliantly and still not get the job. They loved you, you read well, they laughed at your jokes, they said you were the cutest blonde they'd seen all day — but they were looking for a redhead. You can't anticipate that and you can't avoid it. And you can't beat yourself for not being a redhead. You have to have faith that there will be jobs for blondes in the future.

Call-backs

If the job for which you're interviewing is a really important one, you may be recalled for a second or even a third interview. These are called call-backs. It means you're definitely under consideration along with two or three other people. The entire process will become more intense. It will also be just as important for you to remain relaxed and let them see what you can do. You may want to wear the outfit you wore to the first interview to jog their memories.

"Don't think you're no good because you don't get it," advises Virginia Christine, the actress who plays Mrs. Olson in the Folger's Coffee commercials. She now sits in on casting for Folger's commercials. "They will go through maybe 40 or 50 people. It's many times a question of matching a husband and wife, a question of height, should we make her 35 or 22 — all kinds of extraneous things that have nothing at all to do with acting or your ability. So people should never be deflated when they don't get a part in a commercial. It hangs on too many other things that are out of their control, that have nothing to do with ability."

One advertiser-turned-talent gives some insight into how the casting decisions are made: "You would never again let your ego ride on a commercial audition. It has so little to do with your talent. It has to do with whether you remind (the client) of his brother-in-law whom he hates, or whether the woman they're using in a commercial is a blonde and so they have to use a blonde husband. It's not all that professional, because you're dealing with clients who aren't all that attuned artistically. There's a possibility you could be too good and draw focus from the product. In a commercial the product is the star and you're the supporting actor."

There may also be times when one of the factors out of your control is the tension in the group with whom you're interviewing. You may walk into an unpleasant situation and bear the brunt of a strain that's already been created and has nothing to do with you. Under such circumstances, unfortunately, whatever you do may have no impact. Just accept it, get through the interview professionally, and remind yourself that there will be other interviews.

A Note on "Crashing" Auditions

This section would not be complete without a few words about crashing auditions. At some point, you may wonder why your agent isn't sending you on more auditions. You may contemplate sending yourself out on an audition — in effect, "crashing" it — and wonder if you should or should not do it. It's probably a rotten idea, and here's why.

Two women who are both in the business shared rides downtown to make rounds, see agents, shop and have lunch. One day one of them, who had just recently returned to Chicago from New York, asked the other if she was going to audition at a certain production house for a certain client looking for a young mother in a commercial spot. The second actress replied that she hadn't been called for the audition, even though that was her type. She felt somewhat slighted as both women were registered with the same agency. Her companion replied that she ought to go along and "crash" the audition, that it was a common practice in New York and that everyone did it. Who would be the wiser?

So they both went into the audition, and when a production assistant asked the second actress who had sent her, she gave the name of her agency, the one she shared with her friend. The casting director in charge of this audition approached her following her reading and also asked who had sent her, to which she replied the name of her agency and added, "Perhaps my name wasn't included on the list sub-mitted." The next day she received a call from her agency and was asked why she had appeared at the audition when she hadn't been called by them. She replied truthfully that she had heard about it from her friend, had thought "Why not, who will notice one more body anyway?" and had gone through with it. The agent told her how unprofessional her conduct had been, what an embarrassment it had been to the casting director, and that the agency would not call her in the future.

The actress, feeling rotten about the situation at this point, decided to call the casting director and apologize for the incident. Unfortunately, however, this repentance overwhelmed her on a Sunday and the first words out of the casting director's mouth were, "How dare you call me on a Sunday? My business hours are nine to five, Monday through Friday." The casting director further indicated that as far as she was concerned the actress was no longer listed or working in this city. And she hung up.

The actress, on Monday, decided to try the agency one more time. She intended to explain and apologize to another of the agents working there, but after she gave her name to the second agent, the agent said, "I know who you are. I'm sorry, but your files have been discarded." And that was the end of that.

This story is too recent to know what further effect this one incident is going to have on this actress's career. Her lack of experience in this business prompted her to act on a friend's encouragement rather than to consider the lack of professionalism such an act would imply. Given a second chance, of course, she would not have gone to the audition. It was not worth the explaining then and the uncertainty now. Often we don't get second chances. In some situations, no one really would have noticed, but this lady got caught.

It simply isn't worth it to crash auditions. You're telling someone she doesn't know how to do her job.

11 Working

Once you've finally landed a job, you'll probably be as nervous as you are pleased and excited. You'll wonder what will be expected of you and how well you're going to do. This section will familiarize you with the places, people and equipment you're likely to encounter when doing a fashion show, trade show or convention, a job photo session, or when making a commercial, industrial film or voice-over recording. Hopefully, then, the scene won't seem so overwhelming when you actually find yourself in it.

This is also the place to mention again how important it is for you to conduct yourself professionally. A certain level of professionalism was in order when you approached agents and made rounds and when you were having your photos, resumes and tapes made. This is different. Now you're being paid for what you're bringing to the job, so you'd better be able to deliver. If you're unprepared for the job or if you present problems during it, you'll not work again for those clients and professionals. Don't forget that your agent or agency checks your performance with their clients.

Preparing for the Job

When you are notified that you have a job, get all the information. Note the place, time, photographer, director or coordinator, and what you're expected to take to the job. If the job is a convention, trade or industrial show, get the dates of the entire show and check your calendar to see that you have no conflicts for the duration. The client will expect you to work the entire show. If there is a conflict for a photo booking or commercial production, the

client who truly is interested in using you often suggests an alternative date.

Be certain you understand when you're called to set up the booking what you will be expected to do. You may have strong feelings about doing the centerfold for Playboy, but would you feel the same way about doing a nude advertisement for nursing mothers, tub and shower equipment or pharmaceutical packaging? You'd be caught off balance if you arrived at the job expecting to wear a towel and were told that the shot must be nude from waist up. If you are a vegetarian, you might not accept a commercial for McDonald's or Kentucky Fried Chicken. Know the details and accept the conditions of the job before you accept a booking.

Find out if you are expected to provide the wardrobe, and what kinds of clothing they want to see. Since what you're selling is the clothing in a fashion show or fashion photo session, the clothing is provided by the client. You will be asked to shop for certain outfits for certain jobs, particularly trade shows and conventions. Generally you will be reimbursed for these expenditures and permitted to keep the outfit.

If you are providing the clothing, select a wardrobe that offers several choices. Most commercials are done in color, which is not necessarily true of print work. Be sure to include several different colors, as well as styles, from which the producers can make a selection. Solid colors in medium tones — green, blue, brown — work well, and are preferred to solid black or white clothing. Distinct, bold patterns are often too distracting, as is shiny reflective jewelry. Your wardrobe should be on the conservative side; a classic, tailored or casual look will not take focus from the product or "date" the ad. Commercials are often rerun months and even years after their initial use, but the possibility of this happening is limited if your clothing dates the commercial. Whatever you wear, the day of the job the apparel should be clean, well-fitted and neatly pressed.

Gather and pack your accessories. If a certain dress demands a certain belt, be sure to pack the belt. If one of your suits needs a particular tie, take that tie. Shoes, scarves and jewelry are important, as is the proper underwear, including dress shields. If you're going to be on your feet all day, wear good-looking support hose and a pair of stylish yet comfortable shoes. You may even want to pack a second pair of shoes so that you can give your feet a change. Always include an extra pair or two of nylons. If you know that your hair falls fast, include hot rollers or a curling iron.

Be sure to find out if a stylist will be on hand to do your hair or makeup. Often, assistants or professional stylists are brought in for commercial spots and occasionally for printwork where particular focus will be on the hair and face. Otherwise you will be expected to do your own styling and to know how to make corrective changes.

You will want your makeup to be appropriate for the job you are doing. A woman would wear different makeup to sell orange juice than to sell cologne or cosmetics. The look for a high fashion ad differs from the look for a trade show. Some men who do printwork enjoy using bronzers and bases to cover dark shadows; others prefer to go au natural. Whatever job you're doing, arrive makeup ready and be prepared to make necessary adjustments. Carry your makeup with you and be sure to include the translucent powder that covers up that shiny look.

Your hair should be well-styled, clean, fresh and natural looking. Do not have your hair "set" professionally prior to a job and sprayed stiff to keep it in place; it should move, feel and look like real hair. You may be asked to arrive at some jobs with your hair in rollers and a stylist will be on hand to comb it out. However, you should know how to comb out your own hair and how to arrange it in different styles. If you presented a variety of styles in your composite, you may be expected to recreate them.

It is always important to be well-groomed for a job. Many models feel that proper diet, exercise and sufficient rest are essential to constantly looking and feeling good. You should be clean-shaven and use an antiperspirant. Your skin should look good and proper care should be taken to cover temporary blemishes. Your nails and hands should look attractive, particularly if you're going to be handling a product. One model who works a lot of trade shows says that your hands will be noticed whether you're registering a visitor, distributing literature or demonstrating a product. "If you're working with food, you should always wear nail polish. There's nothing yuckier than blue cheese under somebody's nails. If you're going to be into something messy, wear nail polish that will cover so they can't see when you've got food under your nails."

Do not eat, drink or smoke anything prior to the job that will adversely affect your appearance or your performance. Marijuana causes eyes to have a glazed look and a camera does pick this up. Certain liquids can coat your throat or alter your mood, either of which will affect your reading during a commercial or recording session. Liquor is out, no matter how much you think a drink might calm your nerves and smooth out the edges.

Be on time, and be ready to go the moment you arrive. One Los Angeles agent advises that you arrive 20 minutes ahead of time so that you can have time to relax, fix your hair and makeup, and be camera-ready at the time of the shoot. Arriving early shows your willingness to participate in and find out about what is going on. Some agencies have rules that any model who is late must pay for the waiting models' time.

During the job, while on breaks or at times when equipment is being moved and the pace has slowed, be alert and waiting for the announcement to start again. Listen and watch. You will learn a great deal this way and the pros you're working with will appreciate your attentiveness. Even after you have done many jobs and are quite familiar with the scene, you are still smart to listen, watch, and keep your opinions to yourself. Respond to direction and move quickly. Professionals will rehire models and talent who are cooperative and pleasant. Most pros are very helpful to and considerate of newcomers. Be open to their suggestions.

When the job is finished, let everyone know how much you enjoyed working with them. Do not badger anyone for a promise of more work. If there are vouchers to be signed, have them signed. Thank whomever is in charge and know when — and how — to leave.

Modeling in a Fashion Show

Be certain, when accepting the booking, to find out if you are expected to provide accessories or shoes. Most often anything that is seen will be provided for you, but if you do happen to have an extra pair of shoes, boots or a good-looking scarf with you and the fashion coordinator somehow finds herself shorthanded at the last minute, your foresight could save the day and insure future jobs. Definitely take underwear, including a strapless bra, pantyhose (preferably the sandalfoot type), dress shields and a net hood or scarf to protect your hair and the garments as you quickly slip in and out of them.

Arrive a half hour ahead of time. Give yourself a chance to look through your wardrobe, get the zippers, buttons and belts undone, plan the order in which you'll be wearing the outfits and any changes you'll be making with your hair. Ask the coordinator how the clothing is to be worn, whether you should wear or carry a hat, tuck in or leave out a shirt, and how the outfits should be accessorized. Although a "dresser" will probably be on hand to help you make the fast changes, once the show is in progress you will most often be expected to do your own makeup and hair.

On the runway itself, it is your job to show the garment in such a way that all its features are spotlighted. If the skirt has a slit, show it. If the skirt is full, move in such a way that the fullness is beautifully displayed. If the sleeves are Dolman, hold your arms in such a way that the special sleeves are accented. The way you wear and display the clothing should make your audience want to wear that outfit, too.

Coordination, balance and a good sense of timing are essential on the runway, particularly if you are working it with one or two other models. You should be able to adjust your pace and style to whatever music accompanies the show.

Even during a show it is important that you react with your audience. "She can't come across as an aloof vision — the nonsmiling model — not here in Pittsburgh," says a fashion coordinator. "We want our models to relate to the audience, to smile and have life in them." That you enjoy what you're doing and feel good in the garments you're showing must be apparent to your audience. "Models must project their own personalities — that's most important." Enjoy your moments in the spotlight on the runway.

Many stores, if they think you have the potential for runway work, will start you out with other kinds of modeling. You may be asked to hand out samples of new products at their cosmetic counters, or to offer cheese and crackers for a new cheese currently available in their kitchen shop. You must furnish your own clothing and the fees are not terribly attractive, but the work does give you an opportunity to approach people and build up your self-confidence.

You may be asked to model informally, showing a new line to customers as they shop or as they dine in the store's restaurants and tearooms. Here, again, you may have to furnish your own shoes, boots, belts, scarves and other accessories. You may do a trunk show mingling with the shoppers and directing their attention to what you're wearing while the line's representative answers questions and sells the collection.

Several coordinators emphasize the public relations-sales aspect to this kind of modeling. They want the customers to relate to the models, and they want the models to converse with the customers. One Chicago model admits that she "used to think I had to be an aloof, elegant person — my impression from watching the shows at Saks and Marshall Field's years ago." Now she is an aggressive, one-woman sales force. Although shy at the beginning of her career, she now walks up to the shopping women, introduces herself with a smile, and tries to generate some excitement about the clothing she is modeling. "Ladies, I'd like you to know more about the outfit I'm wearing." Her new approach has meant that she is asked to return, because the stores value her style. She also does their style shows now.

Working a Trade Show

As a model or talent working a trade show, you may be serving several functions. You may be introducing a new product, helping the exhibitors you're working for make direct sales, or trying to interest visitors in your product so that your employer can follow up these prospects when the show is over. You may be delivering a memorized script every half hour or distributing sales literature. Performers are also used, so you may be working next to a booth where a singer, dancer, magician, ventriloquist or puppeteer is making a pitch for the product he or she represents.

Combining warmth and salesmanship.

On the first day, arrive in plenty of time to familiarize yourself with the people for whom you'll be working, the booth itself, and the layout of the show at large. You'll want to check in right away with the exhibit manager or whoever is in charge. Ask for your identification badge if you haven't already received it.

There may be a training session on the first day; if not, you'll want to ask your employer for any special instructions regarding your duties. One model takes a clipboard to each show, asks about shipment, weight, time for ordering, and other questions she has noticed most reps will ask, and fills the answers in on a form she designed and had copied.

Also ask for your employer's business cards if they are not in sight. Find out when you and the other models are expected to take your breaks and lunches. If no one else has made a schedule of these times, do so and post it where it can be readily seen.

You'll need some time to memorize the script and study the company's sales literature if it wasn't available prior to the opening of the show. Be certain, particularly if the show is open to the public, to stash your outer clothing, purse and other personal belongings out of sight in a safe place. You'd be wise to leave valuables at home. This is also a good time to check your makeup to see if it looks good in the convention hall lighting and to make appropriate changes discreetly.

Whether you are delivering a prepared speech every few minutes or handing out the company's literature, your purpose is to attract visitors to the booth and to interest them in your product. You're trying to grab their attention, and one model recommends grabbing the visitors, if you do it nicely. "Always with a smile and a twinkle in the eye!"

Walk up to someone who is approaching the booth and smile. You want to simultaneously make eye contact, smile and clearly say what you have to say. Check their identification badges, searching for a company name, hometown or other reference point that will help you to open the conversation.

You want to talk to visitors, not other exhibitors. Address a man as Mr. So and So, even if his first name is on the badge, or as "Sir." Refer to a woman as "Miss or "Ms." unless, of course, her badge indicates she is a "Mrs."

Another way of opening the conversation, particularly if you see that the rep is from out-of-town, is to ask if he or she is enjoying your town. You can then be helpful by providing the names of restaurants, interesting places to go, landmarks, and available public transportation. The rep may return the courtesy by showing interest in your product.

You don't want to let them get away without getting their names and business addresses. A registration book is sometimes provided for this purpose, but few people will sign it unless you direct them to it. You can ask them for their business cards so that your employer can send further information to them, particularly if they have expressed interest in a certain feature or product. You may also be holding a drawing or doing some other gimmick to draw them in and have them write down their names, companies and addresses.

Even though you have familiarized yourself with your product, you won't have the answers to every question. Never leave a visitor with "I don't know." Instead, take the visitor inside the booth and tell him that you are going to find Bob Jones, your company's specialist in that area.

If you are hassled by any visitors, be tactful, and report it to your employer. If you are hassled by your employer, report it to your agent, for she will want to know. If you are working freelance, that's one of the risks you take.

While the show is in progress, keep an eye on the display counter and straighten the literature if it's untidy. Be friendly with your co-workers, but keep the socializing at a minimum. Visitors may be hesitant to interrupt a conversation already in progress.

You should stand, difficult as it might be, at all times. You don't present a high sales profile when you're sitting. Refrain from smoking, drinking or chewing gum while working in the booth; wait until your break to repair your hair and makeup.

It's probably a good idea to refrain from wearing heavy perfume. Some people are bothered by strong odors. Of course you should be certain to wear deodorant. You might also want to think twice before having that spaghetti or a garlic pickle at lunch during the show. You don't want anyone avoiding your booth because of your breath.

When your break does arrive, notify someone in your booth that you are leaving. Never leave your booth unattended. Try to get off your feet. Check your appearance before you go back on the floor. You should look as well-groomed at the end of the day as you did at the beginning. It's not too difficult to do actually, because the work you're doing is not taxing physically. Return by the specified time.

Your employer may ask you to dinner or to make an appearance at the company's hospitality suite following the show. It's really up to you. If you've enjoyed his company during the day and feel up to it, fine. If you are tired and really would like to go home, be honest about that, too. You should be able to tell whether the fellow simply doesn't want to eat dinner by himself or if he has something else in mind.

If your duties do extend beyond the regular work day and you are asked to hostess or serve cocktails, this should have been arranged in advance with your agent. Find out when you accept the job exactly what you will be expected to do and what you will be paid.

Trade shows can be fun and challenging, or they can be painful and boring. The statements of these two models sum it up: "I must say I don't like trade shows. It's a lot of standing and saying the same thing every 10 minutes for four days. By the end of the third day you think, 'My God, either my voice or my feet aren't going to hold out.' It's a rough way to make a living. The pay is good, and to some degree it's fun and I'm not sorry that I did it, but I'm glad that I don't have to any more."

And, "When I first got into modeling, I thought doing trade shows was something you could do if you couldn't do anything else . . . that it was one of the low rungs on the ladder. After doing one or two shows, I realized it wasn't the low rung on the ladder; it was a different spoke on the wheel. If you choose, you can be the best in this field. You can become very well known and have a following and do very well. I look at it with great respect now."

Doing Printwork

You've been through at least one photo session already to get photos for your head shot or composite. You may have been through many sessions in order to build up your portfolio. If you have worked with professionals during these sessions, you already know much of what to expect now.

While a job photo session will basically be the same, there are some important differences. Now you will be paid, instead of paying to be photographed. Your input will be what you do, not what you say you can do or would like to do. You will be expected to take direction and respond quickly. You will be under pressure that did not exist in your first shootings. This, at last, is the real thing. The photos you're shooting now are part of a process that includes many people and much money. Jobs and this particular account may be on the line so you're expected to perform.

Upon arrival, check in with the stylist, assistant or photographer. Display your wardrobe and find out what you should wear. Ask if your hair and makeup are all right or what changes should be made. Dress quickly and make the appropriate touch-ups. Makeup artists, hair stylists and dressers may be provided to create your look or, more commonly, to put on the finishing touches. This will be true whether you are a blushing ingenue selling cosmetics or a character actor portraying a Civil War soldier for a liquor ad. The "look" they want will be created for you.

While you're getting ready, other professionals also are preparing for the shoot. Assistants will be setting up basic lighting and giving the set its final dressing. The photographer will be directing all this or conferring with the advertising people and the client. The atmosphere may be charged with excitement or with unspoken tension. It's your job to get ready as quickly as possible, with no fuss, and to wait for the shoot to begin.

You may be asked to get on the set occasionally so that the lights can be adjusted to you. An actual set, looking like a complete kitchen or living room or restaurant, may have been built in the studio. You may be asked to stand on a sweep. Or you may be doing all this on location.

Shooting sessions done on location outdoors are occasionally tense times, as temperature, lighting conditions, and unexpected rain can cause delays or postponement. The decision to postpone often comes after hours of setting up, adjusting, and waiting for change. It is likely that your agency has a sliding fee scale to cover your time in such cases.

It is essential that you remain uncomplaining and ready to move should the decision be made to begin or continue. Whining about the rain or how cold you are is a certain way to insure that you will not work again with this particular crew. You prove your professionalism by withstanding the unpleasantness and being able to give a convincing performance, no matter what.

While the adjustments are being made, you may ask to see the storyboard if one is available. This is an artist's sketch, usually done by the art director, roughly showing the placement of the models, components of the set and the product. It sometimes indicates where the copy in the finished ad will be superimposed on the photograph. The storyboard should give you a feel for the tone of the ad and an idea of where to position yourself.

Once the shoot is to begin, it is likely that the photographer will tell you what he or she wants from you. If you are doing fashion photography, you may be asked to stand a certain way so that the slit of your skirt is revealed or the detail on the cuffs of the jacket you're modeling is easily seen. You may be asked to go through certain movements to show off the flair of a skirt or the fullness of a sleeve.

Fans may be used to create movement of your hair or the scarf or garment you're wearing. You may be asked to hold a purse, glasses, gloves or an article of jewelry in your hands. Since beginning models often do not know what to do with their hands, holding a prop helps them to appear natural and relaxed. Expertise will come with experience, and the more professionals you work with, the more tricks you will learn. Finally, then, you will develop your own style.

You must remember that these fashion photos are intended to sell the clothing, not you. While it is important you look your best, it is essential that you show the clothing. Your skill will be judged by your ability to make the clothing look good.

You will also be given direction during a commercial print job. You may be asked to say something like "The kids all love Countrytime lemonade!" or "I enjoy my midmorning break with

A product shot with flare . . .

. . . and one with flair.

Studying the storyboard.   *The stylist applies appropriate makeup.*

a cup of Maxwell House Coffee,'' or "Here comes Excedrin headache number 43,'' so that your mouth and face convey the message. Speaking lines often helps models and talent to get into the feel of the ad.

If you are going to be holding the product, you will be shown how to do so in order to minimize lighting flares and to prevent your fingers from covering the product name.

A photo session may go on longer than you anticipate. You may think you have covered every angle and still you'll be asked to do more. More film is shot for one final photograph than you'd believe. It is not unusual to shoot six or seven 36-exposure rolls of film to get that one print that's going to do the job. In a situation where you and all the other professionals are being paid, where a location fee may be involved, where the equipment being used may be rented, where props, costumes and products may have to be returned, film is the least expensive consideration. Re-shooting the entire thing would cost a great deal of money and effort so a quantity of film is shot in order to insure getting the one right photograph.

The photographer will be shooting for different compositions, lense effects, lighting and arrangements. The photographer may be shooting to the specific demands of the storyboard and art director, and then doing it several other ways that satisfy his or her own artistic ideas. It all takes time, and if there are problems, it will take a great deal of time.

You are being paid to be patient and to be ready to go when the shooting continues.

When the shoot is finished, have the photographer or assistant fill out your voucher slip if that is requested by your agency. You will probably be asked to sign a release. Be sure that you understand what you are signing.

If the release is very general, if it does not place limits on the time or ways in which the photo can be used, the photo could show up anywhere at any time. Many models have been embarrassed to see photos they did early in their careers surface and be prominently published years later. Generally, the release is not valid until the model has received payment for the job, but if you are in doubt about it, ask if you can review it with your agent and mail it back to the studio.

It is likely that you will not see proof sheets or prints of the jobs you do. Your opinion is certainly not important and you will not be included in the selection process. Some big name models and talent and their agents do negotiate for inspection rights, but for you that is a long way down the road. Depending on where the print is going to be used, you may never even see the final result. It is not at all unusual for a model to hear from friends across the country that they've seen her in an ad she hasn't even seen.

If you are interested in getting a job print you think would be particularly useful in your portfolio,

Wardrobe is selected on set.

you might call the photographer to see if an extra print is available. You may be told no, but it can't hurt.

Sometimes the art director at the ad agency has extra tear sheets available. These are actual reprints of the entire advertisement, with copy, headline, brand name and product inserts included. Some models, if these tear sheets feature them as well as the product, reproduce the entire ad in their composites. Such usage may cut down interest in you from people with competitive products but does show that you have worked professionally.

Filming a Commercial

There are some ways in which shooting a commercial is like doing print work. The emphasis is still strongly visual with careful attention given to details in makeup, hair and wardrobe. You will still be doing your thing in front of a camera on a set with the same careful attention given to set dressing and lighting setups. There will be numerous takes filmed to provide choices and achieve the desired result.

Now, however, there will be several more activities going on, and you will have a few different skills to master. You must be able to move easily and appear relaxed. You must be able to speak, to memorize a few lines of copy and deliver them in a natural way. You will have to coordinate movement and speech, singing, dancing, frying an egg, mopping a floor, eating cereal, applying mascara, and relating to other talent while maintaining eye contact with the camera. None of these, singly, sounds too difficult, but you're going to have to pull it off in a 10, 20 or 30-second time period in a relaxed and yet persuasive way in front of a crew of busy professionals. Responding to a director, doing take after take with banks of hot lights on you — all this will take practice and endurance.

While you're making the necessary changes, others will be busy setting up. Preparations are not unlike those for still photography; assistants will be busy adjusting lights, wiring and camera position. The camera is larger than most still cameras and is likely to be on a crane. It may follow the action with you if you are moving or remain stationary and zoom in on certain segments. There will be banks of lights to make the lighting appropriate to the scene being photographed and white reflective cards or umbrellas to bounce the light back onto the set.

If the commercial is being videotaped instead of filmed, the lights may be brighter and hotter. As with still photography, the film used to shoot commercials must be developed. With videotape the results can be viewed immediately on a monitor, which means that changes and corrections can be made on-the-spot. This is especially good for beginning talent.

The commercial may be filmed and videotaped simultaneously by two cameras. They may intend to

It's a take.

Virginia Christine of the Folger's Coffee commercials.

use the filmed version, but having a videotape setup working as well insures that what they have on film is exactly what they want. With this setup there are few surprises. For this reason, the number of takes done when videotaping is usually less than when filming a commercial.

While they're setting up for the camera they may also be setting up for sound. Sometimes the audio portion of a commercial is recorded while filming, in which case microphones are included in the setup. Sometimes the sound portion is recorded in a recording studio, at a different time, and added or looped to the film. Recording in a studio affords better control over the process, filtering out inappropriate background noise and allowing numerous takes to be done to insure the right audio sound.

The arranging is likely to take longer than the actual filming and you may arrive long before the crew is actually ready to shoot. You must have patience. One talent comments that "Shooting a commercial is hours and hours of sitting around and waiting for things to get done." She recommends that you take a book or magazine to pass the time, particularly if you are asked to take your place so that the lighting and set can be adjusted to you.

When everything is set the action will be started just like in the movies. Someone yells "Action!" and the clack of a clapboard starts the film. There will be more people working on the set of a commercial shoot than in a photo session. A director will be running things and a camera person will be operating the camera. There is likely to be a technician and an assistant in charge of lighting as well as an assistant following the storyboard and doing the clapboard. It's the scene of much activity.

You may start by shooting a master, which is a print of the commercial from beginning to end shot from one camera angle in just one take. The finished spot won't be seen this way; there will be close-ups and cuts to the product itself or other talent. Shooting the master will provide a sense of the timing the commercial will have.

It is more likely, however, that the commercial will be shot in segments. Everyone will concentrate on a certain line and action, repeating it time after time until the director and camera person are satisfied that they have what they want.

It will not be difficut to memorize the few words shot in each segment, although you may be required to say a line at a certain point and within well-defined time limitations. Some segments will require no lines at all, just reactions to what has been done or said prior to the segment being filmed.

Some segments will have to be done more often than others. It's not because you didn't give a wonderful performance the first time; it's because the creative people give themselves more choices each time a segment is filmed. They can edit and choose what actually will end up on the commercial during the hours of post production.

Unless you have been directed to change something in your action, it is important that you do the same thing each time. For instance, if you end up resting your chin on your hand after the line "I can trust Kraft foods," and the director yells "Cut!", that gesture — resting your chin on your hand — should be where you end up on all subsequent takes. In this way the proper sequence of action is assured.

The professionals you're working with will direct you. If you don't get it quite right one time, they'll just do another take. Remaining relaxed, cooperative and open is the key. People who are "naturals" in this business are just that — natural. Rely on the professionals to direct you, to cue you in on when to speak and where to look, and to instruct you on how to hold the product.

One problem many novices who have acted on stage encounter in commercial work is that they tend to overact. Hold back. You're not projecting golden tones to hundreds of people in a large room with potentially poor accoustics. You are speaking to a camera that may be no more than five feet in front of you. The tone is intimate. Gestures and movements must be minimized and makeup toned down. You're not on a stage; you're in somebody's living room. You're not lamenting the human condition; you're selling corn flakes and life insurance. Making commercials demands different techniques than those needed for theatrical work. It is essential to know the difference.

Ask where you're being framed if you have no sense of it and have not been told. If they're closing in tight on your face, you'll know to pull way back with your facial gestures. Raising an eyebrow could be overwhelming if the camera is in real close. One talent advises that "sometimes it is just as important for you to remain as part of the background as it is in some cases to be the main star. The product, in most cases, is the star. Too much animation can be bad."

The following are some tips on working in commercials from Virginia Christine, also known as Mrs. Olson of the Folger's Coffee commercials.

"Professionalism means, in part, that you come prepared with everything you're going to need. If a girl comes in with her hair hanging, and she knows we have tight schedules, she hasn't made any effort at all and the poor hairdresser has to compensate for her. I never come in without my hair rolled up, and then they comb it, but they don't have to start from scratch. These are just the physical things that, in my opinion, it's taken for granted you'll do. And how many little girls come in bleary-eyed in the morning. They don't care enough.

"Learning lines is not a problem in a commercial. Being on the set all the time is imperative to a professional. If you have to go off the set for a moment, tell the assistant where you can be found. You wouldn't believe the number who just disappear. To be interested, to be actively watching and involved and concerned, not goofing off and giggling, is professionalism.

"Another discipline in making commercials is the timing. Timing is all. If you have to get that copy read in a definite frame — and sometimes we're talking about half seconds — that takes a sense of timing. I remember once we had a little girl, pretty but not accomplished, who simply could not pick up the slack in her dialogue. I had to make up for it. I saw that commercial on the air and I hated myself.

"I'll never do that again. In order to get the thing done and in the can, I picked up what she was unable to do. That will not happen again. My dialogue was much too fast, there was no time to play.

"Another trick in making commercials is to be convincing within this short period of time. You don't have much time to register. If you're playing a leading part in a motion picture or a television show, and one scene is not so hot, the next scene will pick it up. That is not so in that condensed 50 or 60 seconds.

"I resent, deeply resent, the young kids who will come up and say 'Can you get me in a commercial?' And I say 'Can you act? Do you know anything about acting?' This business of thinking that you simply go in and do it, that it's a lucky break — well,

it's a discipline. And a craft. Acting is a craft. But doing commercials is a real discipline. They're harder to do than scenes and television shows, without question. You're dealing with a product that has to be exactly lit, you're dealing with having to repeat the same things all the time. To keep life in them, to make them real each time, you have to — forgive my expression — suck in your gut and say 'Now this is real. This has got to be real.' Otherwise you can very quickly become routine and flat and the sparkle goes out of your eye. And that boredom photographs. That is the pitfall. You must keep it fresh.

"The repetition, the long hours, the demand to still keep it fresh in spite of the physical problems — you're on your feet — it's a discipline just to keep your energy up. You may have to keep doing it over and over and over again. You have to have stamina."

Following are some comments from advertisers and producers of commercials about what they are or are not looking for from talent during the shooting of a commercial.

"I like input from people," says one producer, "but they have to know where to put the input. They have to realize that they're in a situation with a certain structure. A concept or idea has been sold and it is being produced. There is a certain amount of room within all of that for interpretation, but they have to be cognizant of the limits placed on them. It comes from experience and their own sensitivity to the situation. One of the things the amateurs have to understand is that they don't really understand how things go on the camera or on film. When they don't understand and yet want to do a good job, they should realize that they don't understand and just do as they're told. They've got to relax enough to just follow orders completely."

What he's saying is that many beginners don't even know what they don't know. The best policy, given inexperience, is to listen, watch, and be open to advice.

Another advertiser is irritated by fits of temperament from talent during a job. In one case, a New York actor being flown to Pittsburgh had agreed to cut his hair during the filming of a commercial for a hair care product. Between the time he accepted the job and its conditions and the day of production, he was offered a part on a soap opera, which prohibited cutting his hair. Rather than informing his agent and the ad agency in Pittsburgh, he flew to Pittsburgh and hoped to talk the producers out of their need to

cut his hair. It didn't happen, and the ad agency spent about $7,000 on a commercial that wasn't shot. The professionals who set up, rent equipment and buy supplies still have to be paid, whether they work or not. Needless to say, the agency did what they could to hurt the actor's career.

An advertiser in Cleveland says that attitude is very important. His agency had flown in a recognizable face — an actor from New York — to be a construction worker in a commercial. The shoot went longer than it was supposed to, due to weather and lighting conditions. "As the number of takes went on, he got more moany and groany about what a small town operation it was. He came in with his nose in the air, and he was snooty about it. He did an adequate job, what appeared on the film was all right, but he made our lives miserable. He was moody. In fact, he even told us 'I don't need this job!' "

Many professionals comment that talent should not make fun of the copy or make suggestions for changes. The lines you're reading have survived quite a succession of approvals. Ad libs are rarely appreciated.

What one advertiser says he is looking for is talent who can "improve the final product just by being there, just by their ability to look at a script or a situation and read something more into it than what was written. They bring it to life — bring it to a level where most people can identify with it."

Doing a Recording Session

You will probably not be hired for a voice-over job if you have not put out a demo or jingle tape. If you have produced a demo tape, you are fairly familiar with the equipment, people and procedures.

As in graduating from a composite photo session to your first real job, however, there are changes you can expect in your first real recording session.

You may have received a great deal of assistance when making your demo tape and be unaware of the number of seconds it took to get through each segment or why one take was more successful than another. Now the people who hire you expect a professional reading in a defined time space. If a spot is to be read or sung in 28 seconds, they mean 28 seconds; 28½ or 29 is not good enough.

The advertisers or producers are very often not exactly certain of what they want, and they've hired you because they think you can deliver whatever it is they're looking for or lead them to something better. Responding to these very real time pressures and these very broad expectations can be nerve wracking. Unfortunately, tension is immediately recognizable in a voice so it is crucial that you remain relaxed.

Unlike other job situations, appearance is of little consequence during a voice-over session. One very successful pro in New York is quite pleased that "we don't have to conform to anything. I don't sound any better in a tuxedo than I do stark naked." As long as your attire is not offensive to the client, it is of little importance.

It is essential that you arrive at a recording session early enough to give yourself a chance to relax, read through the copy, and find out what is expected of you. Be sure to test the microphone before the actual taping begins. One Chicago voice-over pro says, "You have to learn about microphones. They're not all the same. Some of them are bass-y, and some are terribly sensitive and pop all over the place. They have improved a lot, in terms of not picking up everything, but you still have to learn to work the mike like a friend in order to get the best results."

You may be giving a straight reading for a radio spot or a pre-recorded announcement. You will be expected to read a certain amount of copy or sing so many measures in a certain amount of time. You may be reading the audio portion of a commercial that has already been filmed. "You're watching a picture, you're listening on a headset to the on-camera actors and the music, and you're underneath a big picture screen. There's a frame counter that has a three digit read-out number starting at 000. You use that to

know when to come in. Or you use a music cue or a visual cue. The more there is going on, the more fun!" says a veteran.

You will probably be asked to give several different readings with varying emphasis and inflection. As in filming, the numerous takes do not mean that the producers are displeased with your performance; they're giving themselves more choices.

They may also be hoping that you'll do something unexpected to turn a good piece of copy into a brilliant spot. Feel free to ask questions and experiment. Do what is asked of you and then offer other interpretations. Be slow to commit yourself to a particular way of reading or singing the material.

"No matter what," mentions a New York talent, "do not laugh at the copy." If you know there are grammatical errors or if the reading is awkward and could be improved by moving around a few words, suggest these changes tactfully and only if the atmosphere is such that you feel safe to do so. It takes a pro to "be able to read something inane, and make it sound sensible. To not let people notice that it's really nonsense that you're reading — which a lot of the times it really is — is a career challenge. Sometimes it isn't so much that it's stupid; it's a lot of non-sentences. In one of my accounts, there's rarely a complete sentence in the copy."

Knowing which words or phrases to emphasize and how to fit "X" amount of words or notes into "X" amount of seconds are both skills that can be acquired with experience. "This is all learned. It's all craft," stresses another pro. "Anybody can learn — this part doesn't have anything to do with talent."

12

Getting Your Child into Modeling and Commercials

This section of the book is directed specifically to children and parents. It offers information on how to get started and what to expect. If after reading this section you both decide that you are still interested, read and discuss the guidelines and suggestions offered in the other sections as well. Professionalism and good working tools are expected from children as well as adults. So is union membership. Be sure to read the chapters that cover these aspects of the business. Your participation in this business can be enjoyable if you know what to expect.

Your child might be motivated to pursue this kind of work because he's heard that earnings and residual payments can finance college educations or because he has friends who are involved and successful. Your child's interest may be the result of performing abilities and experience and his or her association with adults who do commercial work, or he or she may be a curious, outgoing person who gets excited about lots of new things. It may start with someone commenting to you that your child is a natural for this kind of work or an outright declaration from your son that he wants to be on television. Whatever your reasons for pursuing modeling and commercial work, you and your child should be informed at the outset about what exactly is involved. It can be a pleasant, profitable, positive experience for both of you or it can be a painful time of disappointment in the business and each other.

Setting Up a Partnership with Your Child

It is imperative that you know whose choice it is before you go about trying to get your child into the business. Your eagerness will not be enough to sustain your child through interviews and jobs in which he really has no interest. If you want to make a success of it, you will have to work as partners who understand from the outset what to expect from each other.

I recall photographing a family of four children several years ago. They ranged in age from thirteen to five, and all had worked professionally prior to our shoot. When the time arrived for the five-year-old to take his turn, he started to whine. At this first sign of contrariness, his mother simply asked him if he wanted to work with his brothers and sister. She reminded him that it was his decision to try to get work, and therefore his responsibility to cooperate during photo sessions. There was no arm pulling or nasty threat. In fact, that was the end of the discussion. The shooting resumed and his natural spontaneity and good humor returned. I've often wondered how many kids, if offered the choice in such black-and-white terms, would actually continue in the business. I've wondered if being in the business was their choice in the first place. But it was quite clear that this mom and her children had negotiated the terms and were sticking to them.

Cooperation and understanding between parent and child are necessary for success in this business. Defining your expectations and setting your terms will help you determine if you're right for this business; you will know what to count on from each other during interviews and job sessions, and it will be readily apparent to you when you both have outgrown your interest and your willingness to be involved.

The Child's Understanding

It is important for kids to know what to expect so that they aren't surprised at what they discover and aren't disappointed with what is not — or can't be — a part of their experience. Even adults have difficulty reconciling the fantasies and the realities in this business.

Here are several points that your child should consider before deciding to pursue this work.

1. It's competitive. There are lots of kids trying to get the same jobs you'll be trying to get. They are just as cute, pretty, freckled, long-haired, buck-toothed, able to sing or talented as you. Some have been in the business for years and have a great deal of experience; some will be as new and nervous as you are. Many of your interviews will be "cattle calls," where you and 20, 50 or 200 other kids are all being considered for the same job. And because you'll sometimes be one of a group that large, you can count on the producers and advertising people taking a great deal of time to see all those kids and make their decisions. You'll have to have patience.

2. You won't always win. In fact, there will be a lot more jobs that you don't get than you do get, particularly as you start. Some pros estimate that they get one of every 11 or 12 jobs. So you'll be putting in a lot of time and energy on interviews that you don't get. One of the worst things about it is that you rarely find out why you weren't selected. Count on having hurt feelings and being disappointed from time to time. It's unavoidable.

3. It can be hard work. It can be boring. You'll be asked to hold poses, stand for long periods of time under hot lights, pay attention to a variety of people giving you directions, get your timing and positioning just right, and sometimes do take after take to get one that's acceptable during the shooting of a commercial. Through all this you'll be expected to be fresh and natural. You'll be given adult responsibilities and asked for the spontaneous reactions of a kid.

4. You'll have to make sacrifices. If you become really busy, you'll have to work hard to keep up at school. There may be times when you have to finish a paper or you want to attend a sports event, and you'll be stuck at a job going into overtime or an interview that is dragging on. You may find that some of your friends act differently toward you as you become successful.

5. The business is fickle. Once you have found a footing, are comfortable in interviews and are working frequently, the amount of work you do and money you make could diminish or stop overnight. Kids grow up, their looks change, they get pimples, wear braces, grow out of the right sizes, and outgrow cuteness. How much do you see these days of Rodney Allen Rippy, the Jack-in-the-Box kid, or Mason Reese, who went from deviled ham to the Carson Show? You may lose interest in the business, or it may lose its interest in you.

6. You could gain a lot. Outside of the obvious rewards of banking a paycheck or seeing yourself in commercials, newspaper ads and on cereal boxes, you'll get the experience of involvement in a very exciting and complex field. You'll understand, at an early age, the responsibilities and rewards of work. You may be asked to travel, all expenses paid, for some jobs. Some kids with high exposure in modeling or commercial work expand into other performing areas, as did Brooke Shields into movies and Gary Coleman into television work. Your experience here can expand into other areas of interest such as theater and advertising. What you experience as a child could be of great value to you as an adult.

The Parent's Understanding

It is important for parents to know what to expect so that there are no surprises for them either. Parents must be as enthusiastic and willing to enter the business as the child is, for your involvement and investment is going to be greater. The spotlight will be on your child, and you will be doing everything necessary to prepare him for it. You will need to have the time, flexibility, patience and understanding adult overview it takes to make your partnership work. Knowing your own limits and those of your child, you will have to establish and enforce the agreements you make with one another. Otherwise, what could be a wonderful and positive experience will be a disappointment.

There are several points that you should consider before you try to get your child into modeling or commercial work.

1. Your days will have to be free or your schedule flexible enough to adapt to the time demands of the business. Interviews and auditions take place after school hours. The actual job, should your child be chosen to do it, is most often completed during normal business hours. It might be a one-hour photo booking or an all-day commercial session. It might start and finish according to schedule or it might run into overtime.

You must adjust to the calls that come the night before or the morning of the audition. That will mean rescheduling your own interests, your job or your bridge game to do the laundry and ironing you hadn't planned on to prepare a wardrobe. Or you may have to arrange for a sitter for other children. There will be nights when you won't get home on time to prepare dinner for the rest of your family. You'll all have to be flexible.

There may be times when it will be necessary for you to travel. Your child may be selected to do a job being shot on location, and you will be expected to accompany him. Your expenses will be paid, but you will have to schedule your child's job into your own plans. You may have to make major adjustments; Gary Coleman's success in commercials led him to Hollywood, accompanied by his mother. His father followed later, having to adjust his own career plans to the skyrocketing career of his son.

2. You will have to put some money into this. Initially you will have to invest in professional photographs and duplications. You will need a dependable source of transportation to get you to interviews and jobs. You may have to spend money on sitters if you have other children. You may occasionally be asked to supply a certain item of clothing that you will have to purchase. There will be incidental and continuing costs throughout the time your child works. All these costs will be speculative, for there is no guarantee that your child will get work.

3. You will have to keep your involvement and your interest at an appropriate level. Your reason for being active in the business should always be that your child wants to be involved. It is his choice, his motivation, his sustaining interest. Moms have been known to take kids who are ill to interviews and jobs. Whose

interests are being considered in such cases? Certainly not the child's, for he cannot perform his best under such conditions. Agents and producers resent it as well. You should support your child in his decision to become involved in this business, but certainly not at the cost of his health or happiness. When it becomes obvious that he is no longer interested in being involved, support him also in his decision to drop out. You can lead a horse to water, but you can't force him to interview well or enjoy performing. Know when to make your exit.

4. It will be necessary for you to make judgments throughout the time you are both involved. If you aren't comfortable making decisions, and sometimes making them on the spot, it will be difficult. Whether you must decide what clothing to take to the job, whether to accept a job advertising a product you don't believe in or which calls for your child to use language you find unacceptable at home, or whether the gain is worth taking your child out of school, you will constantly be making decisions. At the beginning you may be approached by people offering to teach your child or manage his career. It will be difficult but it will be necessary for you to realize that they are appealing to your vanity and pride. Investigate such offers before you sign on the dotted line. You know your child is wonderful, but most legitimate agents and photographers wait for you to approach them. Just don't forget — there is one born every minute. You will need to make the choices that are best for your child.

5. Be there. Perhaps this is the most important pointer. You're both preparing to enter a highly competitive and pressurized business. Rejection is inevitable. Most often you won't know why he was right or wrong for the job. Be there to celebrate his achievements, and be there to help him through his defeats and disappointments. Help him to understand why some jobs are worth doing, and why you must turn down others. Use your mutual experience to grow and learn.

The Next Step: Approaching the People Who Have Work To Offer You

Once you've both decided that you are interested and would like further information, approach legitimate modeling and talent agencies who have work to offer you. Ask friends who have jobs in advertising or who have children involved in the business for the names of agencies. If there are no such agencies in your hometown, you will have to approach department stores, commercial photographers, production facilities and advertising agencies on your own.

The ideal solution, however, is to register your child with the legitimate agencies in your hometown. Call first to see if they handle children and what their procedures are for registration. You may be asked to send several snapshots with the child's name, address, phone number and date the picture was taken clearly printed on the back. That may be the basis for their decision to see you in person or that may be all they need to keep on file. Particularly in cities that don't have many jobs to offer, it is likely that a snapshot sent through the mail will suffice. Be sure to send in photographs, complete with current information, on a regular basis so the agent can update her files.

This is especially likely to be all that is necessary if your child is an infant. By the time you have completed the professional 8'' x 10'' photographs and duplicates, your baby has grown three inches and gained a full head of hair. Many of the agents interviewed for this book expressed amazement at the number of mothers who call who want their months-old infants to be professional models. One agent in Washington, D.C., even recalls one woman, six months pregnant, calling to register her unborn child. That mother certainly had plans for that baby. Most often, even the agents in big cities call their models and talent who have recently had babies when they need infants for commercials and printwork.

If you have twins, triplets or quadruplets and the inclination to try your hand at this business, you really ought to register your kids. You never know when some ad agency will come up with a campaign that simply will not work unless they can find twin girls or triplet boys. There may not be a great deal of work in which such kids are necessary, but there aren't all that many who are right for what work is available. You have nothing to lose but the cost of the snapshots and postage.

Many agencies set aside a few hours of a particular day each week to see the children and mothers who want to get into the business. You may be given an appointment time or you may find yourself in a long line of people crowded into the agent's waiting room and reception area.

What are the agents looking for? They'll be watching for certain qualities in your child, in you, and in how you relate to each other. What happens in the reception room, while you're waiting to be interviewed, will be observed as well. If you have difficul-ty keeping your kid under control, if he is rummaging wildly through whatever is around, snooping into closets and open office doors, it will be noted. If your four-year-old has her fingers in her mouth and is looking wide-eyed in apprehension at everyone who passes, unable to speak, it will be noted.

One commercial agent in Los Angeles says that he looks for kids with energy and a real "kid" look. Especially in California, where there are thousands of blonde, blue-eyed, good-looking children, kids with a unique look "will work like crazy." Kids in minority groups work a lot as well. Another agent says, "I look for precociousness. When you deal with children, you need a child who will not freeze up in front of the camera. You need someone who is just a little bit adventurous and will be willing to mug and fool around."

These kids are going to be working in studios where expensive equipment is set up. The time of the other professionals involved is valuable. Sometimes an account or even a job is on the line. The pressure can be quite intense. For these reasons and because their professional judgment is involved, agents are looking for children who are cooperative and responsive. They want kids who have the right look and right personality, and who are able to follow direction. They want children who are not shy with strangers or sensitive to criticism. They want kids who are outgoing, resilient, polite and yet precocious. Couple such a child with a mother who is cooperative, prepared, on time and realizes she is not the director, and you have any agent's winning combination.

Here's what agents don't want to see: children who are shy, who have missing, broken, chipped or discolored teeth, children who are very large for their age, have complexion problems or who are unruly in the office. Some say they don't want to see kids who have gone through charm courses, who have learned to replace spontaneity with plastic smiles. "Training a four-year-old is just dreadful. We think it's the worst thing people can do," they add.

Another agent reveals that "The biggest problem is not with the children, it's with the mothers. I don't want to see photographs of their daughters winning beauty pageants, I don't want to have children tap dance in my office, and I don't want to be serenaded by an eight-year-old girl. A lot of mothers are reliving their youths through their children. It really perturbs me to see some seven-year-old child come in here and perform. I just don't like it. It's not natural. I think the child is already on the road to destruction. I resent it. Just show me some photographs and let me talk with the child.''

Producers and advertising people, the ones who audition and actually work with the children, also resent pushy mothers. In interview situations, one advertising executive says, ''We are not casting the mother, we are casting the child. Let the child answer for herself or himself.'' They have had to audition and try to work with sick children who are complaining and whiny and unable to perform simply because they don't feel good and should have been kept at home. Schedules and advertising pressures being what they are, directors and photographers are often forced to use these kids.

Agents and photographers mention that a mother's presence during interviews and photo sessions changes the child, often drastically and in a negative way. Girls who are quiet and withdrawn when Mom is watching become exciting photographic models when Mom leaves the room. Don't force the agent, client or photographer to ask you to leave. Realize from the beginning that this career is your child's. You can be supportive, but you can't always be present.

The Keefe Family: An Interview with Six Successful Kids and Their Parents

The Keefe family of Northbrook, Illinois, entered the business in 1977. The family's six children — Katie, 17; Colleen, 16; Kelly, 14; Kara, 12; Larry, 10; and Michael, 8 — enjoy the work and have appeared for Sears' Winnie-the-Pooh collection, Gee, Your Hair Smells Terrific shampoo, the Holly Hobbie line, McDonald's, Cookie Factory Stores, Kelloggs cereals, Seventeen magazine, soft drinks and fruit juice accounts, local banks, department stores, and in numerous clothing catalogs. Kelly has also appeard in a movie starring Robert Conrad, which was filmed in Chicago.

Q. I understand you were contacted by an agency that told you your kids might be successful in television commercials.
A. *Mrs. Keefe: Initially we received a letter. Then an agency representative interviewed the family. He went ape over us. He told us what an extremely lovely family we were and that the kids would work. He was very high pressure, saying that an exclusive contract would be signed committing us for five years and that we would have three days to cancel after we had*

signed. We — all of us — sat in the room and he said, ''I have to know. I have to have the answer now.'' He wanted us to sign that very morning. That's part of the razzle dazzle. In Illinois you are protected in that you do have three days in which to cancel legally. I called the Better Business Bureau to check on him right after he left because we were not used to anyone coming on that strong.

You feel complimented. ''You want my children? Oh, isn't that wonderful.'' They can give you a line of baloney and any parent is so prejudiced toward their kids that they'll believe all of it. I didn't like what the Better Business Bureau reported; the agency had several court cases pending. We didn't sign then.

Q. How did you finally get into modeling?
A. *Mrs. Keefe: For years people had told me to get the children into modeling. I didn't want to get involved until I was ready because if the parent isn't ready, it's not going to work. I wanted to wait until the kids were of an age where they wanted to do it. I wanted it to be their ideas, too. That was about two years ago. I got advice from a parent who was already in the business. She said, ''There's one thing you do — you go to a reputable agency. And you don't pay to register.'' She recommended several agencies downtown.*

You do not pay to get into this business. You go to an agency; show them the children. If they see any promise, they will tell you to have composites made. If they do not see any promise, they are not going to tell you to spend money for photography.

Q. How did your first interview go?
A. *Mrs. Keefe: I dressed all my little ones up. You just don't do that to go to these agencies. You wear jeans...everyday American clothes...but you look cleancut. In spite of the fact that we were overdressed, however, they liked us, and we're still working with that agent.*

Q. What was the next step?
A. *Mrs. Keefe: We were told to get composites. Including a family group shot was a terrific idea. We have gotten a lot of jobs as a result of it. When one comp is sent out and it is turned over revealing all the children, the client often decides to use several of the children.*

Q. Are pictures really important?
A. *Mrs. Keefe: Yes. Once agencies all over the city were looking for a girl. They searched everywhere and finally chose Colleen from her comp. It's an in-*

The Keefe family: Michael, Colleen, Kelly, Larry, Kara, Katie.

Kelly in a quiet moment . . .

teresting story that taught me something else. The job was for a hair product: a good job. I opened my mouth and told our agent that Colleen had a little pimple on her nose. We know now that you don't have to say those things because it frightens the client. It was a dumb thing for me to say because in five days, on the day the shot was scheduled, her face was clear and it wouldn't have made any difference. The job was lost because I scared the client.

Q. Any other comments on getting ready for the pictures?
A. Mrs. Keefe: If your children don't have teeth yet, wait until the teeth come in. Generally, toothless kids aren't appreciated.

Q. How do you get out-of-town jobs?
A. Mrs. Keefe: Our good jobs have come from composites. A four-day job in Cleveland for Holly Hobbie resulted from the comp. We also got a job for John Deere from a comp.

Q. Then the kids do travel?
A. Mr. Keefe: Oh sure, after they're hired.

Q. What is the expense situation?
A. Mrs. Keefe: All expenses are paid. We have a ball on our out-of-town jobs. We're flown there, put up in great hotels, and taken out to dinner.

Q. Have you had to put much money into this?
A. Mr. Keefe: You need a bonus to get started. Kelly's first commercial for Sears' Winnie-the-Pooh line paid for the first comps. The family who thinks it will start into the business on a shoestring is wrong. It takes 30-90 days to get the cash in the bank.

Q. Have you experienced any "cattle calls"?
A. Mr. Keefe: That's the unfortunate part about it; cattle calls are extremely inconvenient. It's not very selective. Katie was just involved in a cattle call.

Q. How many kids were at that particular audition?
A. Mrs. Keefe: Twenty. And this is just for an hour's work. It was for a national ad in Seventeen magazine. We were thrilled with it. It was print work and that means just so much per hour, but print rates are going up. When we first started, I would go downtown in a blizzard for $35 an hour taking just one child.

Q. How about commercials?
A. Mrs. Keefe: For national ads you make at least several thousand dollars.

Q. All at once or on residuals?
A. On the residuals.

Q. How is voice-over for kids handled?

A. *Mrs. Keefe: The agency does a tape of the kids there in the agency. Sometimes it's for a particular job.*

Q. How do you feel about auditions?
A. *Mrs. Keefe: I hate auditions. It's not fun unless you get the job, but it does make the kids outgoing.*

Larry: It's okay, but it's sure a waste of time if you don't get the job.

Q. What happened to you on your last audition?
A. *Mrs. Keefe: There were 50 kids on this audition for Kelloggs. They said they were very interested in Larry, but he was the wrong size. When it's close like that, it's a bitter disappointment.*

Q. Do you usually find out the results that day?
A. *Mrs. Keefe: Usually you find out that day. Twice we have found out at the audition. All the other times we found out at home.*

Q. Who calls you?
A. *Mrs. Keefe: The client calls the agent and the agent calls you.*

Q. Kara, what are your feelings about auditioning?
A. *Kara: Well, the first one I tried out for I was real nervous. Very, very nervous. And then later it got easier. Sometimes there are a lot of people sitting there and sometimes there aren't.*

Kelly: Most of the time they take you in individually and ask you do to something with their product. You might say some lines or sing some lines.

Q. What do you do when you first go in?
A. *Kara: You say "Hi" and introduce yourself. Sometimes they give you a little slip of paper with lines and you have to read them, and sometimes they just tell you to do what you want.*

Q. Do they ask you to do silly things?
A. *Kelly: One time a job was embarrassing because they asked me to pucker up and act like I was being kissed. Stuff like that.*

Mr. Keefe: And we've turned down the lingerie type of things.

Mrs. Keefe: The kids don't want to do that. They don't want to model underpants or underwear. Once an agent called and asked if Kelly would do an industrial film. The producer was right there in the agent's office and wanted her to do it, but she had to say some words she really wasn't interested in saying. She was supposed to be attacked, raped by a school-

teacher. *I'm going to take this little 12-year-old downtown, and she's going to go through that on film? I said "no." I said I would like her to see the film, I was not against the film being made, but I don't want her to be the one that's going through it. And the agent said, "Don't get Midwestern on me, Mrs. Keefe." I said, "Sorry." Actually I got her on the phone and said "Kelly, you talk to this agent. You tell him how you feel."*

Kelly: So I got on and told him, "No, I don't think I'd be interested in making that film."

Q. What percentage of your work has been fashion and what commercial?
A. *Mrs. Keefe: We're much more fashion oriented than we are commercial. One of the agents said "I can see why your girls do fashion. But they're not going to do much television with me because television mostly is character look. They don't really want pretty kids." She's the only one who came out and said that to us. I think she's been the most honest.*

Q. Do the kids wear makeup for jobs?
A. *Mrs. Keefe: The young girls don't wear makeup to the jobs, but the older girls enjoy applying makup now. I usually put blusher on and powder them to remove shine before a job — even the boys, who hate it. Not all studios demand that they have even that slight amount of makeup. I also usually take a curling iron along for last minute touchups or changes. And sometimes I am asked to bring the children in curlers and the stylist fixes their hair.*

Q. Was there anything else you've learned in your first year?
A. *Mr. Keefe: We didn't do any favors for the agents the first year and it may have hurt us because there are a lot of people who try to entice the agents.*

Mrs. Keefe: Parents often give Christmas gifts. They'll ask me what I'm giving my agent. There are some parents who push their children and they have absolutely no childhood. If you get them in too young and all they're geared to is modeling, it can be destructive.

Q. How do you all feel now about performing?
A. *Mrs. Keefe: That's one spin-off of this business that we could never have gotten into before. This is a positive of the business. The kids are much more creative. We enjoy plays; we enjoy new family activities. The kids have play practice. Colleen signed up for a play, and we went as a family last weekend to see her. Now we're much more involved as a fami-*

. . . and Kara having fun.

ly with fun things like this. They go to an acting class and they enjoy professional theater.

Q. Has anyone done a fashion show?

A. *Kara:* Yes, me. It was through the agency. It was fun when you walked out and showed off the clothes. I didn't like it when I always had to change the clothes.

Mrs. Keefe: The dressing rooms were a rage, because everyone was hustling in a tiny area. The back scene of a fashion show is horrendous.

Q. Do you feel that the kids who are small for their age have an advantage?

A. *Mrs. Keefe:* The little kids in the business have it made. That's why Kara does so many commercials. She is eleven years old but she looks nine. The disadvantage is looking too old for your age. The reason Kelly hasn't gotten many commercials is that she looks much older than she is. She doesn't look twelve years old. They once wanted her as a 17-year-old. In fact, the photographer said that Katie's strongest competition was Kelly.

Q. Financially, are you ahead?

A. *Mrs. Keefe:* There are a lot of expenses in this business and it is not nearly as glamorous as the mothers who are not involved believe it is. There are a lot of hidden costs. You are not paid for auditions; you are not paid for parking; you are not paid for gas. Monetarily, we're ahead of the game. I spend a lot of time at it, but it's certainly better than a part-time job because it is mostly at home. I would say a one hour job takes three or four hours minimum of preparation. It's an hour to get down there, an hour there, an hour to get back in good traffic, and at least an hour to prepare.

Q. Most of the auditions for kids are after school, and that puts you downtown during rush hour?

A. *Mrs. Keefe:* It's a law that the auditions have to be after school. I have turned down lots of work because of school. I won't take the kids out regularly. I will if it's an extra super job or if they haven't been out in a while. Our agent knows that school is a priority.

If there is a really good job, I'm not going to be fool enough not to take them out. We're ahead of the game financially, not so much because of print work, but because of voice-over and television.

Q. Do you have any other comments?

A. *Mrs. Keefe:* Yes. I want to let mothers know that unless they are going to be committed to this, they might as well forget it. It will only be frustration for the kids and for themselves. You cannot have your bridge, you cannot have your own activities at set times, because this is a very "night-before" business. You cannot have your set thing to do every day, because you are going to be terribly frustrated when something comes up and you cannot do it.

Plus you have to learn to be decisive, which is something I really didn't have to do before. Can he or she do this or will it interfere with this class or that class or can I get them there or should I say "yes" or "no." I had a terrible time in the beginning figuring what to say. It can drive you crazy unless you learn. Once the decision is made, it's over. But you do have to learn to be decisive.

I love going on set, and every time I feel good because I know we can deliver. Each child is very good at it. I am not living vicariously, either.

I do not regret for one moment that we got into this business. It's been developmental for the kids — they're not on super ego trips because they've had enough rejections not to be. Yet they are competent because they've gone to enough auditions and had enough compliments to know that they're fine. Not only fine, but really, really good.

Comments From an Agent

Claudia Black is the Director of the Children's Division at Eileen Ford's Modeling Agency in New York City. One of the department's "discoveries" is Brooke Shields. In these excerpts of an interview, Ms. Black discusses the qualities she looks for in prospective models, how Ford's Children's Division makes its decisions, how the business runs in New York, and what concerns she has about the children with whom she works.

Claudia Black — "It's a very difficult business, especially in New York, because the competition is so fierce. I must get at least 50 phone calls and 50 to 75 letters a week from all over the states. I got one phone call from a woman in Ohio whose husband was so wealthy that they were going to Lear Jet the kids back and forth whenever they had an appointment. That was ridiculous. There is work in every state. If there is a local department store, there is work.

"If you want to be a New York model, then you've got to make the sacrifice and move to New York. There's just too much going on at such short notice, especially with the kids. We have a requirement of a half hour transportation time from home to agency, which we will bend if we know the child is exceptional. We'll also have to know that both child and parent are willing enough to sacrifice social life after school and be here at exactly 3:00 or 3:30. Then we'll take a chance.

"We screen first in the mail. I couldn't tell anybody specifically what I look for. We ask people to send in recent snapshots. And it's something that jumps out of that picture. Maybe it's a personality or a funny looking kid — it just has to strike me right. We get lots of pictures of really pretty children but there is nothing unusual. Even the beautiful children who are with us have something about them that makes people want to say, 'Oh, look at that child!' There's something there. I couldn't pinpoint it for you if my life depended on it.

"You can never pass up a pretty face because you never know — it might be your next star. Often it's the one who's got a little crooked tooth that you're interested in.

"The hardest thing I can do in this business is say no to a parent, because I know it's going to affect that child. So I try to pick out something — either she's not the right size or her teeth are bucked or whatever — to make her realize it is not her personally.

"My mother took me to be a model when I was a little girl and the woman said, 'Oh, she's too tall.' She didn't even look at me.

"I remember that experience. I was seven years old. I wouldn't do that to a kid. I find out what they're interested in even if I'm going to turn them down. You're adorable but you're just not right. It's as simple as that. You should never make anyone feel that they're ugly or wrong. You should make them feel good when they walk out. That's the most important thing.

"There are so many things in this business to learn. Being young, they pick up everything. They watch the older girls, the older guys — I've even seen the little boys at six hold their cuffs just like the male fashion models when they're wearing a jacket.

"When we get a booking for them, the mother has to know where she is going, how to make out her voucher, what she has to take with her and what is expected — if the child should be a little imp, if it's a character shot or if it's just a fashion shot, whatever it is. We tell them beforehand. The only thing we expect of them is to get there on time, to have everything they were supposed to take with them, to fill out the vouchers properly and to let us know if the child works overtime.

"Specifically with children, one client may want short hair while another client doesn't want anyone with short hair. J. C. Penney, Sears, stores like that — they want ears. Some agencies work more with catalogs. They like funky kids. The people who do ads — Tide, Downy, products like that — they want kids with character looks. So each agency will specialize in different things, certain looks.

"The average size 10 girl, who is a top model, gets out of school about two days a week, on an average, for a full day booking. Our rates depend on the job.

"Mrs. Ford does not believe in modeling schools. If you've got 'it,' no matter how minor it is, someone will be able to tell you how to bring it out. Personality or whatever that 'it' might be — there are so many different ways to describe it.

"Our first concern is that the child is happy. Because if the child is happy, the parent is happy, we're happy and, most important, the client is happy, which means we're going to keep getting business. Once the child is unhappy, it's a hassle for the mother because it means bribing and doing anything to get the child to smile. Most of these kids really like what they're doing. One point we always make is that if the child doesn't want to do it — let us know. I'd rather know than have this kid going out and the client calling me later to say this kid should not be working.

"A lot of kids get very nervous. They're cute, but they just don't have what it takes to be in front of a camera. We don't know; what we do is try to second guess. You see a face that you think is going to do well, and it might be beautiful, but it might not give anything in front of the camera. The personality might not come out, or the child might not want it. Sometimes too much exposure is detrimental, especially with children. I don't want any of that on my conscience.

"I had one situation where I was getting complaints about a child, and I asked the parent and child to come in. I asked the mother to excuse herself and I asked the child, 'Do you want to work? It's okay if you don't want to.' She said, 'Yes, I do, but my mom makes me nervous.' Fine. From now on, Mom is not allowed in the studio. The child is now working fine. She loves it. There are ways of telling. You have to realize that a stylist is going to know if a mother is being too pushy. She will tell me, 'Look, I love the kid, but you have to keep the mother out of the dressing room!'

"It's when they stop being natural that you have to worry. It's when the moves are calculated and when the tilt of the head is always the same and the smile is always the same — that's when you have to worry. We've had kids four years old who were played out at four.

"But I would say the most important thing is to make sure that they understand what the business is about.

"They participate in a go-see and there are 100 kids sitting outside and there's only one garment and it's an hour job and 50 of them have been there before and worked with the client before and here's this one kid and it's his first time and he's very ex-

cited. The client says, 'You're perfect, Yes, we're going to use you. Can you be here tomorrow at 3:00?' The kid leaves and someone comes in after him and they decide to use the other kid. You have to realize that it's not you. We stress that. When I take a child on, he's in here for at least 45 minutes. I tell him, 'Do not take anything personally. This is a business. It's your first introduction to the business world, and the advertising business is the toughest business. There is no personal element. It's either the garment looks good on you, or it doesn't. You're the right look or you're not.'

"It's very hard work. It's not as easy as everybody thinks. It's not just standing in front of a camera and smiling and getting your picture taken. It's leaving social life after school which is very important for children, especially between the ages of six and twelve. That's a very important factor. And you have to have a mother who's willing to run around. Most of our kids don't live in the city, so the mothers have to do what they have to do in the morning and pick the kids up from school and run to New York. It's always hitting traffic in rush hour and always being stuck. And sometimes they have the wrong addresses, or the clothes didn't come in, or the photographer is late. It's a very hectic schedule. And if you've got more than one child to deal with, and we do have people with six working children, then you've got to be a very together lady to keep it nice and simple during the day.

"Don't do it unless you've got the time, energy and understanding to let this child know that it's business. It's very difficult to do that at an early age. Kids can confuse business with pleasure. If our kids have a good time, fine, they don't realize they're working. When it gets to the point where it's 'Oh, do I have to work today?' then it's time for Mommy to say either 'Ok, we're going to call it quits' or to have a discussion. You've got to have a very good rapport with your child in order to do that. You've got to know yourself very well and how much you can take. A child is going to react to what you do and what you say.''

13 Money

How much money you make will vary from city to city, agency to agency, and will also be determined by your experience and the demand for you. Hourly photo rates range from $5 to $100 and more, depending on whether you're working in Charleston, West Virginia, or New York, New York. Children's rates range from $5 to $45 and up. If you are very much in demand or have established a "name," your agent will negotiate each job and hourly rates will not apply.

A day rate for photography is usually based on an eight-hour working day and is generally billed at five times the hourly rate. In other words, if your hourly rate is $45, even if you worked eight hours in one day at the same job, you would be paid a day rate of $225. Some "stars" in New York make as much as $1,000 a day.

You will be paid more for advertising certain products. Underwear — bras, panties, girdles, pantyhose, shorts — is often booked at twice the hourly rate. Personal hygiene products are often booked at twice the hourly rate. Lingerie, such as slips, camisoles and peignoirs, might be booked at one and a half times your hourly rate, while nudes might be booked at three times your hourly rate. Your agent sets these rates.

You will probably also earn an established fee for fittings, polaroids, travel time, speculation jobs, go-sees, cancellations or postponements if not made within a certain time limit, jobs called on weather, tentative jobs (on ice) not confirmed by a certain time, evening or weekend jobs. Time and expense of having a manicure or hair styling to client's specifications, wardrobe use (you supply the fur or formal wear), shopping time, and other services are compensated, too.

Your agent is likely to negotiate your booking fee for photography used in a national advertisement, product packaging, billboard and point-of-purchase displays. You should earn more for this kind of usage because you can quickly become overexposed and reduce your chances of getting work with competitive products.

You may live in a city where your agent has one fee for all photo work for all models and talent. There is no sliding scale, no rate determined by experience and demand. It's great for a beginner, but it may be rather insulting to the seasoned pro. One model working in such a setup admits that "I make, after 15 years of modeling, as much as the girl who walks in on the set to her first job. I will give her half my wardrobe, put her makeup on for her, fix her hair and tell her what to do, where to look. I won't look good if we both don't look good. I think I'm doing twice the work, and this girl is getting paid as much as I am. It's frustrating, it's somewhat insulting, and it hurts. I don't mind teaching her, in fact I enjoy that, but it's the idea that in any other business you move up the pay scale according to your experience, assuming you're doing a good job.''

Your agent probably has established fees for other kinds of work as well. Trade show or convention work will earn you $50 to $125 per day, perhaps more if narration or product demonstration is required. Promotion, the distribution of product samples in stores or on the street, ranges from $7 to $25 per day.

Fashion shows booked by your agent will probably be booked at your hourly rate. The fee will depend on the length of the show, the location, rehearsal, fittings and required accessories.

How much are you going to make doing fashion shows and informal modeling? Unless you live in New York, not much. For all the time you'll put into the fittings, the shows themselves and the travel, you'll either have to do a great deal of live modeling, supplement it with other work, or do the shows for the pure love of doing them.

In some cities the rates will be set, city-wide, by a Manikins' Guild, a professional association of live models. In one small city, you'd make $5 an hour whether you were doing a fashion show, fashion photography or a television commercial for a particular department store.

Some jobs will pay travel expenses and travel time. Some stores will supplement your paycheck by giving you a discount on clothing purchased from their store. Informal modeling is generally $15 per hour for three or four-hour periods. A daytime fashion show might be $40, an evening show, $50, with $10 allowed for travel. If a fitting is required, fitting fees will be paid also.

The rates for films, industrial films, radio and television voice-over, narration and voice on-camera work that does not fall under union jurisdiction will also be set by your agent. Again, these rates vary from city to city. The rates for work done under union jurisdiction are established by regularly negotiated contracts. Union rates, residual payments, benefits and policy are discussed further in chapter 15, *The Unions*.

You will be very eager, of course, to receive your financial rewards. In only a very few instances, however, will your gratification be immediate. I was present at one photo session for a brand-name cereal where the parents walked off the set with their children when they were told that they would have to bill the advertising agency for their photo fees. They actually had expected to be paid in cash immediately following the shoot. Very, very rarely do things ever happen that fast in this industry.

Payment: How, When and By Whom

How, when and by whom you will be paid will vary from job to job, city to city. Models in fashion shows are often paid immediately following the show. Women in trade shows and conventions are often paid at the conclusion of the show. A few photographers will pay you directly following the shoot.

Sometimes direct or cash payments, as immediately gratifying as they might seem to you, are made to avoid going through more professional channels. It may cost the producer, photographer or client an additional fee to go through an agent. A producer independent of the unions will definitely save himself a great deal of money by paying you direct. The only party who might be hurt by this method of payment is you. If you are new to the business and are not aware of the rates a professional should receive, you will very likely be thrilled to receive whatever amount of money is offered. While it is not always the case that a producer will try to take advantage of your inexperience, protect yourself by checking with an agency or other professionals who have experience in the field.

The freelance model or talent should define his or her terms with a producer or photographer before the job begins. You should know how much money you will be receiving for what work, and when payment will be made. If possible, get this agreement in writing. Find out also what the terms will be if the job has to be re-recorded or photographed. This would apply to models and talent in many small cities where the unions have no jurisdiction and there are no agencies. There are freelance talent in unionized cities who make six-figure incomes. These are obviously people who know how to protect themselves as freelancers, and who are existing quite well without agency representation. If you are hired directly by an ad agency or producer, you will very likely be paid directly by them and any problems of collection will be handled by you.

In most cities, however, a newcomer is well-advised to sign with an agent who will protect his or her interests. The agency will see that you earn the established rates or bargain for better rates, press the client for payment, and sometimes issue your checks to you. In return for this and the other services that the agent offers, a commission or percentage will be deducted from your earnings.

This is not to say that you can totally entrust your financial matters to an individual or group of individuals who are representing a number of models and talent. You have an obligation as an individual in business for yourself to report other additional charges and to keep a record of what you've earned and what you've received. If you feel that too long a period of time has passed since the completion of the job, it is up to you to call the agent or the client to see about collecting your money. You must be responsible enough to keep records and insist on what is due you.

What is a reasonable length of time to wait for payment? That, too, varies from city to city and agency to agency. One producer in Charleston, West Virginia, prefers to pay his people on the spot. Since the work he does is non-union, this is possible. An agent in Louisville, Kentucky, says that her people are generally paid within 10 days, although it can stretch to 30 days. In Chicago, it is not uncommon to wait 90 days for payment on certain jobs, and some models and talent have waited as long as six months.

Some agencies work on a voucher system, issuing checks on a certain day of the week or month to those who have turned in vouchers by a set time. Most often, however, you will be paid by the agency when the agency has received payment from the client.

The point is that this is a business where, most often, you will not receive your money until some time after the job. "Modeling is the type of business where, if you do a job, don't count on that money to make a car payment the following week, because it is not that fast," admits a Cleveland agent. "Count on it as spending money when it comes in." For most people in most cities, this is good advice.

Collecting money for jobs done under SAG and AFTRA jurisdiction is a bit more complex. You, individually, can't really keep track of the use the client has made of your commercial. The unions and other agencies do this for you. Checks for union jobs may come to you from the union, your agent, the client or advertising agency. There are also companies, such as Talent and Residuals, which has offices in Chicago, New York and Los Angeles, that are used by the larger advertising agencies to keep track of use and send checks to talent.

Managing Your Finances

Whether your involvement in modeling and commercial work is part time or full time, it is advisable that you keep records of what you have spent in pursuing this work and what income you have received. Open at least one checking account and attempt to pay for everything by check. You might consider a second and separate account to deal with business expenses only. The checkbook provides a record of your expenses which is most beneficial to you in preparing taxes. You should maintain a record of each job you do, where and for whom it was done, and how much and when you were paid.

Tax Deductions

Following is a list of items you may be entitled to deduct when filing your income tax. Know how much you have spent on these items when you see your accountant. He or she will determine what is deductible and ask you about other expenditures not included in this list. The IRS (Internal Revenue Service) makes changes every year, so be certain to consult with them or your accountant about what expenses you are entitled to deduct.

Business Expenses

- Rent and utilities — a fraction
- Phone
- Answering machine or answering service
- Postage for mailings related to business
- Promotional material
- Business cards and stationery
- Accountant and tax preparation fees
- Legal fees for business related matters
- Secretarial services

Professional Costs

- Fees and commissions paid to agents, managers, and advisors
- Union dues, initiation fees, and expenses
- Subscriptions to trade journals, magazines, and newsletters
- Inclusion in trade promotional directories
- Transportation costs to auditions and jobs — mileage, tolls, parking, car depreciation, cab fares, train or airfare to location jobs

Professional Tools

- Photographic session fees
- Reproductions of photos — glossies or composites
- Voicetape recording session fees
- Duplicate copies of voice tapes
- Packaging for voicetapes
- Typing and reproductions of resumes
- Portfolio
- Camera (still or movie), AM-FM radio, tape recorder, television, stereo, home video recording machine

Appearance Costs

- Makeup
- Wigs, wiglets, mustaches, beards, toupes
- Haircuts
- Hairdos required for special jobs
- Dry cleaning
- Cost and maintenance of clothing required for special job
- Rental of costumes and props for jobs or test shoots

Educational Expenses

- Classes and private coaching which maintain or improve your skills as an actor or model — scene study, dancing, singing, speech, improvisation, commercial acting
- Seminars — and the expenses of travel, meals and lodging if overnight stay is required
- Cost of tickets for plays, readings, recitals, etc.
- Purchase of reading material or albums related to the business

Entertainment Expenses

- Business meals
- Dues or fees for social, athletic or sporting clubs

Medical and Dental Expenses

- Medical insurance
- Medicine, drugs, birth control pills, prescribed vitamins
- Doctor and dentist appointments
- Medical examinations, X-rays and lab services
- Eyeglasses, contact lenses, corrective braces
- Travel costs to get to medical care — mileage, parking and tolls
- Cosmetic surgery
- Electrolysis
- Psychoanalysis or therapy

Other Expenses

- Child care — nursery school, governess or baby-sitter
- Contributions — to religious, charitable, educational, scientific, or literary organizations, those that work to prevent cruelty to animals and children, political candidates and campaigns. Fair market value of used clothing and furniture
- Interest — paid on revolving charge accounts, finance charges on bank and charge cards, home mortgage including points

Reporting Income

You may be asked, particularly when hired by an advertising agency or production facility, to fill out a W-4 form. If you do many jobs for many advertising agencies and production houses, you will fill out many W-4 forms. In the W-4, you claim a certain number of dependents, which determines how much will be withheld from your earnings. All federal and state deductions will be made. In other work situations, no forms will be filled out at all.

At the end of the year you should receive all your W-2 forms, which state what wages you have earned from each company and what tax has been withheld, as well as the 1099 forms from companies that reported but made no deductions from your earnings. They will not all arrive at the same time, and some, of which you should have a record, may not arrive at all. If they do not arrive by January 31, make some phone calls. Collect all of these forms, as well as other statements of income you have received or listed and the list you have made of your deductible expenses, and make an appointment to see an accountant. The income tax return of an actor or model is complicated. You are wise to invest a small amount in an accountant's fee to save yourself hundreds or even thousands in taxes.

Unemployment Compensation

It is not uncommon for actors to draw unemployment. Even when the unions strike, many professionals who continue to work in jurisdictions not affected by the strike draw unemployment. What qualifies you for unemployment and what determines how much you will receive varies from state to state.

In Illinois, you must have worked at least 4 or 5 months — two quarters — of the previous year. You will then be entitled to approximately one-half of your highest quarter's earnings. You will be entitled to draw this for a maximum of 26 weeks.

In the event that you are concerned about unemployment and wonder if you are entitled to it, call the Unemployment Claims office. It will be listed under the Labor Department for each state.

14

Why You May Need an Accountant

At some point, when you are starting to make between $10,000 and $15,000 annually in this business, you will be faced with preparing a very complex income tax form. Because you are your own business and because you work for many employers during the course of the year, you will very likely have a number of questions about all the W-2 and 1099 forms you receive at the end of the year. You may not be aware of the many deductions an actor or model is entitled to take.

Even if this work is only part time for you, providing income that is additional to what you earn in other or more regular employment, you may be entitled to deduct expenses associated with your occasional modeling or commercial work. This assumes, of course, that you do not file the Short Form.

At this point you should seek the services of an accountant, preferably one who is particularly knowledgeable in preparing the returns of people in this business.

One such authority is Barry R. Steiner, C.P.A., and author of *How To Pay Less Tax Legally*. The following is Barry's message to actors and models about preparing income taxes and handling financial matters.

Barry R. Steiner — *"When should someone go out of his way to get an accountant? I think almost anyone who is in acting or modeling, when he gets to a position of earning more than $10,000-$15,000 per year, would be wise to spend an extra couple of bucks to find an accountant or an attorney who specializes in people of that profession. Where do you get someone like that? Word-of-mouth from someone who is pleased. Talk to your friends over a cup of coffee. It may very well turn out that there is one accountant in a particular town who has the 'inside track' when it*

comes to income tax returns. The reason why it is important to find a person on the inside track is because that person may turn out to be very helpful after a period of time. Perhaps he has a contact, perhaps he also does work for producers or directors who are looking for your talent — there's always an outside chance that he'll mention your name to someone and perhaps put two parties together where otherwise you'd never stand a chance if you were just going to your own accountant.

"When we start talking about accountants, I strongly recommend you find someone who is a CPA (Certified Public Accountant) because that is one way of being able to tell if he has had any experience in preparing taxes. If you can find someone who worked for the IRS, so much the better. If you can find someone who is a CPA and worked for the IRS, you're in like Flynn!

"You'll find that most accountants understand enough about investments and managing money without actually managing your money to be able to advise you when you've crossed the point where you no longer can handle it yourself. When you have more money than you know what to do with, and the telephone calls to the accountant and the attorney don't get you any more response, you're in a very prime position to be taken, in terms of some type of investment. Someone might call you and say, 'We'd

like you to bankroll this play,' or 'Perhaps you should invest in this stock,' and you're pretty much of a babe in the woods when it comes to those kind of investments. You know acting or modeling and that's about it. When you reach the point where you feel that they know more about what they're doing with your money than you do, then you know that that's the time to find someone who is trustworthy.

"The same thing holds true in finding a professional money manager as in finding a good accountant. Find someone on the basis of word-of-mouth. But I caution — you'd better be earning a great deal of money before you take that step. There are a number of attorneys, at least in Chicago, who handle their clients' money, negotiate contracts, and provide a certain amount of advice; it is important to ferret out these people. Find out who they are, find out who some of the top people in the profession use and who handles their money. But you better be making a heck of a lot more than $50,000 to a $100,000 a year before you consider that step. Otherwise, the fees they'll wind up charging are going to eat up much of your income.

"As a general rule of thumb, if actors or models are making more than $10,000, chances are that they're going to have a number of very unusual expenses that are going to be deductible for income tax purposes. Most expenses that deal with modeling, fashion, the arts, drama, taking classes and things of that nature would be tax deductible, even if withholding taxes have been taken out of the model's pay. It's important to keep this in mind. I advise my acting clients to go ahead and get a checking account in order to pay for everything possible by check.

"The question of wardrobe is frequently a problem area as far as the IRS is concerned. The IRS feels that if the person buys an article of clothing that is adaptable to everyday wear, it can't be deducted on an income tax return. We know that it is necessary to buy particular things for auditions. I had an unusual case about five or six years ago. An actress whose income tax I prepared had sought to deduct two white party dresses and we wrote them off her income tax return. She had done a Dracula movie, on speculation, and she was supposed to be the victim. Part of the deal was that she was to have been bitten through the neck and stabbed in the heart with a knife, bleeding all over the first dress for dress rehearsal, and all over the second dress for the actual filming of the movie. She showed pictures she had from the movie of her, lying dead, with blood all over the party dress. The IRS agent said, 'Yeah, but it's still adaptable to everyday wear.' Can you imagine some-

one walking around in a white party dress stained with blood? But that will give you an idea of how far the IRS is prepared to carry this.

"I suggest that an actor or model buying an article of clothing have the bill describe the article as being something so weird that a person would not wear it on the street. If it has sequins or beads, have them go out of their way to specify them. There is also another way around this. If you buy ordinary clothes for an ordinary shooting session or an ordinary modeling assignment you can still get a write-off if there is a place that you can leave the clothes and have a wardrobe mistress take care of them. If you wear these particular clothes only for shooting, and leave them with the wardrobe mistress afterwards, it's all tax deductible.

"Something as unusual as a nurse's uniform would be tax deductible if purchased for a photo session or a commercial. There is an interesting case that involved Liberace. You know he spends a great deal of money on those crazy clothes — the IRS disallowed it. They disallowed it, and he said, 'But I can't wear my stuff in everyday use.' And they said, 'Yes, you can.' So what he decided to do when he had an appointment at the IRS office in Los Angeles, about five or six years ago, was to deliberately park his car a block away from the office, and wearing one of his sequined jackets, he proceeded to walk to the IRS office, bringing with him an enormous crowd of fans. They pulled into the IRS office, they all ran in there at the same time, and the agent said, 'Okay, we'll allow it, just get all these people the heck out of here!'

"Dry cleaning of those outfits you use for rounds will be tax deductible. It would include facial makeup, getting haircuts, buying hair pieces, wigs and wiglets. I even had one case where a fellow bought a pretend beard for a shoot that he was on. If you are a woman having your hair done, if you can key it into a particular modeling assignment or to particular rounds that you are making, it's a lot easier to write off than your regular weekly hairdo.

"Another thing that is important for aspiring actors and actresses to keep track of is the use of cabs to go to auditions. Ask for a receipt. Keep track of your mileage if you're using your car to make rounds. Get a hold of one of those small inexpensive notebooks and record all of your job assignments and all of your rounds. Going from step one to step two was 10 miles, the second interview was this many miles. Also, if you attend plays, readings or go out of your way to buy record albums, keep receipts. It isn't inconceivable that someone who is involved with the art would go so far as to buy a color television set to see what kind of commercial work is going on. If you assume that line of reasoning, then you could also justify a radio to hear the commercial voice-overs. It doesn't have to be an ordinary radio — it can be an AM-FM stereo with tape deck, tape recorder and video recorder. Get a video recorder with a camera — what's more natural for someone who is involved in modeling or acting?

"If you take an out-of-town trip the primary purpose of which is business, such as seeing directors or making rounds, or other activities with commercial potential, then you can write off the entire business expense, even if you incidentally visit your Aunt Mathilda. Any extra expense on your side trip to Auntie is not, however, deductible.

"Don't have lunch by yourself. If you have lunch by yourself, in your own home town where you live, it's not deductible. If you entertain someone — you're talking to someone who may be influential in getting you a part, and you have lunch with him and you pay $10 in order to take him out — you don't need the receipt if it is $25 or less. But you should carry with you a little diary where you list the name of the person you took out, the business relationship, the business purpose, where you took him, and the amount of money you spent. Get into the habit of looking for receipts wherever and whenever you can get them.

"Most, if not all, of your telephone bill will be tax deductible. I would suggest you deduct all of it. What the IRS may say is that you've got a minimum call pack of $10 or $12 a month that you won't be able to deduct, but anything over and above that is tax deductible. I've never run into an actor or model who just limited themselves to the call pack. Telephone calls are a big part of their business. It's their bread and butter.

"Telephones, telephone answering machines and telephone answering services all are tax deductible. The IRS has generally put the kabosh on home offices as a tax deduction unless it's your only place of business. It is for most actors and models, who are not furnished any office or desk space elsewhere and who use their apartments as their base. Figure out how much total rent you pay, assuming that like most actors you rent as opposed to own your home, and if you have a four-room apartment, divide by four.If you have a five room apartment, divide all the expenses, including the rent and utilities, by five. Then deduct it. But don't call it a home office expense, call it a rent. If you call it a home office, you'll probably get called in to the IRS.

"Other deductions would be dancing or singing lessons, private or class coaching, photography sessions, the cost of printing the comps or reproducing the glossies, promotional material, postage, business cards, accounting fees, and other items your accountant will help you remember.

"Save the W-2 forms. Stick them in a cigar box or file. It's not inconceivable that someone might do one job per week and end up with 52 W-2 forms. They'll sometimes come through the agent and sometimes directly from the client. You'll get all the forms at the end of the year. That's why it is important to keep records of all the jobs that were done and the amount of money you received. What happens, 99 percent of the time, is that you're not going to receive all of your W-2 forms. There's always going to be someone who didn't send you one and you won't be able to get in touch with him. Then you're faced with giving that information to the accountant and he's got to decide what he wants to do. The more jobs you do, the more W-2 forms you're going to receive. Unless you're working in the theater for one particular employer all year round, you're going to get more than one W-2.

"I don't think that actors or models should try to prepare their own tax returns. I study enough tax law for all of us, and most good accountants do as well. That should be one less thing you have to worry about. So if you're making over $10,000 to $15,000, go ahead and get an accountant. But be suspicious of some of the accountants who are with the unions, because they have a minimum fee of $250. It's incredible! That's why if you can find a good accountant who specializes in it for $35 to $45, grab him. I've always felt not exactly sorry for my acting and modeling clients, but I try to be encouraging to these clients to the point where I've worked with them and spent whatever time was necessary to prepare their income tax returns. They may only have an income of $10,000, but they might have the most complicated return I've prepared all year because they come in with 2,700 W-2 forms. I've always thought in the back of my mind that this guy really needs money, and he doesn't need to spend a lot of money on accountants. I try to give the additional service thinking that maybe, one day, this will be the guy who makes it. If you can find someone who takes that same attitude and is willing to answer your questions during the year and perhaps act somewhat as a guidance counselor when it comes to money matters — not that very many actors or models have that kind of money to worry about — grab him.''

15

The Unions:
What You Need to Know

The Union offices receive hundreds of calls each week from curious beginners interested in finding out about the business and puzzled professionals with questions about their check vouchers or the legitimacy and status of potential employers. This chapter seeks to answer the questions most commonly asked.

Q. When they say I'll have to join the union, what union are they talking about?

A. *The union that represents you is the Associated Actors and Artistes of America, which is comprised of several branches that represent performers in different performing arts. Also known as the "four A's," they are AGMA (American Guild of Musical Artists), AGVA (American Guild of Variety Artists), AEA (Actors Equity Association), AFTRA (American Federation of Television and Radio Artists), SAG (Screen Actors Guild), SEG (Screen Extras Guild), and several small specialty unions.*

The contracts most likely to affect you as someone working in commercials are those negotiated by SAG and AFTRA. Broadly speaking, SAG has jurisdiction over work that is filmed (television commercials, motion pictures, industrial and educational films), and AFTRA covers work that is videotaped (television and radio commercials, live television and radio programs, including entertainment shows, slide films, industrial films recorded on videotape, and phonograph recordings).

Q. How do I choose which one to join?

A. *You don't actually choose; you'll join the one that has jurisdiction over the job you're hired to do.*

SAG represents those performers (including actors, narrators, announcers, singers, specialty dancers, specialty acts, puppeteers, stunt men and airplane and helicopter pilots) who are employed in filmed commercials (and the motion picture industry at large) and AFTRA represents those performers (including actors, singers, announcers and sound effects people) who are employed in videotaped commercials (and other recorded material).

This jurisdiction is technical, not based on your performance. Many performers are members of several branches of the union, and it is likely that, as you become successful, you will join both SAG and AFTRA.

So, if you're hired to sing a radio jingle, you'll join AFTRA, and if you're asked to do a commercial that will be filmed, you'll most likely join SAG.

Q. Is there a union that represents models who do print work?

A. *No. No union has been established to regulate still photography, although several cities have models' associations or guilds that attempt to set wage guidelines and establish working conditions. You'll have to check in your city to see if such organizations exist.*

Q. What happens when I'm hired for my first union job and I'm non-union?

A. *You can join the union right away. However, you may be encouraged to sign the Taft-Hartley waiver, permitting you to do this first job and as* many jobs as you can get in a 30-day period (starting with the day you sign the waiver) without joining the union. This means you will be entitled to wages at union scale and residual payments for all the sessions you do in this 30-day period, and you don't have to put out a cent in initiation fees and union dues.

This is particularly beneficial to people who participate in the testimonial or interview-type commercials, who most likely will never make another commercial.

The producer who wants to employ you must report your name, Social Security number, and the first date of employment to the union shortly before hiring you. A producer will be penalized with a stiff fine for hiring you (if you're still non-union) after your 30-day waiver period has elapsed.

Q. How many commercials can I do before joining the union?
A. As many as you can get in the 30-day waiver period. You may also work for as many different union-affiliated producers as you can convince to hire you during this waiver period.

Q. When do I have to join the union?
A. Membership in the union cannot be required as a condition for hiring you until 30 days after your first employment under union jurisdiction. If more than 30 days have elapsed since you signed the waiver, you can sign up just prior to doing your next job. You will have to join after the 30 days have elapsed whether you are working for the same employer who initially hired you or for a different producer.

Agents can and do submit non-union talent for jobs under union jurisdiction, which is how the beginner is given a chance to overcome the Catch-22 ("I need a card to get a job, I need a job to get the card") nature of trying to get work.

Q. What does it mean if I live in a right-to-work state?
A. Under federal law, each state has the right to determine whether it will permit a union shop. A few states prohibit such agreements, meaning that a person need not join or maintain membership in the union unless he or she wants to. The union usually cannot maintain locals and protect the performers in such situations.

Q. Is it easier to join the union in some cities?
A. Although the same contracts, agreements and membership qualifications apply to all locals, different locals interpret these regulations differently. Actors denied membership in one city may be more easily accepted in another city.

Many models and talent feel that is is easier to break into the business and get union cards in smaller union cities than it is in New York and Los Angeles. Many advise that you have your cards before transferring into these cities, both of which have enormous numbers of experienced and union-affiliated talent.

Q. How do I go about joining?
A. The factors that are taken into consideration when you apply for union membership are whether you have a union job lined up and whether you have been a member of another branch of the four A's.

In order to join SAG, you must have been hired for a job within SAG's jurisdiction. You may sign the waiver, if it is your first job, exempting you for 30 days, or you may join immediately. You must join in order to work within SAG's jurisdiction once your 30 days have elapsed.

There are no work qualifications for membership in AFTRA, which technically means that you can join if you have the cash to meet the initiation fee and dues. This, too, will be interpreted differently by various locals.

The several branches within the four A's have an interchangeability agreement, which means that you may be given a break upon joining a second union if you are a paid-up member and have worked at least once within your first or parent union's jurisdiction. The agreement between any two of the branches will likely be different than for any other two; there is an understanding between SAG and AFTRA, and that understanding is different than the one between SAG and AGMA. The rules concerning this interchangeability change from time to time, so check with your local about current practice.

If you are a paid-up member of one of the four A's, make that fact clear when applying to a second union and ask to receive the best possible break on dues and fees.

You will be given a packet of documents to sign, an application for membership, cards that will be sent to the Pension and Welfare offices, and an agreement indicating that you are aware of your right to sign the Taft-Hartley, that it is your (and not the union's) responsibility to find work for yourself, and that you will agree to change your professional name should a duplicate name already be on file with the union. You can see how there might be some confusion if your legal name is Rock Hudson, right?

You are strongly encouraged to read the material in this packet. The information in the Member Handbook and the various union contracts is invaluable to you as a new member. The contracts list the working conditions that the union has negotiated for you and give you an overview of the concept of payment. It is important that you be aware of the rules established to protect you.

Q. Do I have to audition or perform in order to be accepted to SAG or AFTRA?
A. No. Neither SAG nor AFTRA tests or judges your ability to perform. There are no experience or educational requirements.

Q. How old do I have to be to join?
A. If you are 16 years old or younger, you are a minor. As a minor, you must have your parent or guardian sign the membership application and forms.

The union, by the way, regulates the hours and conditions in which children are allowed to work. Auditions and fittings, for instance, must occur after school hours and prior to 8 p.m. Actual jobs, however, are not limited to those hours. For more information, contact your agent and union local.

Q. How much does it cost to join?
A. The initiation fee to join SAG is currently $500, and dues payable upon joining are $25, half the yearly fee of $50. For AFTRA, the initiation fee in most locals is $300, although a few have a lower fee. (This is not the case with SAG, which has set nation-wide figures.) Semiannual dues in the lowest bracket that you can join are $30.40. Dues for both SAG and AFTRA are payable semiannualy on May 1 and November 1.

If you are a paid-up member of an associated union at the time of application, you likely are eligible for a reduction of initiation fee and/or dues. Ask for it.

Q. Can I spread out my initiation fee and dues payment as I earn money?
A. No. The initiation fee is due when you join, and the dues are due every May 1 and Novembr 1.

Q. What happens if I join and then don't work for a while?
A. If you hit or anticipate a "dry spell," and if you have been a paid-up member for at least 18 months, you can apply for a temporary withdrawal from the union. You should do so at the beginning of any dues period (May 1 or November 1). If approved, you will not be charged dues for that or subsequent periods until you work or receive residuals again under union jurisdiction.

Q. What does the union do for me?
A. The unions were organized to protect performers, who, in some cases, were grossly exploited prior to the existence of these unions. In collective bargaining, the union negotiates to establish equitable minimum wage scales and use compensation rates, as well as better working conditions. You, as a performer working in commercials, work under Commercials contracts negotiated by the union and the advertising industry. The current contract is in effect from 1979-1982, at which time it will be renegotiated.

The AFTRA contract states that it seeks to "protect and secure your rights, abolish and prevent abuses, assist you in securing just and equitable contracts, agreements, working conditions and minimum compensation in your business dealings; investigate and/or take action against those who deal with you in an unfair or discriminating way." This covers your dealings with employers, whether they are "producers, networks, stations, advertising agencies, sponsors, independent packagers, transcription companies, phonograph recording companies, slide film companies, agents, managers, impresarios and others connected directly or indirectly with the radio, television, phonograph record or slide film businesses." That's pretty comprehensive coverage, and SAG offers similar protection within its somewhat more limited jurisdiction.

The union sees that you're paid properly and promptly for the services you perform. It imposes penalties on producers who are late with their payments to you and on producers who are decreasing your opportunity to work by using non-union talent in an illegal manner. When you are required to travel to a job, the contracts provide that you be transported in a more than adequate basis, which often is first class air transportation, and that you be compensated for the time spent in travel. It sees that you are compensated for fittings, certain makeup, wardrobe and rehearsal calls, and that you aren't kept an unreasonable amount of time at audition sessions.

Although state licensing requirements are not uniform, agents who become union-franchised have to meet certain standards. They must provide character, business and banking references and pay a nominal franchise fee. The annual franchise fee is based on what the agent has made in commissions during the year. Agents can and do lose their franchises if they act in a way which the unions deem harmful to their members. The union protects your interests by initially screening and then regulating those agents who are franchised by it.

The franchise agreement protects you at the beginning of your career (when you have so much to learn) and later (when you have so much to lose). If your career takes off and you're constantly in demand, agents will want to sign you exclusively to their agencies. The union protects you by regulating the length of exclusivity for which you can contract, limiting and governing the types of contracts, and establishing the percentage of your earnings an agent can take in commission.

The agent also agrees to act fairly in your behalf, keeping accurate records and paying you promptly. The agent must actively try to generate work for you, acting as more than a telephone answering service.

The agreement also allows you to break your contract. What if you sign on exclusively — say, for a year — with an agent who promised much and delivers nothing or very little? If your agent does not get you "X" amount of jobs or generate "X" amount of income, you are entitled to break your contract and look elsewhere for representation.

Producers, too, must become signator to union regulations in order to use union talent. They must maintain records and keep current with union transactions, as well as handling Social Security, withholding, unemployment and disability payments. Further, producers contribute a percentage of your gross compensation — above and beyond what you make in session fees, holding and use fees — to the union Pension and Welfare Plans.

You can call your union any time with any question about any job, and you don't have to give your name. The union urges you to make inquiries whenever you have questions or doubts. The union offices will not, however, find work for you. That is up to you and your agent.

Q. What about the Pension and Welfare Plans?
A. These benefits are offered at absolutely no cost to you. They are financed by producers, not performers. The producer contributes nine percent (his percentage is renegotiated with each contract) of your talent fee directly to the union funds, so it costs you nothing and involves no paperwork.

The Pension plan offers benefits to those who have been with the union for 10 years, making $2,000 or more in each of 10 years, although those years need

not be continuous. You are entitled to the Pension at age 55.

The Welfare Fund offers Major Medical, Blue Cross, life insurance and other hospitalization coverage to you and your dependents if you have earned at least $1,000 (for AFTRA) or $1,800 (for SAG) in a year's time.

For further information on benefits and eligibility, contact union offices in New York, Los Angeles or Chicago.

Q. What do I have to do for the union?
A. You have to keep current with your dues. You will want to cast ballots in the elections of officers and for strike votes.

On a job basis, you should carry your union card with you when you go on a job. The producer may ask to see it. You may be asked to initial the producer's time report. Although different locals have different procedures and different forms, you may be expected to file a Member Report within 48 hours of each job, stating the date, studio (production facility), ad agency, producer, use category, sponsor and product name, talent agent, hours worked, how many spots were done, etc. It is a good idea to fill the report out at the job so you can ask questions of the production staff and have it initialed. Some producers will have these forms on hand, but you should carry one with you to each job. Filling it out is your responsibility, and you may be fined if you fail to do so.

Most important is that you **not** work for any producer who is not signator with the union. SAG's Guild Rule One "provides that no member shall work as an actor for any producer who is not signed to a Guild contract." It is your obligation and responsibility to make certain that the producer wishing to employ you is a union signatory. Always telephone the nearest union office to check on an employer's status. Union members are subject to disciplinary action by the union if they work for a nonsignatory.

Most locals regularly issue lists of currently unfair producers. You are strongly warned not to accept employment from these or from talent agents not franchised with AFTRA or SAG.

Q. How do I know which companies to work with?
A. If you have any doubt about a company's status, call the union office.

Companies that are signatory with the union have signed an agreement, at no cost to them, stating that they will abide by the rules set forth in the contracts.

Signators agree to the conditions stated in the contracts, provide assurance of their ability to meet the payroll for actors, and agree to do the necessary paperwork. They also agree to contribute to the Pension and Welfare funds.

Q. How much will I make?

A. At the beginning of your career, you will make scale wages — the minimum — as established in the current contract. Many highly successful performers who make their livings doing commercials work at union scale throughout their careers. At some point, your agent may negotiate over-scale wages for you. The big names in the business do not work for scale, although you are entitled to exactly the same pension and welfare benefits they have.

It is stated in the SAG and AFTRA constitutions that the union shall never regulate or fix the maximum rate of compensation for any performer, so the sky's the limit!

Q. How is payment figured?

A. Your wages are based on the **services** you have rendered during the production of a commercial, and the **use** of that commercial. You will be paid a session fee for being in the commercial. You will be paid additionally depending on the extent of use of the commercial. This will be determined by the number of times your spot is played on a network basis, the number of cycles it is used (a cycle is 13 weeks), or how many and in what cities your commercial is aired. The use fee for a city the size of Chicago would be greater than for a smaller market, such as Springfield.

Residual payments will result in far greater monies to you than the required basic session fee.

Your participation in the commercial will also determine what you're paid. If you are a singer or announcer, a solo or part of a group, on or off camera, a principal or an extra, what you do and whether it appears in the finished spot will affect how much you earn. If you are asked to work on holidays or weekends, if you must have a wardrobe fitting prior to the shooting, or if you must travel, these work conditions and a list of others discussed in the union contracts can affect your paycheck. The length of the finished commercial, whether it is 20, 30 or 60 seconds, does not affect what you will be paid.

Industrial films and other nonbroadcast work may be paid on a per hour, per day, per week or per finished footage basis. The different contracts covering the different useages establish individual wage guidelines.

Q. How are residuals figured?

A. Very broadly, residuals are based on how often the commercial is aired and in what markets it is seen.

When working in commercials for television, you must receive a payment every 13 weeks or you can assume the commercial has been released. You should receive a holding fee or a use fee; if you do not receive either one, consider your commercial released and yourself available for commercials for competitive products.

There are four basic types of commercials: The wildspot, the network program, the local program, and the dealer and seasonal spots.

The **wildspot** is played on a local non-network basis. The advertiser or client may stipulate at what times it is to play, because, of course, certain time spots are more desirable than others. Compensation is based on unlimited use within a cycle of 13 consecutive weeks, and the use can be continued for additional 13-week cycles. The fee is paid once every 13 weeks and is computed by determining the number of units in which the spot is played during the cycle (each city is given a certain number of units, the number being determined by the size of population), applying the appropriate unit rates (which are listed in the Commercials contract) and totaling.

The unit weight for any city changes as the population changes. Boston and San Francisco moved from four to five units in the most recent contract.

The **Network or Class A program** is a commercial aired on interconnected programs and seen at the same time in all cities. A fee is paid every time the commercial runs. Each time it runs within the 13-week cycle, however, the fee decreases. It returns to its highest value again at the beginning of each new 13-week cycle. For example, if the commercial is shown six times, you will be compensated for six uses.

Local or regional program commercials, classified as Class B and C, are telecast on a program entirely sponsored by one advertiser. Payment is based on unlimited use in each 13-week cycle.

There are also **seasonal** spots — commercials done for short-term use during particular holidays or seasons — and **dealer** spots, which are commercials made, paid for and placed by individual dealers or dealer associations. Station time is set up and paid for by the dealer instead of an ad agency.

The prime reason you are paid residuals for commercials that continue to play is that your identification with the product you are advertising increases proportionately with the continued telecasting of the commercial and could reduce your opportunity for further employment within the field.

Compensation for radio is similar, but is not figured on exactly the same formula as for television. You do not get a check every 13 weeks for work done for radio. You are paid only when they use your spot. There are also no holding fees for radio, because you do not grant any rights of exclusivity.

Q. Who is eligible to receive residuals?
A. Again, your participation in the commercial determines how and what you will be paid. If you are a principal, you are entitled to session and continuing use fees. If you are an on-camera performer, you will receive somewhat more than an off-camera (voice-over) performer, and what you earn as a group singer is determined by the size of the group you're in and if you're on or off camera.

An extra player who does not speak, is not identifiable and who would not be missed if, as an individual, he were removed from the commercial is likely to receive just one initial payment and no residuals. Extras who often are entitled to use fees are hand models and some general and group extras.

Q. When will I be paid?
A. Both the SAG and AFTRA contracts stipulate a certain, fixed amount of time in which producers should issue checks. If the payment is late, a late payment fee paid by the producer will be due you.

The session fees for television commercials should be paid within 12 working days. The payment of a holding fee should come within 12 working days after the commencement of the fixed cycle for which it is payable. Payment for local programs, Class B and C, is due within 15 working days after the date of first use, and the payment for a wildspot is due within 15 days after the date of the first use in each cycle. For all uses that occur within a single week from Monday through Sunday on a Class A program, payment is due within 15 days after the end of such week.

Payment is by check, and your check is accompanied by a voucher identifying the commercial(s), advertiser, dates and numbers of sessions, type of use, dates of use, and expiration date of the maximum period of use. Checks for AFTRA jobs are made out to you and sent to the AFTRA office; checks for most SAG jobs are sent to your agent or directly to you.

Some cities do a sufficient volume of work to support check-writing firms that issue talent checks for the ad agencies and producers. These firms figure Social Security, withholding, unemployment insurance, disability insurance taxes, and pension and welfare payments and note the cycles. The ad agencies and producers pay fees to these firms to handle this complicated bookkeeping task.

Q. How do I know when they're playing my commercial?
A. You don't, really. Needless to say, when a commercial is airing nationally, regionally or even locally, you can't keep track of each place and each time it is used. There are monitoring services that do air checks, spot checks and occasional audits of advertisers' and producers' books. None of these systems is foolproof, however, so the honor system generally prevails. There really is no conflict of interest between the advertising agencies and the performers. The ad agencies are paid a percentage on the amount of talent payments they make, so it is not in their interest to conceal or fail to report use. The business of broadcasting is complex, however, and errors do occur.

A union official mentions one actress and union member "who had postcards printed with her picture on one side and 'Date,' 'Station,' 'Commercial' and 'Comments' printed on the back. She sent these to friends and relatives all over the country and asked them to please keep the cards by their television sets and drop one in the mail to her if they saw her on television. This woman wound up with substantial residual claims; some commercials were played in error and some may have been aired intentionally. It was a tremendous idea. We had another fellow who had done a commercial for a beer in Ohio. Many actors have part-time jobs, and he worked in the toll booth on the turnpike. This fellow was a character actor, small and roly-poly and you wouldn't forget him. So this beer truck goes through and the driver leans out and says, 'Hey, I saw you on TV last night in my motel room!' The actor asked where, and the driver told him and also mentioned the TV station. The actor called us, and we got him a tremendous amount of back pay." So ask your friends and relatives to keep an eye out for you!

Q. Who is watching out for me?
A. Your agent should be keeping track of holding fee cycles, use payments, and dates of cycle beginnings. You, too, have to watch out for yourself. And the union does, too, by its own methods.

Q. How long am I held to a commercial for a certain product?

A. When you agree to do a television commercial for "X" shampoo, you are bound not to do a commercial for "Y" or any other shampoo for a period of at least 21 months. This exclusivity is an agreement by you, the talent, not to accept employment in commercials advertising any competitive product.

If you are being paid a holding fee (which means your commercial is in a holding cycle), then the producer, agency and/or client is retaining the rights to the commercial and the talent on it even if the commercial isn't running.

Q. *What is the procedure for getting released from a commercial?*

A. If you are receiving use or holding fees, the only way out of a commercial is to wait for the maximum period of use (21 months from the date of the session) to elapse. Not more than 120 days and not less than 60 days prior to the end of the 21 months, you must notify the ad agency in writing that you do not wish to renegotiate your contract — that you want out. However, if you have written permission from both agencies or clients, you may be permitted to do a commercial for a competitive product.

Q. *Are there any union traditions I should know about?*

A. Not really. As a rookie in the field, you may be the butt of a few jokes or made to feel as if you really don't know the ropes. It doesn't happen too often. But if someone tells you that only the experienced pros and old-timers can sit while eating lunch (a lunch provided for you by union contract), don't believe it. All you need to know is spelled out in the contracts.

Q. *Where are the union offices located?*

A. There are union locals in 40 to 50 of the nation's largest cities, with new ones organizing when there is sufficient interest and need. Check your phone book to see if there is a listing for Screen Actors Guild or American Federation of Television and Radio Artists. Don't hesitate to call them if you have any questions. They're there to help you.

16 ■■■■■■■■■■■■■■■■■■■■■■■■■■■■■

Expanding Your Career

■■■■■■■■■■■■■■■■■■■■■■■■■■■■■■■

Many of you will be quite satisfied doing an occasional photo job or fashion show right in your hometown. You will have no desire to uproot your family, leave your regular job, or face the challenges of living and trying to find work in a big city. Or you may, at some point, decide to expand your career by moving to a city which has more to offer you. Some of you won't have a choice. The bug will have bitten you, and you'll have to respond.

You'll have accepted the fact that you'll be spending most of your life looking for work, never certain of your next job. The only thing that you will be certain of, and that certainty will occasionally be shaken, is that you have the right look and skills and the know-how to market them. You'll have made a commitment to yourself and to the business.

"Smaller city modeling endeavors are not really big business," says a spokesperson for Wilhelmina's Agency in New York. An art director in Pittsburgh comments that "Most models who have anything to offer in fashion are not in Pittsburgh. They cannot make a living in Pittsburgh and so they've left." A producer of commercials in Cleveland says that "Success in Cleveland is leaving it."

What all these people are saying is that truly ambitious, experienced models and talent cannot survive in small cities. They will be broke and bored. They will be permitted to do what they are good at only on a part-time basis. Whichever cliche you choose to describe it, the big duck in the little pond has to check out being a little duck in the big pond. At some point, you may have to accept the challenge of the larger city, the larger talent pool, the bigger business.

If you really want to make a career of it, few cities other than Chicago, Los Angeles and New York have the volume and variety of work to support many full-time professionals. Once you do decide to

see if you can play in the major leagues, once you have made the commitment to move, there is still no guarantee that you'll be successful.

If you are going to relocate, give yourself time to make preparations. This is essential. You just will not be taken seriously otherwise. While exposure, experience and contacts in the business in one city is no guarantee of a welcome mat in another city, without them — or a very interested and protective sponsor — your chances are nil. "You have so many good, talented people who will never make it. I do not take anyone on unless they have been in the business and are professional. If they haven't done anything, unless it's a very unusual type that walks in and just carries a spark, I am not interested." That statement from a Los Angeles agent could apply to you.

Before you leave for the big city, exhaust the resources and potential of your hometown. Test with as many photographers as possible, have tear sheets from jobs, have clips of commercial work you've done, tape of any voice-over jobs, evidence of anything you've done that is professional. Study with well-known professionals and take classes at respected schools, universities, and theaters. Do as much theater as you can. One commercial talent from Chicago, commenting on her transfer to Los Angeles, says "I had made no preparation and yes, indeed, one should make preparations. Don't rush out here. Take advantage, as much as you can, of what you have where you are.''

Save money. No matter where you go, it's going to take time to knock 'em dead. Have a sufficient amount to get through at least two months' expenses. Some insiders recommend that you have enough saved to get you through six months; it could take that long to break in. Don't forget that the cost of living in large cities is high. The more money you have going in the more secure you'll feel, and it will be important to feel secure about something. A marketable skill, like typing or bookkeeping, is a hedge against poverty, as is the knowledge that you can tend bar, wait on tables, drive a taxi or pump gas if you have to. Whether it's yourself, your parents, an encouraging aunt, a supportive spouse or a generous patron, you need to have a regular and dependable source of income.

Find out what you can about the city before you move there. Ask people who have been there or lived there about restaurants, affordable, good places to live, public transportation and about the things that are going to affect your daily life. If out-of-town papers are available to you at newsstands or in a library, read them.

Have people who are excited about you call industry people in the city to which you're moving. Let the agents, photographers, producers, directors, advertising people and fashion coordinators you've worked well with know that you're leaving and ask them if they have any contacts in the city you're going to. If they do, it is important that they call for you, as opposed to writing a letter or giving you the contact's name and number. Anyone can drop a name, anyone often has, and it rarely does any good.

Unfortunately, many agents have no idea what is going on in other cities, even ones that are nearby or the ones in the ''Big Time.'' If you use their names, you could look foolish. Many ''Big Time'' agents don't care about what you did and whom you knew back home; they've been burnt or bored by too many minor league agents and talent. Even an enthusiastic call, however, is no guarantee that the contact will be interested in you or willing to see you.

Be prepared for some changes. Things are going to be different. One agent in Dayton, Ohio, says that he tells his departing models and talent to ''expect criticism from the agents. 'You have some potential but your hair is a mess, your makeup is all wrong and those pictures are just atrocious.' Don't be upset by what you take with you in terms of your materials or your appearance. What you have was fine for Dayton. If you really want to be a pro and want a shot at the Big Time, then you're going to have to learn to change to do it their way. I have never had anyone in New York or Chicago like what my people brought. So there is that first put-down. You're from the boonies, and this is the big city. The best advice I can give is don't be defensive. 'That was small-town stuff and I loved it. It made me a little money and it got me here.' But be willing and ready to change.''

When you arrive in your new city, you'll need to find a place to stay and have a phone installed or hire an answering service as soon as possible. The service will be every bit as essential now as it was when you first started looking for work in your hometown. Your photos and resume should be current. If not, have new photos done and print new resumes. Look up those contacts and get yourself established. Find out what classes are available, who is teaching them and if they are valuable. They could provide a place for you to make friends, make contacts, learn something and get support at a time when it will be needed.

No matter who you are, no matter what you've done, no matter where you've come from, be prepared for a period of re-integration.

The ''Big Time''

What can you expect to find in Chicago, Los Angeles and New York? If you're arriving in any of these cities for the first time, you can expect to find a different pace and attitude. You may have been the belle of the ball, the cream of the smalltown crop, the apple of your agent's eye in your hometown; it won't mean a thing in the ''Big Time.'' Your agent had the time to chat with you, to admire your new way of making up, to ask about your family or how your new car was running. The business of modeling and making commercials becomes big business in these cities.

If you are transferring from one of these cities to another of them, you must still expect changes. The business operates differently in Chicago than it does in New York, and New York operates differently than Los Angeles. You may have been a big wheel in Chicago or New York, but you will still need time to establish yourself with agents and begin to work in Los Angeles. Even big names in New York cannot be guaranteed success in Los Angeles. Admits one transplanted talent in Los Angeles, ''We've all started in differnt places, but when we first come here we are neophytes. People are here because they want to work. This town is about business.''

You may have had one or two agents who pretty much ran things in the city where you started out. In New York and Los Angeles, and recently in Chicago, casting directors are actually the people in charge of auditions and interviews. They are the ones who decide who reads for what commercials. They are independent of agents, producers, advertising agencies and talent. They call the agents in order to see the right talent and run the auditions. Therefore, it is important that you or your agent sell you to the casting directors. Your agent still negotiates contracts for you and collects a commission, but the casting directors are the ones in positions to request you for interviews and auditions.

You can still use your composite for print and modeling work, but in some places it earmarks you as a model, rather than as a talent, when you're looking for commercial or film work. Actors use headshots or glossies. Your agent, your career goals, your abilities and local custom will determine your photographic needs. Ask your agent or other professionals what the protocol is concerning pictures and resumes.

Many agents in these cities work out of larger agencies. You may have one agent handling you for all work or several agents handling your work in different job areas. You may be listed with several agencies whose interest in and work for you overlaps. Some agents have offices in New York and Los Angeles. Even if an agent promises you representation on both coasts, however, there is no guarantee that a look that sells in New York will sell in Los Angeles.

Because of the volume of work that is done in these cities for out-of-town clients whose schedules, budgets and concepts may change from day to day, some of the jobs you'll interview for and win will never go through. You'll face occasional disappointment. You may also find yourself competing with recognizable faces, people in the soaps and television series, for commercial spots. The general increase in volume over what was available to you in your hometown should offset these drawbacks.

Chicago

Chicago may be an intermediate step for some — a nice place in which to live and build a career. The city itself is clean and safe, compared with New York, and has a clearly defined city center, as opposed to Los Angeles. With a few exceptions, the industry — photographers, agents, production houses, union office and advertising agencies — is centered in an approximate 10-block radius that is negotiable on foot. You can easily check in with agents, make rounds to several photographers and ad agencies, and hit the major department stores within a day.

One professor of drama at Northwestern University, located in Evanston, Illinois (the first suburb north of Chicago), notes that Chicago is an ideal place for theater students to learn about the business. "More and more of our kids are staying here for three months, even six months, after they graduate. They're beginning to go downtown during their senior year, at my encouragement, so that the blast of reality that comes when they step out of the hallowed halls is not quite so terrifying. In Chicago they can make mistakes, ridiculous errors, and no one will ever know and no one will ever care. By the time they get to New York, they won't be wet behind the ears anymore because the basic process is the same. An audition is an audition is an audition. The adjustment they get rid of in Chicago is, 'My God, I'm auditioning,' and all the nerves that go with that. They learn to read commercial copy."

Chicago has experienced some significant changes in the business in recent years. Casting directors now run some of the auditions, several New York and Los Angeles agents have at least considered maintaining offices in Chicago, and the major voice-over talent have radically changed the scope of their freelancing. They have banded together in groups of seven to 10 different commercial talents, produced master reels with spots from each talent, hired representatives to carry these reels, and approached freelancing on a serious basis. The representatives do not negotiate contracts; they are strictly promotional. Energy and money is invested in hiring this rep rather than convincing an agent to represent them or to increase representation. While each talent may spend up to $2,000 annually to pay the salary for the rep — they are not commissioned — one talent reports that his earnings increased $17,000 in the first year he was in a group.

One union official in Chicago estimates that 75 percent of the dollars generated in Chicago is in voice-over work. Chicago produces more voice-over for radio, television and non-broadcast recordings — slide film, educational and industrial film — than Los Angeles. The city offers a variety of other work as well.

Chicago is a city that encourages multiple listing. There are many union-franchised agents, and a newcomer to the city or to the business is well-advised to register with all of them. The decisions about whether to go exclusive and with whom to go exclusive should be put off until you see how you fare with each of the agents.

One agent feels that "for the kind of work where you're looking for new faces every day for the big advertising accounts we have here, the multiple listing pool provides a large number of faces. We can use a face once." Another professional favors the multiple listing system because "it's easier to get into the business and it's easier to get thrown out if you're no good. It's more fair."

But many of Chicago's models and talent, beginners and established pros, are not satisfied with this kind of agency representation. Says one of them, "The agencies don't really do much work for you. They act more or less as a clearing house. They sometimes can give you a foot up or recommend you to people in the business, but that's rare. That's usually only during the 'wooing' period when they're trying to get you to sign an exclusive contract or when you've just signed it and you have gotten six commercials in six weeks. After that, it drops off appreciably because they have to give their attention to so many other people. In New York or Hollywood you have to be a little more special to get an agent, but then you also get special treatment. I wish the agencies here were better."

Another talent is dissatisfied because the models and talent who are good and have potential are not developed into professionals. He feels that actors and models need management. In New York and Los Angeles, an actor with potential is managed; in Chicago you are left to your own devices to do what you can. Another talent flatly comments that "The problem with the Chicago agents is that they think of the buyer as the client. The models and talent are their clients!"

Because the agents are licensed with the state as employment agencies, they are legally obligated to register anyone who comes in seeking work. They are not obligated to find work for someone who has no skills or potential; they owe nothing to the thousands of people registered with them. With so many hopefuls in their files, it is difficult for them to develop any one person's career.

Some professionals are also dissatisfied with the treatment they're given by the advertising agencies. They feel they're not being treated the way talent on either coast is treated; they're not being dealt with as professionals. One talent charges that "The advertising people think the talent are overpaid, that the work is easy and could be done by they themselves as well or better, and that the talent are doing similar work for all the other ad agencies in town."

More than that, the talent feel that a lot of work that could be done in Chicago is going to New York and Los Angeles. A long-time talent in Chicago and the voice of Morris the Cat's mom, Dorothy Jordan relates, "Not a year or so ago I was making rounds and met a guy at Leo Burnett I'd not met before. He was very impressed with me and said, 'I don't know why I haven't come across you before.' And I said, 'Probably because you don't see talent — you just got through telling me that.' And he said, 'Well, are there very many people like you out there? I haven't cast anything here in Chicago for 15 years.' And I said, 'Well, yes, there is a nucleus of voice talent in Chicago which is very good. However, with people like you going out of town to cast spots that could easily be produced here, you are eventually going to drive us all someplace else to work. Then, when you get in a tight place, there's not going to be anybody to save you!' Because that is what they do. They go someplace else and track things and then when it doesn't work out they call us to come in and re-do it. I'm tired of that. I'm tired of being treated like a second-class citizen. I have been treatening to go to Los Angeles because more and more of the commercial work is going there."

When you go in to see an agent, be prepared. One pro's advice is that "you ought to present yourself as a ready-to-go professional, because the agents here are not like those in New York and Los Angeles. They're meatshops. There are lots and lots of people who go through each agency. When you go to them, you ought to have in hand a good tape if you intend to work in commercials or do voice-over, and any materials that indicate your commitment. They get thousands of people who come into their offices and everybody wants to be a star. They get people who come in and say, 'Hey, I want to be in the business, you tell me what to do.' They haven't got time for that. If you are committed to going into the business and you want to impress the agents, you must have your materials ready."

Another says, "Being new is wonderful. Everybody in Chicago is looking for new faces. When you're new, one of the agents will want to grab you for whatever potential you have. If you hang around the agencies and make yourself very visible and do a little courting, you get called. If you don't put that time in, you don't."

Many of the professionals working in Chicago enjoy the city. They are able to make good livings and breathe relatively fresh air, walk on relatively safe streets, and lead pleasant lives. Some want to build their resumes in Chicago and get their union cards. For others, however, the excitement and challenge simply isn't there.

One who moved to New York comments that "sooner or later you've got to see if you can play ball with the big kids in the big kids' ball park. I think Chicago is an excellent place to start, but you get to a certain point where you've done what there is to do in Chicago. New York is a hundred times more exciting; there is more work here and more money to be made. Yes, there are talented people in Chicago, but there are 10, 20, 100 times more talented people here. There are two reasons. First, there are simply more bodies in this town — twice as many. Therefore the percentage of professional actors is much higher. Also, a lot of the professionals in Chicago become successful and leave, so there is never the same talent pool in Chicago that there is here."

Another, who left for Los Angeles, felt that he would feel successful only if he found that he was competitive in that ball park. "Chicago is still, in a lot of ways, the minor leagues. The money isn't the same, although there are a few making a lot of money. I'm making double what I ever made in Chicago, and this is only my second year here. And it only stands to look better; here longevity works for you."

Los Angeles

If you do decide to go to Los Angeles, be prepared for a city with polluted air, no public transporation and no central downtown area in which the business is concentrated. Be prepared for lethargic, mellow, laid-back people, and an abundance of that which is slick, plastic and shiny new. Be prepared for lavish parties, big productions into which a lot of money, a lot of time and a whole lot of frustrated creative energy are invested. There are few other diversions and few other opportunities for people to meet and make connections, so a great deal of business is mixed with pleasure in this town. Also be prepared for an almost constantly pleasant climate, a place of eternal summer — a producer's delight.

Because of the setup of the city and the industry, there is a feeling of expansiveness in which many people lose themselves. Some professionals describe it as a land of Lotus Eaters: people who have lost their drive, their energy, their ability to self-start. One casting person in Los Angeles says that many profes-sionals balance on a tightrope between how stoned they can get and still function.

There are agents who will handle you just for commercial work (commercial agents), television and film work (theatrical agents), and stage work (legit agents). Some theatrical agents handle commercial work as well. The large agencies, in which you are represented by one agent, handle your work in all media.

The Los Angeles agents are reputed to be inac-cessible. One agent with offices in both New York and Los Angeles says, "I do think agents in New York are more accessible than agents in California, that they are more interested in and more willing to see new, young, talented people." One Los Angeles agent states that she sees new people only if they are signed with a competitive agency or she is familiar with their work. Others will see new people who are strongly recommended by professionals in the business. Others don't see anyone new; they are too busy working with people who are already signed.

It is for this reason that connections are essen-tial. Go to Los Angeles with your contacts already made, your union cards in hand, and a dependable car. Comments one talent who made the transfer, "I wouldn't come out here without contacts or a definite connection. It's impossible to get in the front door. A decent agency just won't see you off the street. It's much better if a casting person out here or an agent from Chicago or Dallas or wherever calls and says, 'This person has worked for me; he is good.' There are so many people out here who are waiting tables and still trying to get an agent after four years. You must have an agent!"

Even if a connection is set up, there is no guarantee that the agent will be interested in signing you or even seeing you. You'll still have to get an agent as soon as possible. There are services that send out your photo and resume to different people on a weekly or monthly basis, or you can prepare a pro-motional mailing to recommended agents. Some agents permit you to drop off photos and resumes in their offices; some encourage you to leave your port-folio overnight as well. Some casting directors see talent who do not have agents; it has happened that an actor has landed a job and then, through that job, landed an agent. If you are intending an office visit, call first to see when and if you will be welcome.

The only other good way to have agents and casting people see you is in a showcase, which re-quires that you have sufficient performing experience or talent to get into one. There are a lot of these live theater performances, the exposure is good, and the agents and casting people do attend.

Whether you're trying to get an agent or impress a casting director, it is important that you continue to promote yourself. "Hustling is different here. I'm not out making rounds, but I'm out rehearsing scenes, doing a showcase, preparing a mailing, auditioning or taking classes. Do not fall into the sloth syndrome — it's easy to do," advises one talent. Carefully selected classes are valuable — you learn, you stay in tune, you find out what is important from lectures given by agents, casting directors and producers.

There is not a lot of still photography shot in Los Angeles. Notes one agent, "Most people do not get into print work out here. It is a business where you have to work around the clock and on weekends to make a good living from it. A lot of people just don't want to start it; it's not worth it. And there are no residuals." So, if you have been accustomed to doing a lot of print work, you would be well advised to expand your skills to include movement and speech. Film, television and commercials are where it's at in Los Angeles.

One commercial talent estimates that 90 percent of the commercials produced in Los Angeles are network, national spots. "You can plan to make at least $3,000 on 9 out of 10 of the commercials you do here." A great deal of national work that used to be shot locally, particularly in the Midwest, is currently being done in Los Angeles. A production person with Young and Rubicam Advertising Agency in Detroit says the car commercials left that city because of the favorable weather conditions in L.A. Not having to wait for weather conditions to clear means saved dollars. With its predictable climate and large talent pool, many producers go to Los Angeles for their commercials.

New York

New York, on the other hand, is a dirty, crowded city with a crime rate and a cost of living that are high. A place so peopled and so small may get to you if sizing up your competition does not. One actress says that her two strongest memories of New York are the smell of urine and the old men living in cardboard boxes on the sidewalks. There is much to contend with in New York.

But in spite of how it looks or smells, there is a vitality to New York that makes her residents love her. So much of what is going on in America finds its origins in New York; many industries are headquartered there. The big advertising agencies have offices there, as do most of the European and American designers. Its proximity to Europe makes it the first to receive imports. The garment center is there; the big money in America is there.

Most important to the modeling business is the presence of most of the prestigious fashion publications. A spokesperson for Eileen Ford's agency says that "the exposure a girl gets from a magazine is really what launches her. The ones we know as stars or name models usually achieve fame through magazine exposure and covers on *Vogue* and *Glamour*. (The modeling business) wouldn't work as well in Los Angeles, as there are no vehicles for them as there are here. This is really where it's happening."

Most important to advertisers and producers, there is a huge pool of professional talent, many of whom have extensive Broadway and television experience. The talent and production facilities are the finest the nation has to offer, and they attract many smaller city advertisers and producers to New York.

One advertiser from Pittsburgh says "we use local folks for radio spots, and they are adequate, but you can tell. The quality of their delivery is less than what we can count on getting in New York. Commercial production is a combination of talent and time — mostly time, which translates into money. You have a certain amount of time in which to shoot a TV spot or record a radio commercial. If you go over that time, it comes out of your wallet. The client pays. You can count on getting what you want from talent in New York well within the time frame. Not only that — you get what is down on paper, and then they always go beyond that to give you two or three different readings. They go that one step farther than your material goes. Maybe five times out of ten, the client will hear the spot and say, 'You know, that's better than what we had written. I like the way that guy did it.' I can't think of a shoot that I've ever been on in New York that was not made better by the talent. That's the real value of professional talent. I go to New York to get a production that makes the client feel good, doesn't make him embarrassed about what is on the air, and does not exceed the production estimate he signed."

Models and talent who have worked in both Los Angeles and New York comment that it is easier to see agents in New York. The modeling agencies in particular are likely to have hours set up for new people to drop by. Even without an appointment, you will be seen during these times.

As in Los Angeles, there are some large agencies that have many agents working for them. The large modeling agencies have television and commercial departments as well as extensive print departments. These agents are interested in building careers, helping you develop, and will handle you for all media. There are strictly theatrical agents and strictly commercial agents. In New York it is possible to freelance with several agents until you find one with whom you want to sign and who wants to sign you.

The agents strongly recommend that you have experience, knowledge and realistic expectations before you come to New York. One agent who manages commercial talent says, "We get so many people with no experience, who have never worked, who have no concept of the business but think it's all glamorous and wonderful. Somebody told them once they were funny at a party, and now they think they have a great career. It's those kind of people I object to. I think agents in New York are very tired of people with no background and no credits coming to New York, feeling that they are going to become important and talented people when they have no experience, no training and no background. They come here and they have nothing to offer."

The modeling agents suggest that professionals working in other cities who are seeking representation in New York send their portfolios or composites and plan on going to New York to interview with several agencies. Wilhelmina's, if interested in you, will recommend that you come for a month or six weeks during one of three hot times during the year to see how things work out before you commit yourself to the move. Both commercial and modeling agents strongly urge that beginners put off their dreams of New York until they have experienced the business elsewhere and are confident and knowledgeable.

It is also essential that you give yourself at least a year to get established. It may not take that long but be prepared for the worst. "Anyone coming to New York, from any town and any situation, should have a great deal of money saved, have some kind of income, or some kind of job ability where money can be made immediately. Maybe one percent of the new talent that comes into New York gets picked up right away. So be prepared for that period of time, which can be up to a year in length," recommends a commercial agent. A spokesperson from Wilhelmina's adds that "it takes a while to meet new clients and be approved by them. Even people who are going to do

very well, if they don't arrive at the right time of the year, will have to wait several weeks or several months before they start to get in motion."

Rounds or go-sees are encouraged in New York, although an agent who is interested in developing you is likely to exercise tight control over whom you meet and when. Such agents will set up these appointments for you at the right time with their clients most likely to be interested in you. These are important opportunities and not as casual as they might appear. Testing is encouraged and may also be set up for you by your agent with those photographers who might be excited by your look and have jobs for you. If you're with a well-known agency, many designers will loan you their garments for your testing sessions.

The financial rewards for a professional working in New York are great. Many voice-over specialists make over $100,000 each year. One male model, signed with Wilhelmina's feels he is just surviving making $900 a week; he looks forward to being one of the successful models who makes six figure incomes. The top models can make in the vicinity of $250,000 covering several media each year.

While you are likely to make good money if you are successful, you are also likely to receive it faster than you did in your hometown. Many modeling agencies handle such a dollar volume that they can afford to pay on a weekly basis, using a voucher system. (Even if you are in the $100,000 bracket for your work in commercials, the work falls under union jurisdiction. Payment will be handled by the advertising agency, producer, an independent talent payment company or the union. Your money will not be collectable in a week's time for commercial work.)

The system may be such that you receive 80 percent, and the agent takes a flat 20 percent, or you receive 70 percent in your first payment, and an additional 15 percent when the agency receives payment from the client. The agent's percentage then is 15 percent. At one of the well-known agencies, if you have your voucher in by 9 a.m. Tuesday, you will be paid on Friday. Quick and dependable payment is one of the advantages to being signed with an established agent in a big city.

Models will sometimes trade their $75 to $100 hourly rate or $600 to $750 day rate for exposure in the magazines. Someone who appears on the cover of a magazine may be paid very little for the job but the investment she makes in terms of exposure and future work is tremendous.

There is no guarantee, even if you do sign with a prestigious agency, that you will work out and remain with the agency. Newcomers are often signed on a trial basis. A spokesperson for the Eileen Ford agency describes the process this way: "We see on the average of at least 100 girls a week. It's not unlikely that nobody makes it. Out of seeing 100 we may try five. Maybe one out of those five will go beyond the trying stage, the testing stage, where either they don't like it and might drop out or we feel that they're not right for our agency or don't have potential for the business. You do try, at some point, to build the girl up and groom her and then get her out to the right clients. If the clients don't respond and there's not enough work coming in, at some point you have to say 'Well, we tried our best, maybe another agency can do more' or 'We've promoted you once, we can't do it again.' Some girls do have a limit as to how much they can work. Some little thing might be lacking; not everybody makes it to the same level of success. Sometimes, early in the career or even a year or two into it, we have to end it, just for mere business purposes. It's financial. It's very painful. Sometimes you're doing somebody a favor, I feel. You're helping them make a decision to move on to another area of the business, or to find an area in which they are stronger. Some girls just want to linger on and say that they're models, but if they're not working, they're not modeling. It doesn't pay to stay in it under those circumstances."

There is also no guarantee that a successful model will remain successful, even if she has been in the quarter million dollar bracket. "This is the major leagues. It is a difficult business; the amounts of money are big. The old timers feel, often, as if they are being disregarded and overlooked, but they chose to come into a business that's sudden death. We're not talking about people getting a job for $200 or $300 a week, we're talking about someone who's earning $6,000, $7,000 or $10,000 a week. If people venture into this situation, if they want to play a game this deadly, they have to be prepared for all the circumstances that are involved in it," warns an agent with Wilhelmina.

While the amount of time you've been around may eventually count against you as a model, it will work *for* you as a commercial talent. Whether you're in Chicago, Los Angeles or New York, the time you put into meeting people, working with them, building up your resume, and learning about the business is time well spent. One actor says that "your longevity works for you. The more the casting directors know you, the more they call you in. The most important thing is to keep your nose clean. If they have worked with you before and you haven't been a problem — you've done your homework, you know your lines,

when they call you to the set you're not off on the phone talking to your agent or somebody else, you're always there, you don't cost them any time or money, you do your job and you're not a neurotic personality — they will hire you next time. Even if there is someone else who is possibly more exciting, they won't want to take a chance. Once I work for somebody, I work for him again."

The Industry In Other Countries

Commercials are made and the business of modeling does go on in countries other than the United States. Other fashion centers, such as Paris, Milan, London and Tokyo offer a great deal of work. The industry works in much the same way in many of these countries as it does here. You sign or are listed with agents, you need photographs in composite or card format, you need to build up an impressive portfolio, you may possibly make rounds, and there may be unions to protect your interests.

Of course, some things will be different. There will be different "looks" and priorities in merchandising the garments. In Europe the look is casual, editorial, unconcerned with total neatness and showing each feature of the garment. The look is not stiff or posed the way some American catalog photography is.

One European male model now established in New York has these comparisons to make: "In Italy you do find that they're much more interested in pictures with a lot of atmosphere. I would say they are more artistic in their work. Maybe they don't show the garments as well, but they go more for atmosphere. Here it's the hard sell. The catalogs are very straightforward. In America pictures are much cleaner cut. Nudes are very rare in New York, because America is still quite straight. In Europe, they get away with a lot more. They go in more for exotic-type models, too. Here, they prefer the all-American type. If you're exotic, you might get more work in countries where they go for a wilder type of clothing and advertisement. That's from a woman's point of view. For a man clothes are much the same. It's just the way they shoot it that differs. It depends on budgets, too, and the state of the country's economy. In London, they really don't go on location much because of tight budgets. They're not so affluent as their New York counterparts. In certain countries, Germany, for example, the business is very good. I didn't work there myself, because they go for an older type of man, and they're not so big on youthful types. In Paris, the taxes are crippling. They take a lot of taxes out of your paycheck if you're not a French citizen. In Milan, you might not even get your money. There are a lot of problems with clients not paying. I lived in London for three years working this business. There really isn't the volume, and the work itself doesn't pay half as well as in this country. I came to New York because I was confident that I would be all right here. I was determined to come regardless.''

Success in Eruopean fashion modeling is also reputed to be based largely on who you know and what you do with them. A spokesperson for Eileen Ford's says that the question of mixing intimacy with professional work "does come up from time to time. Probably more so in Europe than here. A major portion of the girls have experience working in Paris or Milan before or during their careers here and it just comes back to us that they are pressured more often there.'' Another agent adds that "I've heard success, especially in Milan, is largely dependent on your social life.''

It is quite probable, if you sign with a New York modeling agency, that you will be sent to one or several of Europe's fashion centers to "season" you. A few agents in other cities might suggest it. One New York agent says, "Many of our new girls are better off starting in Europe because there are more magazines there, and they work with newer girls much more readily than the magazines here do. Then the girls get the sophistication of being in a foreign country and being surrounded by professionals. They learn a lot more than they might learn here. Sometimes it's not necessary at all to go there but it would fill out their books. The clients here are very impressed by European tearsheets. They feel a girl has a lot more experience if they see those tearsheets rather than black-and-white test photographs.'' A

new model may spend two or three months in Europe and then six to eight months testing in New York before a decision is made to sign.

An agent in Washington, D.C., says that she has European connections and promotes a European experience for girls who are interested and have potential. "We send each other copies of books that we think the other might be interested in and they may or may not like the girl. If they do, they say they're willing to take her and she can come in February and stay until June. Then I will say, 'Fine, I'd like one of yours.' It's like a camp. They will come over here and I will get them work with my clients, and get them some tearsheets. My models go over there and get European tearsheets. It's a little different for the people who come here. They will acquire more work experience for commercial-type things as opposed to my people who go there and are more likely to do a lot of live shows or editorial fashion photography. Models actually acquire experience that they would not get as readily in their home countries. And, of course, it's a wonderful way to get more modeling experience. In Europe the money to be had is not too great. It's definitely a way to survive while being in Europe, and to build up your book towards your career here. To come back with European tearsheets is impressive.''

Some agents, however, feel that the European experience for American beginners is merely an ego trip and a fantastic way to put off the real test. "I'm not particularly fond of sending people *anywhere* to be seasoned,'' says one. "I think if they're going to do it, they can do it right here and now. A lot will say it's just for fun and the experience, but I think there's more to it.'' She feels that those few months are a safeguard against failure and an insecure way to approach the business. Remember, a look that sells in Europe might not do at all well back home.

17

New Horizons

Now you're familiar with the places to which this business can take you: Europe, a runway, a recording studio, New York, the floor of a trade show, Chicago, a production house or photography studio, Los Angeles, the fashion department of your local department store, the offices of the people who have work to offer you. The business can provide excitement, glamour, big bucks and fame for a few, and satisfaction and extra spending money for most of you. It is a business that offers a great deal to a wide range of people.

The day may come, however, when you realize that you're not going to make it as a model or commercial talent. You might lose interest in the kind of work you are doing. You may be forced to seek a different direction due to age or the passing of your certain "look," or your natural curiosity may simply lead you onto new pathways.

Regardless, your knowledge of the field and your experience in it can serve as stepping stones to other areas of the business. For example, the skills you learn as a model can be utilized in positions such as fashion coordinator, editor of a fashion magazine or the fashion section of a magazine or newspaper, or fashion consultant for stores and companies. Your sense of style and the salesmanship you develop while modeling are assets as a sales representative. An interest in hair care and cosmetics can pave the way to positions with companies who make and market these products. You could become a buyer for a boutique, a production assistant, or a creative director in an advertising agency.

Experience gained reacting in front of a camera, behind a microphone or on a runway may spur your interest in developing acting skills. Many who begin their careers as models move into commercial work and use the contacts and skills they acquire to advance into television and film. A spokesperson for Wilhelmina's in New York says, "Pam Dawber started out by modeling and was also interested in acting. Pam had a real spurt of success in commercials and was just a natural for this (Mork and Mindy) show." This is a business in which you can develop theatrical and film acting abilities while you are working and making money.

It is not uncommon for models and actors and actresses to try out their skills behind the camera as well. Some of them become photographers to supplement their incomes; a few become full-time professionals. Associations with other models, talent and agents make the transition fairly easy; friends and co-workers are eager first customers.

Knowledge of the business and familiarity with a city's talent pool encourages some models and talent to become casting directors or agents. "This business opens many doors," says a successful model in New York. "You meet a lot of people — things open up for you. You just have to be a bit of an opportunist."

Whatever your goals, now or in the future, I hope this book helps you to succeed. I know that I've punctured a few balloons and shattered a few illu-

169

sions, but aren't you glad you know what it really takes to enter the business, get jobs, and develop a career for yourself? It's far better to have realistic expectations of how far you can go and what you can do than to hang onto dreams that simply can't come true. There is a great deal of work out there for those of you who care enough to learn the business, find your niche, develop your skills, and promote yourself. Good luck to you as you explore your horizons, and do let me hear from you somewhere along the way.

P.S. One of the interesting aspects of publishing is that even as a book is going into production, plans for a sequel are already being discussed.

Do you have information or tips you think would be valuable to other people getting started or trying to succeed in the business? If you have had an experience — good or bad — that you'd like to share with other potential models and commercial talent, or with the parents of children who are trying to get work, I'd welcome a letter from you. There is so much we can learn from shared experiences, and your comments would be helpful to me in my continuing research into this field.

You may write to me at any time in care of the publisher, Van Nostrand Reinhold Company, 135 West 50th Street, New York, NY 10020.

Index